THE SOCIAL CONSTRUCTION OF MIND

By the same author
APPROACHES TO INSANITY

THE SOCIAL CONSTRUCTION OF MIND

Studies in Ethnomethodology and Linguistic Philosophy

JEFF COULTER

Associate Professor of Sociology
Boston University

MACMILLAN PRESS

First edition 1979
Reprinted 1987

Published by
THE MACMILLAN PRESS LTD
Houndmills, Basingstoke, Hampshire RG21 2XS
and London
Companies and representatives
throughout the world

Printed in Hong Kong

British Library Cataloguing in Publication Data
Coulter, Jeff
The social construction of mind: studies
in ethnomethodology and linguistic
philosophy.
1. Intellect
I.Title
128′.2   BF 161
ISBN 0–333–23882–6 (hardcover)
ISBN 0–333–43772–1 (paperback)

FOR LENA

Contents

Contents

Acknowledgements

I wish to thank Ms. Joan Nashawaty of Boston University for her generous help in the preparation of this manuscript for publication. I am also grateful to the Editors of PHILOSOPHY OF THE SOCIAL SCIENCES for their kind permission to reproduce, with minor modifications, my paper 'Transparency of Mind' which appears here as Chapter Two. (*Phil. Soc. Sci.*, December 1977). Unless otherwise stated, the data extracts are taken from research with mental welfare officers and patients, and I am deeply grateful to them for allowing me to tape-record, and reproduce, episodes from their naturally-occurring social interaction. For the patients especially, these were episodes of serious moment in their lives. Sociological inquiry is made possible only by such generous co-operation and trust.

JEFF COULTER
Boston, USA

Introduction

This book comprises a collection of essays organized around the theme of subjectivity. The aim of the collection is to undermine the empty dualism of behaviorism and mentalism as it has traditionally, up to this time, been applied to problems in conceptualizing and studying 'psychological' phenomena. I believe that the Cartesian 'subject/object' dichotomy has wrought conceptual havoc in sociological and psychological thinking, and has even influenced some of the formulations of scholars whose basic purpose has been to transcend it (e.g. Schutz). In its place, I want to propose a different account of the 'mental' concepts, drawing heavily on the Wittgensteinian tradition in the philosophy of mind. I shall try to show that, when taken together, currents in both linguistic philosophy and ethnomethodology provide for the possibility of making genuinely sociological propositions about subjective phenomena in ways which demystify and dereify the latter.

I had hoped in this work to lay out some principles for the construction of a sociology of mind; that ambition has not been fulfilled, but I believe that in the ensuing arguments and analytical essays the reader can locate various general directions in which further work could be done. Much of the present book has been devoted to theoretical and ·illustrative issues which are intertwined with each other; it turned out that establishing some foundations was to be more than a modest attempt. However, I think that the research value of the anti-psychologistic stance defended here is clear.

The basic problems addressed include the following. Is it necessary to postulate or to impute determinate mental contents to persons as a part of studying action sociologically? What are the relationships between social circumstances and 'mental' states and processes as these are elucidated? Is there anything essentially private about minds? At what analytical level can inquiry into subjective phenomena best proceed?

Since a good deal of what I have to say turns on the use of logico-grammatical analysis, I want to outline this method briefly before inviting the reader to proceed to the essays themselves.

Logical Grammar and Mind

The analysis of the mental-conduct concepts and predicates to be discussed derives from inspecting reasoned, linguistic uses in ordinary sorts of circumstances; the aim of logico-grammatical analysis is to show how various concepts relate meaningfully, or intelligibly, to some particular other concepts whilst not to yet other ones. Logical grammar does not connect a name to an object by setting out the 'distinctive', 'necessary-and-sufficient' or 'essential' features of the object, but by relating

> . . . various concepts to the concept [in question—JC]. Here the test of your possession of a concept (e.g. of a chair, or a bird; of the meaning of a word; of what it is to know something) would be your ability to use the concept in conjunction with other concepts, your knowledge of which concepts are relevant to the one in question and which are not; your knowledge of how various relevant concepts, used in conjunction with the concepts of different kinds of objects, require different kinds of contexts for their competent employment.[1]

For instance, grasping the concept of 'chair' (knowing what a chair is) involves knowing how it can be related to concepts like 'wood', 'legs', 'sitting', 'broken', 'repaired', 'furniture' and so on, in distinctive ways and in different sorts of contexts. Grasping the concept of 'broken' would involve knowing how it signals different states of affairs when related to 'chair', 'promise' and 'marriage'. Many of our conceptual errors consist in making the wrong connections, or the wrong sorts of inferences to states of affairs on the basis of given connections, between concepts. Although there are always latitudes in usages found intelligible, there are normatively enforceable limits to such latitudes. Cavell notes a simple case in point: 'If someone says we haven't played all of the Brahms concerto on the ground that we only played the *violin* part, then we probably won't feel for a moment that he has a *different* concept of "playing a concerto", but simply that he has no concept of *that* at all.'[2] Ordinary language is normatively organized, not determinatively controlled; we can, if we like, or out of ignorance, misuse and abuse it. Often, our judgments about the misuse of a concept will depend upon a very sensitive analysis of the particular environment of circumstances surrounding its employment, whereas in other cases it will be quite obvious on cursory inspection. The same holds for standard sorts of expressions. Circumstances of use form *part of* the logical grammar of categories and expressions.

Members of a natural-language community may make mistakes when they engage in idle or isolated reflection upon the meanings of words actually in use or when they try to set out the 'normal circumstances' for their employment or their relationship to other concepts. Members are not infallible *theorists* of their own conventional linguistic practices, even though we must turn to members' reasoned, practical linguistic uses for our understanding of the informal logic of their categories and expressions. To put the matter simply: while an intelligent speaker of English (or any natural language rich enough to express the concept) can employ the phrase: 'I thought that . . .', he may nonetheless cling to a metaphysics in which, e.g. 'thought is the name of a mental event', thereby misconstruing the possibilities of intelligible use of the word *already* embodied in his own pre-theoretical speech. This distinction—between analytical elucidation of language-use and its practical mastery—has been caught nicely by Vendler in the following: consider the case of a relatively competent chess-player who can also (naturally enough) speak his native language well. Vendler observes:

. . . Unfortunately, not all *a priori* truths arising out of chess or out of language are easy to discern. Can you checkmate a lone King with a Knight and Bishop alone? You can, and this is an *a priori* truth. Yet it takes an expert to show you why. But then you will see it for yourself, much the same way as you see the truth of a theorem of geometry that has just been proved for you. . . . It stands to reason, therefore, that certain truths that arise out of the very structure of language may remain hidden to the native speaker, not only because of the remoteness of their connection with the linguistic rules, but simply because some of these rules themselves remain unnoticed by the speaker.[3]

One kind of *a priori* truth which arises out of the very orderliness of our reasoned use of our natural language (whatever it may happen to be)[4] is that 'mind' is not the name of any kind of entity, space or object. We have sought to transcend the subject/object duality as it affects our conceptualization of mind and other mental predicates in this work by showing how they can be employed to make intelligible statements in ordinary discourse, and by showing that if a mentalistic metaphysics were adhered to, this would entail absurdities in the ways in which such concepts could be learned and used.

Consider the similar problem that arises in the case of the concept of 'voice'. Dennett has argued, convincingly in my view, that a voice is not an organ, disposition, process, event, capacity or mere sound.[5] There is no discrete portion of the physical world that makes up a referent for the concept of 'voice' in its customary range of applications:

> We say 'I hear a voice', 'he has a tenor voice', 'you'll strain your voice' and 'I have lost my voice'. Now is a voice a thing? If so, just what thing is a voice? The voice we strain may seem to be as unproblematic a physical part of the body as the back we strain, perhaps the vocal cords; but surely one does not have tenor vocal cords or enjoy Sutherland's vocal cords, or lose one's vocal cords, and one's voice, unlike one's vocal cords, can be sent by radio across the seas and survive one's death on magnetic tape. Nor does one strain or recognize or lose any vibrations in the air or manifold of frequencies.[6]

This is an example of basic logico-grammatical analysis; it shows what concepts are relevantly related to the concept in question ('loss', 'strain', 'recognize', 'enjoy' connect with 'voice', but only 'strain' conventionally connects with 'vocal cords', etc.) and it shows how the concept of 'voice', when used in conjunction with any of these other concepts, requires different sorts of contexts for reasoned use and signals different sorts of states of affairs. It is in this way that Dennett can demonstrate his thesis that 'voice' does not function as a category on the model of label-for-object, and that it has no invariant sense across substitution instances. The case of 'mind' may be given a similar analysis. We can say: 'He has an untrained mind', where we may mean that he cannot perform intelligently on the complex tasks at issue; we can say: 'My mind is a blank', where we may mean that we cannot recall something; we can say: 'What's going on in your mind?' where we may mean to inquire as to the plans or intentions being left undisclosed but about which we may have some suspicion; and we can say: 'She lost her mind', where we may mean that she began to behave irrationally or violently. There is, in short, no point in postulating any common referential core to each use of 'mind', in the above and elsewhere. That search is idle and inappropriate. We need to examine the combinatorial tolerances for the concept and its communicative functions in various occasions of use.

The Limits of Operationalism

The principal difficulties facing attempts to operationalize the concept of mind and other mental predicates involve the preservation of the phenomena and the connection with the problems that initiated inquiry in the first place. If we define mind as a set of transformational functions operating upon input from the physical world, we have immediately set boundaries to the concept that do not match those obtaining in the world of discourse where it functions, and we can end up specifying properties and relations between our own theoretical artefacts without knowing how our specifications correspond to the sense of the concept with which we began. We can invent ways of simplifying the meanings and/or conventional extensions of mental concepts, but only at the cost of losing sight of their rich, original senses and sense-related difficulties. We can end up solving nothing when we redefine our subject matter so as to facilitate a pre-ordained way of thinking and investigating. In this collection, I try to minimize the stipulative aspects of inquiry, and this means that some 'problems' will be found to have been problems only for a misguided method of conceiving of the phenomena, whereas some of the things I see as problems may be thought of as unproblematic if the stipulative approach is sustained. The abandonment of operationalism in this area entails the abandonment of traditional orders of problems (an abandonment based upon detailed argument, however) and the institution of different problems in their place.

Just as the operationalist is sometimes charged with removing his inquiry away from the problem-area that inspired it (a charge which is clearly unjust for *some* orders of operationalization), so also is it charged that much ordinary-language analysis amounts to no more than an inquiry into words, not into the world. However, it is always possible to transform the material mode of discourse (e.g. 'What is a table?') into the formal mode of discourse (e.g. 'What is the meaning of the concept of "table"?'); the so-called 'semantic transformation' of 'ontological problems' is made viable by the simple observation that the concepts we have provide for us what there really is (and isn't) in the universe. That we can change and develop concepts only makes the task a continuing one of explication and analysis. However, for the most part, our mental concepts remain fairly constant, and although attempts at innovation are made, only some are sustained intelligibly, and those are the ones which genuinely extend upon the bedrock of logical uses already available for thinking about mind (and the rest) in the first place. Pseudo-innovations are conceptual constructions which either (i) violate the logical grammar of available concepts and/or (ii) presuppose a version of some concept or concepts which subverts the newly 'innovated' claims. I believe that Chomsky's account of reading falls under the first error-category, whilst Smart's mind/brain identity hypothesis falls under the second. There are, in fact, very few genuine conceptual innovations in the non-biological human sciences that are not guilty of misconstruing the conceptual structures of key categories. However, since I must argue this in detail in connection with some actual work, I shall postpone discussion until then.

It is my belief that most of the puzzles, problems and confusions about mind, subjectivity and associated concepts in sociology and social psychology have derived from the attempt to impose a logically inappropriate methodological and explanatory program onto the subject matter of the field. (This holds also for behaviorist psychology, which I treat as the other side of the mentalist coin.) In so far as social scientists conceive of their enterprize as one of furnishing generalized sorts of explanations for social actions, collective phenomena and historical developments, they have necessarily been constrained to work with distorted and over-simplified models of the relationship between consciousness and social context. Although this issue is addressed in my first, second and sixth essays most directly, it informs the bulk of the arguments presented in the collection which, together, point toward a different direction for analytical work, one which would be more consistent with the explicated conceptual structures of mental predicates. I should note here that any criticism, implied and direct, of positivistic sociological thought holds also for its Marxist variety, *except* in so far as Marxist analysis ceases having pretensions to 'a science of history and social structure' and is self-understood to be a moral, practical form of critical reasoning (as, I believe, Marx himself was committed to, not least in his *Theses on Feuerbach*).[7]

I claim in this book to be dealing with mental or subjective phenomena, *as such*, by dealing with ordinary discourse, sometimes employing sociolinguistic data. Moreover, the thrust of these essays is to make the point that the social world and its organization of social activities is *basic* to any understanding we might derive about mental life. Real intentions, real motives, real thoughts and real understandings are social phenomena through and through, even though in various *particular* cases the negotiability of first-person mental-predicate ascriptions (avowals) remains unsettled, and sometimes people keep their thoughts, intentions, etc. to themselves. Whilst the latter has always constituted a problem for positivistic styles of investigation, I believe that it can be shown that the 'concealment' or 'non-disclosure' problem is not a problem *in principle or in practice* for the research-guiding conceptualizations proposed here, and that the concealability of thoughts, intentions and so on does not in the least undermine the argument for their genuinely sociological analyzability.

1 The Normative Accountability of Human Action

The mutual accountability of human conduct is one of the most significant features of organized social existence. Human beings can describe and explain their own and others' activities for practical purposes and in the light of a host of relevances in everyday life. This poses a dilemma for the student of the social world, a dilemma articulated by Alfred Schutz in the following terms:

> It is up to the natural scientist and to him alone to define, in accordance with the procedural rules of his science, his observational field, and to determine the facts, data, and events within it which are relevant for his problems or scientific purpose at hand. Neither are those facts and events pre-selected, nor is the observational field pre-interpreted. The world of nature, as explored by the natural scientist, does not 'mean' anything to the molecules, atoms, and electrons therein. The observational field of the social scientist, however, namely the social reality, has a specific meaning and relevance structure for the human beings living, acting, and thinking therein. By a series of common-sense constructs they have pre-selected and pre-interpreted this world which they experience as the reality of their daily lives.[1]

Speaking from within a different tradition, Peter Winch has made essentially the same point:

> ... whereas in the case of the natural scientist we have to deal with only one set of rules, namely those governing the scientist's

investigation itself, here (in the study of society) *what the sociologist is studying*, as well as his study of it, is a human activity and is therefore carried on according to rules. And it is these rules, rather than those which govern the sociologist's investigation, which specify what is to count as 'doing the same kind of thing' in relation to that kind of activity.[2]

For Winch, social relations 'exist only in and through their (people's) ideas',[3] and for Schutz, 'it is these thought objects of theirs which determine their behavior by motivating it'.[4]

Such observations render equivocal the claims of social science to be able to describe and explain human behavior with an objectivity comparable to that claimed for much of the work in the physical sciences. What relationship is there between the 'first-order' descriptive and explanatory constructions of commonsense reasoning and those of sociological inquiry? This is especially pertinent, not because sociologists are in need of ways to 'read minds' but because the actual, conventional reasonings and judgments of interacting persons are so often neglected in the functionalist, causal or 'dialectical' schemes entertained in sociology.

We need to reconsider three inter-related issues in some detail: the problem of the description of human action; the problem of causal explanations of human action, and the problem of the level of analysis of social interaction. It will be found that 'psychologism' plays no part in the proposed solutions to these problems.

Action Ascription and Individuation

The description of an action is informed, constitutively, by its circumstances of occurrence if it is to be judged adequate, and this holds for layman and sociologist alike. It is the circumstances of my verbal remarks and pacing around that make of what I am doing 'lecturing' rather than, say, 'rehearsing a speech'. It is the circumstances of my raising my hand with a glass in it which make of what I am doing 'toasting the Queen' rather than 'obeying the barman's order to finish my drink'. There can be no simple story of one-to-one mapping in which an action-description has a neat behavioral referent. The sociologist who is engaged in describing *any* activity must do so *from within* the culture; i.e. if his descriptions are to be intelligible and appropriate as action-descriptions they must be formulated with the range of action-concepts available in the shared culture and natural-language of his subjects and readers and must respect the constraints and conventions involved in constructing such descriptions available to any competent member of the culture. Sociologists have been somewhat reticent, however, to come to terms with the fact that to claim of some activity that it counts as 'doing the same kind of thing' as another activity involves much more than a simple matching operation. For example, the physical act of fellation between two adult males who have just paired off in a gay bar is not 'the same thing as' the physical act of fellation between the delinquent peer and the adult homosexual prior to an exchange of money in a tea-room.[5] Examples abound in the literature of activities charged with very different significance for the participants where the very description of the action in which they are engaged is seen as a moral issue of serious consequence. The delinquent peers of Reiss' study may accept to have their activity described as facilitating a blow-job, but would see a threat to their carefully preserved masculine self-image in the description of what they are doing as 'engaging in homosexual fellation'. Descriptive asymmetries of this sort are highly political (in the most extended sense of the term); the 'rioting behavior of a mob' iṣ often, for the members themselves, a 'political confrontation with the state power', and the 'communist agitation of pickets' is often, for the pickets, 'defending their collective-bargaining rights', and so on. The description and comparison of some course of action is very much a normative enterprise. It reaches down to the heart of moral dispute. Yet sociologists have rarely considered themselves committed to anything normative just in virtue of their descriptions of actions. They need to be reminded of the integral link between the description of an action and the contextual purpose(s) for which the description is formulated. Perhaps it will be conceded that 'elaborate' action-descriptions run the risk of concealed normative position-taking, but surely there is a level of action-description which escapes this difficulty? The fault here is to think that *any* description of human activity can be (a) context-free and (b) incorrigible. Let us examine it more closely.

For a host of basic action concepts, the describer who employs them is unavoidably engaged in ascriptions, imputations or appraisals. It is not a logical option to cancel the commitments entailed in the various forms of description of actions. This holds even where the describer is using 'technical' categories of action-description (e.g. 'anomic suicide', 'retreatist reaction', 'negotiating responsibility' or 'sublimating the sex-drive') because the *sense* of these 'technical' categories is available to us only in the terms of 'untechnical' action concepts which they presuppose and upon which they were constructed. To employ such 'operational' or 'theory-laden' categories is not to escape the ascriptive or imputative work that ordinary action-concept usages carry with them; it merely transposes the issue to a level where it reappears in a less perspicuous form (with its attendant dangers of self-deluding 'neutrality'). We know from the large number of studies of deviance that, not only is the category of 'deviant' seriously problematic in terms of concealed normative commitments, but so also are the ascriptions of concepts such as 'suicide', 'delinquent', 'alcoholic' and 'mentally ill' to people's behavior.[6] Moreover, at the most elementary level of description, we find that we are bound to produce some ascriptions or imputations of a 'subjective' sort when we use any of a large range of action-concepts:

> ... the matter depends to a considerable extent on what sort of action we take as an example; some (of what we ordinarily call) actions are much more dependent on the actor's intentions and concepts than others. Thus, we might agree that one cannot promise without intending to promise (though we could argue even this point), but who would want to maintain that one cannot offend without intending to offend? One may have to intend to lie in order to lie, but one need not intend to deceive in order to deceive. ... The more, conversely, an action is complex, abstract, governed by social conventions, compounded out of a variety of not entirely consistent language games, the less we can ascribe it to someone lacking the relevant concept, awareness, intention.[7]

One can be described as having killed without either the concept or the intention of killing thereby also ascribed, but murder? One can be described as having escaped without the concept, intention or even awareness of escaping presupposed in the description, but flee? Douglas, Atkinson and others[8] have noted that to describe an act as a 'suicide' (and perhaps include it in a statistical count of suicides) can involve colluding with the officially-ratified ascription of suicidal intention to the person who is now dead, just as to describe someone as 'having died' in a hospital setting at a certain time is, as Sudnow has documented,[9] tacitly to collude with the judgment of official 'death-definers' in that setting. From action-descriptions as individual as 'using a bookmark' to those as broad as 'planning a campaign', intention-ascriptions are presupposed; however, as Pitkin makes clear:

> Neither intentions nor observed results are *a priori* definitive of action. Their relative roles depend very much on the situation, our interest in it, and the particular action at issue. The real point about action and intentionality is not that action can be identified only according to intention, and therefore by the actor himself; but that with respect to human action, intention and

the actor's views are always potentially relevant and must be taken into account.[10]

We do not have to accept that intentions are only identifiable by their 'owners' themselves (an argument that is clearly fallacious) to agree that in describing actions of all sorts we cannot escape—either as lay or professional analysts of activities—making commitments, taking positions, engaging in potentially argumentative observations, imputing responsibility, intention, awareness, motive and so on. To demand of any action-describer that he describe members' doings in such a way as to avoid commitments etc. is to ask that he transcend his membership of the social world and still, *per impossibile*, describe actions in recognizable ways.

Descriptions of actions in ethnographic accounts of any kind cannot have a different logical status from descriptions of actions made by ordinary participants in social settings. All such descriptions are defeasible by the course of events, and none have their objectivity vouchsafed by decontextualized criteria. Descriptive *closure* is achieved by *fiat*, where the point of closure can betray a normative preference. Perhaps we need access to people's minds in order to find there the grounds for an incorrigible action-description? Of course, this assumes that an individual is normatively entitled to be sovereign with respect to decisions on how his action is to be described: but social relations do not, could not, work like this. We often need to over-rule people's self-descriptions for a variety of practical and moral purposes, but our over-ruling is itself still a normatively committed practice. As to hoping to find 'the true description' by looking into someone's mind, the only response which this suggestion merits is that it is based upon a misconception of the concept of 'mind'. 'Mind' can be a generic term for our various abilities, dispositions and their relationships (just as 'British Constitution' is used to refer to the ways in which other things, such as Parliament, the Church, the Judicature, etc. are related together). It is not the name of a place at all. (In metaphors such as: 'I cannot get her out of my mind', the speaker hardly specifies the *location* of the girl in question.) White has remarked that the conception of minds as repositories was due to the supposed necessity of finding locations for such alleged objects as images, thoughts, memories and so on.[11] Each of these concepts has been shown to function differently from concepts belonging to our material-object language-games, and thence the problem of their 'location' has been dissipated, along with the entelechistic model of mind. Much as stage-murders do not have victims and are not murders, argued Ryle, so seeing things with one's mind's eye does not involve the existence of the things seen nor the occurrence of acts of seeing them; so no asylum is needed to accommodate them. Imagining is *as if* seeing, not real seeing in a mysterious medium.[12] Malcolm, addressing himself to the question of the 'location' of thoughts, has this to say:

> . . . is this sudden thought . . . literally inside my skull? I think that in our ordinary use of the terms 'thought' and 'thinking', we attach no meaning to the notion of determining the bodily location of a thought. We do not seriously debate whether someone's sudden thought occurred in his heart, or his throat, or his brain. Indeed, we should not know what the question meant. We should have no idea what to look for to settle this 'question' . . . Suppose we had determined, by means of some instrument, that a certain process occurred inside my skull at the exact moment I had the sudden thought about the milk bottles. How do we make the further test of whether my *thought* occurred inside my skull?[13]

Let us postpone for now the vexed question of the nature of thoughts and thinking; suffice to say, neither minds nor brains can literally be thought of as the repositories of indefeasible notions about what we are observably doing. Contrary to Steven Lukes' remark that 'neuro-physiology may be the queen of the social sciences, but her claim remains entirely speculative',[14] I would want to say that her claim must remain wholly irrelevant. Even the most sincere self-description of an action can be, in some context, defeated; undisclosed sincere self-descriptions are in a similar situation. And we should not think that an undisclosed thought has the same ontological status as an object hidden in a box, awaiting penetration by some conjectured future instrumentation of brain science.

The description of an action is an occasioned event, itself an action, undertaken for some purpose, or guided by some particular interest, which informs our judgments about its adequacy. To describe an action can be to perform what Austin called a 'speech-act'.[15] Often, the subject of the speech-act of describing is another speech-act. So, one can describe someone's complaining, thanking, asking, insulting, promising, and a host of other activities performed in and through the use of language. Like all other actions, speech-acts depend upon their context of occurrence for their possible recognition *as* complaints, excuses, insults, jokes and the rest. And, like other actions, they are ascribable independently of psychic or neurological determinations by observers. Their ascription carries commitments, implications and imputations similarly defeasible, arguable and potentially asymmetrical for the parties concerned.

At this point, the counter-argument usually turns to address itself to the question of action-*consequences* (intended, and, more especially, unintended) in the hope that *their* objective describability will be vouchsafed. (Remember that we are still without any clear understanding of the meaning of 'objectivity' in this counter-argument.) We are immediately confronted with the problem of the warrantable *individuation* of actions.

Take as an example the problem of distinguishing between the termination of an action and the commencement of its consequences in a description. An action such as murdering Jones can, under a redescription, be referred to as an action of firing a gun with the (unintended) consequence of killing Jones, where the reformulated action-description is now usable in a manoeuvre against the ascription of intention embodied in the use of the descriptor 'murder'. As Austin has remarked, 'it is very evident that the problem of excuses and those of the different descriptions of actions are throughout bound up with each other'.[16] Excuses are almost paradigmatically contestable speech-acts, so here again we are faced with a difficulty of tacit normative commitment.

There is often a range of choices available for 'splitting up' conduct into 'actions', where the purposes informing the demarcations are normative and quite unlike the purposes informing the physicist's demarcations of phenomena. Often, we have little to go on when we want to decide what counts—*in isolation* from practical purposes—as 'an', 'one' or 'the' action observed. The fruitless, abstract debate in the philosophy of action on the question of whether there can be several correct descriptions of the *same* action, or whether each of these descriptions is necessarily the description of a *different* action, glosses over the fact that in describing we are not invariantly representing connections already present in the world but we are frequently engaged in *making* connections in our description. To claim that 'X' is the same action as 'Y' can be to make a connection between them rather than simply to record a pre-existing relationship.

It should be clear that the fundamental issue in the 'scientific' description of human activities lies not in the direction of mentalistic puzzles but rather is a problem of concealed, commonsense commitments. If the preceding arguments are correct, such a 'problem' cannot be resolved in terms of the development of normatively uncontaminated action-descriptions, since the appraising character of action-descriptions is not so much a 'contaminant' as a constitutive feature. We have to abandon the attempt to purge our descriptions of this characteristic, and instead look for a different line of attack in our search for ways of studying the social world that go beyond the unacknowledged partisan accounting of that world.

The Causal Explanation of Action

So far, we have argued that the description of various actions involves appraisals which are context-bound and defeasible. Action-descriptions, in this light, hardly seem to be proper candidates for incorporation into the propositional format of a deductive-nomological scheme of explanation. For not only is it impossible to codify the circumstantiality of actions into finite lists of (antecedent) 'conditions', their negotiability in normative description renders them ineligible as 'discrete phenomena' for such lawlike explanation.

A. R. Louch, commenting upon the failure of determinate models in this area, observed:

> Both conventions and actions, except in rule-book cases, are characterized by the sort of ambiguity that would require patient observation and study to diagnose. If diagnoses are tentative, it must be remembered that behavior is often tentative; to suppose that such ambiguity cries out for scientific procedure is thus to misconstrue the kind of account that is given.[17]

One has only to examine a detailed transcription of ordinary talk in an attempt determinately to identify which speech-acts are being performed in the exchange of utterances to realize that Louch's comment is on the mark. Yet surely the explanation of actions by reference to causal antecedents is not thereby rendered *logically* impossible? Difficult, not-yet-achieved, perhaps, but logically ruled out?

Consider MacIntyre's attempt to reinstate causal explanation in sociology as a conceptually respectable undertaking (revoking his own, and Winch's, early attempts to reveal its logical fallacies in respect of actions).[18] First of all, he proposes that we begin by thinking of a case in which an agent performs an action (presumably describable in some rule-book, 'unproblematic' fashion) with several quite different reasons for performing it. 'How can he as agent know whether it was the conjoining of all the different reasons that was sufficient for him to perform the action or whether just one of the reasons was by itself sufficient or whether the action was over-determined in the sense that there were two or more reasons, each of which would by itself alone have been sufficient?' he asks.[19] From here, MacIntyre contends that we need to distinguish between the agent's having a reason for performing the action (and being aware of this reason, rather than there merely being such a reason) and the agent's actually being moved to action by his having such a reason. He goes on to claim:

> . . . *the agent's possessing a reason* may be a state of affairs identifiable independently of the event which is *the agent's performance of the action.* Thus it does seem as if the possession of a reason by an agent is an item of a suitable type to figure as a cause, or an effect. But if this is so then to ask whether it was the agent's reason that roused him to act is to ask a causal question, the true answer to which depends upon what causal generalizations we have been able to establish.[20]

This constitutes the first part of MacIntyre's series of arguments. Let us review what we have. The most striking ambiguity here is in the expression 'sufficient' applied to reasons for action. Does this mean 'sufficiently justified' in the light of group culture or does it mean 'sufficient condition' in the Humean causal sense? Presumably, given what is subsequently argued, MacIntyre is treating *the state of possessing a reason* as causally operative, and not the reason itself, so it would appear that the causal argument has not yet properly begun—nonetheless, MacIntyre's use of the expression 'over-determined' with reference to the relationship of reasons to an action seems to betray a causal commitment to reasons *per se*, and not just to the having of them. But let us proceed. The main point is that the agent's possessing a reason is to be thought of as a candidate for either a cause or an effect. Certainly, by this move MacIntyre avoids the problem of treating reasons themselves as contingent rather than logically tied to the actions they inform; he is prepared to admit that for something to count as a reason it must be logically (and hence not contingently) tied to an action (-description). Yet this shift to 'possessing' a reason is not without difficulties. He remarks:

> . . . the question inevitably arises as to whether *the possession of a given reason* may not be the cause of an action in precisely the same sense in which hypnotic suggestion may be the cause of an action.[21]

It seems clear, however, that my possessing a reason is something that others may ascribe to me; it may be said of me that I have every reason to get angry about having been insulted at the party, where this ascription of a good reason to get angry does not match anything I have ever avowed to myself. So, possessing a reason for doing something hardly constitutes a *state* in the sense in which we can speak of a hypnotic state.[22] If my having a reason is not necessarily a state of my mind, then *a fortiori* it cannot be claimed as a causally efficient state. Even in those cases in which I am well aware of a given reason *prior* to performing the action (which seems rather different from the case of hypnotic suggestion, at least in MacIntyre's description of it), how is this to be known about me? If it is to be through my avowals, then surely there is something circular going on, because the truthfulness of my avowal of the reason I have may in part be ratified by observing the action which I subsequently perform. Furthermore, where an agent avows that his reason to act 'moved' him to act, surely he is saying that he felt his reason to be *morally* compelling. Acting from moral conviction is scarcely to be paraphrased as a deterministic process.

MacIntyre moves on to consider a slightly different paradigm for the causal explanation of actions. He cites Goffman's work on total institutions[23] as furnishing support for a causal model of human action:

> Goffman concludes that the behavior of patients (in mental hospitals) is determined to a considerable degree by institutional arrangements which provide a severely limited set of possible roles both for patients and for the doctors and orderlies with whom they have to deal. Thus the behavior of individual patients of a given type might be explained as the effect of the role arrangements open to a person of this type.[24]

MacIntyre does not want this case assimilated to that of Winch's example of the 'berserk lunatic' admitted already not to follow rules and perhaps open to behavioristic explanation at some level; he notes that Goffman's findings work also for soldiers in the armed services and monks in monasteries.[25] However, what does it mean to say that the behavior of patients is 'determined' (to some degree) by limited institutional arrangements? Surely it is not the same as saying that what they actually do is causally compelled by these abstractly describable arrangements? There is, perhaps, a subtle equivocality being exploited in the use of 'determined' here. It might be agreed that the institutional arrangements (rules, practices of enforcement, etc.) determine in the sense of *set limits to what is allowed to be done*, but this is not at all the same as arguing that the arrangements themselves cause some specific conduct. They may *entitle* some kinds of activity and prohibit others, but this is to speak in a normative vocabulary, not a deterministic one. MacIntyre also claims that the patients' conduct could be explained as the *effect* of given role-arrangements in the hospital. But surely a more logically appropriate way of speaking of their conduct in this regard is to depict it as the *enactment* of some role-arrangement, again quite a different conceptualization from that expressible in a causal vocabulary.

MacIntyre's final defense of causality in the explanation of human action consists in arguing that agents may have a variety of reasons for their deviance from some rules, and yet deviate uniformly, this uniformity being independent of their reasons.[26] However, any uniformity in conduct that is independent of agents' avowed or ascribed reasons would only constitute a statistical *description* of that conduct. No one has argued, to my knowledge, that there cannot be uniformities independent of agents' reasons; what has been argued is that such uniformities cannot be used to *explain* agents' activities. (*Pace* Durkheim, one cannot move from ecological correlations to explanations of individual cases by simple inference.)

In everyday life, causal explanation *does* have a part to play. And yet the part it plays in no way signals any philosophical commitment on the part of ordinary people in explaining their own and other people's actions for practical purposes, and in no sense betrays an implicit determinism in their reasoning. Causal explanations play a part in the provision of *excuses* for conduct, but are generally absent in other contexts. (Think of remarks such as: 'I had no choice but to . . .', 'He was compelled to obey . . .', 'He caused them to change their minds by waving a gun in their faces', and so on.) Often, we say of someone that he was caused to do something in contexts where we mean that what he did was the only sensible (or right) thing to do. Occasionally, it is argued that situations of extreme threat are causally efficient in the production of certain kinds of action. But note that here we are not speaking of the sort of causal automaticity peculiar to causal accounts in the physical sciences, because we know that a proper response to a situation of extreme threat on the part of a person presupposes that he has recognized the situation *as* a threatening one. Recognition, reasoning and judgment are not properties intelligibly ascribable to the phenomena for which causal laws are formulated in classical physics, mechanics and chemistry. And from a claim that people are caused to protect themselves in recognized situations of threat one cannot extrapolate to a causal *law*; after all, some people prefer to die than yield to certain kinds of threats. All we have, then, is a rule. We would create havoc in our pre-theoretical conceptual frameworks if we sought to adopt a causal or deterministic form of reasoning for all human actions under all circumstances. What would happen to the concepts of choice, freedom, creativity, responsibility, deviance, convention, appropriateness? We cannot simply dispense with them, because they form the grounds or baseline for any serious thinking which we do in analyzing activities in the real world.

The Reasoned Character of Ordinary Actions

Substantive descriptions and explanations of most ordinary actions and courses of action which figure in ethnographic work omit systematically any reference to the organization of those actions as ongoing, reasoned achievements. The normative orientations and reciprocal analytic work on the part of acting individuals are either assumed to be irrelevant or posited as constants in causal models. Social-systems accounts of organized life rarely penetrate beyond concepts like role, value, general norm and functional contribution, to articulate anything at all about the complex reasoning and analytical competences presupposed in the activities under study. If we seek to transcend stipulations and over-simplified attributions in the analytic study of practical actions, we must alter the analytical level at which we have been working in ethnography and constructive analysis. The product of such a switch in levels would look more like a 'methodography' of action, in Zimmerman and Pollner's terms.[27] This switch would also involve the reformulation of our analytical problems. Instead of seeking to generate predictively inadequate causal models or unacknowledgedly partisan activity-ascriptions, our aim would be to work out analyses of the reasoning structures and conventional member-orientations involved in various empirically observed courses of social interaction. This is, of course, the basic approach of most ethnomethodological inquiry.

Social reality is a reality of communicative relationships. Intersubjective understandings are what constitute this reality. Such understandings are facilitated by commonsense knowledge and reasoning with their normative features. However, to sociologists immersed in studies of 'cultural variation', 'pluralism', 'subcultural organization', 'diversity in belief-systems', '*Weltanschaaungen*' and 'the differential distribution of types of knowledge and ignorance in a social system', talk of 'commonsense' of almost any kind by fellow professionals seems to incur a reaction of incredulity or dismissal. References are conjured up to such theoretically-formulated phenomena as 'finite provinces of meaning', 'epistemic collectivities', 'uneven distributions of knowledge' and so on. Commonsense knowledge of social structures becomes a chimera, a kind of non-phenomenon. Alternatively, sociologists with an unshakeable training in the scientific glosses of their enterprise sometimes react by charging trivialization or by casting students of practical reasoning into the role of the cultural conservative, as if to study the conventional methods of ordinary reasoning amounted to baptizing any layman's *substantive* opinions, prejudices, idle talk or moral convictions about matters on which sociologists have made pronouncements. So profound is the contempt which some social scientists hold for 'commonsense' that, ignoring their daily, practical experiences as participants in mundane activities, they will picture it as all of a piece with myth and legend, or as so wholly malleable as to be subject in its entirety to the arbitrary manipulations of cognitive elites who appear miraculously endowed with the capacity, extraneously, to 'impose their definitions of reality' on the comparatively powerless. Whatever we may think of the paucity of intellectual and moral resources made available to people through the mass communications media and educational systems, this rhetorical overstatement is frequently taken so literally as to inhibit any meaningful appreciation of the complex resources available to people as indeed comprising their 'commonsense'.

The aspects of what can be called 'commonsense' which interest the ethnomethodologist are those which *enable* anyone possessing it to perform their ordinary activities in ways that are recognizably appropriate, rational, intelligible, proper, correct or reasonable for all *practical* purposes. Members possessing common-sense knowledge possess the *means* whereby they can behave in orderly ways; since a part of that 'knowledge' is non-propositional and unformulated for them, we can speak of it as 'practical knowledge'—expressible in terms such as 'knowing how to . . .' in contrast to 'knowing that . . .'. For example, to borrow from Polanyi's discussion of tacit knowledge, it is clear that many people know how to ride bicycles without in the least having formulable, propositional knowledge of the geometric and ergonomic allignments involved. Expressed as a principle, a cyclist must keep his balance by adjusting the curvature of his forward path in proportion to the ratio of his unbalance over the square of his speed.[28] Clearly, knowledge of this propositional form is not available to most people who manage to keep their balance very well, just as detailed knowledge of syntactical principles is unavailable to speakers of English whose speech can nonetheless be found to accord with them. Ethnomethodologists studying the reasoned structures of ordinary activities seek to reveal, or explicate, in propositional form, much of the presupposed or tacit reasoning informing their orderly production. Thus, common-sense amounts to a set of culturally-furnished *abilities*. Such abilities constitute the doing of any mundane activity, such as transmitting information in various contexts, recommending something to someone, persuading someone about something, enumerating, grading, complaining, insulting, warning, apologizing, thanking, promising, ascribing statuses, and countless other practical actions. To say of someone that he is *able to* do such things means that he *knows how to* do them, and this practical knowledge forms the central core of what is here being described as 'commonsense knowledge of social structures'. The tie between such knowledge and mastery of natural language becomes clear when it is recognized that an overwhelming number of our ordinary, everyday activities are performed in and through *speaking*, and most of the rest presuppose linguistic abilities. To have grasped a natural language *is* to have grasped practical knowledge of more than vocabulary and word-order constraints; it is to have mastered a range of socially-required skills along with a great deal of propositional knowledge as well. The common-sense competence in which the ethnomethodologist has an interest, then, is in large measure *co-extensive* with natural-language competence; the one varies with the other insofar as they are mutually constitutive. We learn a language and common culture together and *pari passu*, and we discover, through speaking to others, where, and to what extent, that common culture of a natural language fragments and where it is sustained between us. In saying things, we partake of a system of rights, obligations and sanctions; if I say 'I know it' in most ordinary contexts I *entitle others* to make certain inferences, to draw certain conclusions, to the effect that I felt great confidence in what I was asserting.[29] And those whom I entitle are not so entitled on grounds such as common class, race, urban origin, religious conviction, political persuasion and many other varying features that may divide us at other levels and in other ways; they are entitled solely in virtue of their command of and participation in the *same* natural language. There is, then, a kind of solidarity built into the orderly functioning of talk which goes beyond a basic commonality of syntax and vocabulary sufficient for minimal comprehension: there is a solidarity in the organization of speaking, in the monitoring of presupposition, in the inference-tickets I write with my words, wherever and whenever mutually intelligible and orderly communication is taking place. Asymmetries are always possible here, but they cannot be the rule.

The conventional sociologist of culture may still be feeling some unease; nothing has been said about 'technical' language-use, specialized and esoteric ways of speaking bound up with scientific, medical, religious, technological and other differentiated forms of discourse. Surely, the argument could run, here we have variations directly pertinent to the issue, and some of them quite extreme variations at that. However, before we get carried away with a rhetoric of 'discrete languages' (e.g. 'the language of science'), let us remember that those who have come to command technical and other 'esoteric' linguistic resources had to acquire their command from a position of *ordinary*-language competence, and can only transmit their technical resources to the uninitiated, can only teach and train novices, students and lay persons generally, by translating back into the structure of ordinary idiom, into the pre-existing terms of the natural-language (which was how *their* teachers taught *them*). An unteachable expression is without sense; the intertranslatability of the technical *metier* and the untechnical resources of ordinary language is rather too often forgotten by those who would treat science, for instance, as a wholly autonomous domain of knowledge and practice. Everyday language-use remains the bedrock for meaningful reasoning.

I noted earlier that, in analyzing social reality (a reality of communicative interactions) we have to find some way of transcending the unacknowledged partisanship of our substantive descriptions and explanations of empirical courses of action. We need to locate a different level at which to work. It seems to me that the study of the abstract structures of reasoning and presupposition informing ordinary communicative interaction offers the most generative promise for a sociology free of internally-generated normative commitments. Instead of using our commonsense with its irremediably normative features as an unacknowledged resource for studying the social world, we can now begin to study commonsense itself as constitutive of the construction of that world by all of us. Now, to be sure, this enterprize will itself be made possible by the use of and reliance upon forms of practical reasoning and commonsense knowledge, but wherever possible such resources can be explicated; the fact that residual features of such explications will not themselves be explicated does not so much constitute a theoretical difficulty as a practical one, having to do with exigencies of time and the limits to analytical patience and competence. Using practical reasoning to explicate practical reasoning is no more of a regress than using one's natural language to formulate features of that same natural language or than using precision tools to make precision tools.[30]

Analytical work of this sort makes use of transcribed recordings of naturally occurring social interaction as its data base. This provides for the reproducibility of empirical observations, and facilitates competing analyses of reasoning structures, whilst also neutralizing the 'commitments' implicit in the first-order commonsense readings of the data. Since 'what is going on', 'what the parties are doing, speaking about, etc.' are subject to descriptive variation, the benefit of presenting transcriptions is that the analyst's unavoidably committed rendition of the data into commonsense categories can be scrutinized in the light of the transcription. Wherever a different characterization of such data is to be preferred, then some different reasoning structure must be worked out commensurate with the newly-constituted data. Perhaps, indeed, the term 'data' should be used to refer not just to the transcribed record, but to the transcription-plus-first-order-characterization.

Nothing in this program commits us to a view of human conduct as beyond the categories of the public, social world; reasoning structures are *cultural* and the abstract categories of ethnomethodology consist in categories alien to psychologism. There are no 'egos', no irreducible 'impulses', no 'subjective meanings', no 'interior states', no individualizing ontology and no interest in the 'private domain', whatever that could mean. There is no *uncontrolled* intuiting, even though the exercise of commonsense, reasoned intuition forms a necessary first-order step toward getting analysis off the ground. There is no stipulation about 'the real course of events'; only modal specifications. The normative character of committed activity descriptions does not interfere in unrecognized ways with the analytic work, because the aim of analysis here is not to *settle* the matter of who is right about what is going on, nor to ascribe grounds or 'causes' to actions or types of activity, and certainly not to collect up and get on record the (often transient) perspectives of participants. The goal is to locate what appear to be conventional presuppositions and member-orientations informing the construction of courses of action commonsensically depicted, where to change the depiction sets a new task for the analyst. Divergent intuitions are not, however, an omnipresent problem for ethnomethodology, as can be shown by the increasingly cumulative and consensual regard for various analyses already effected. Moreover, divergencies have to be *argued for*; arbitrary attempts to multiply descriptive variations for transcribed materials simply are not fertile intellectual exercises. We have here an art, but a disciplined one.

The notion of 'conventional procedure of reasoning', or 'conventional presupposition', is clearly not identical to the idea of invariant rules of action. Conventionality and contextual variation are two sides of the same conceptual coin. It is recognized that the sense of utterances and actions is *indexical*—varying with contextual particulars—but this does not mean that each and every utterance or action has a *unique* sense (although obviously many *will* have a sense unique to one context of production). What is being noticed by the use of the concept of indexicality is the failure of context-insensitive, invariant models for the treatment of conduct generally. It is not being claimed that there are no 'trans-situational meanings', if this means that the same utterance or action cannot be understood in the same way in more than one situation. Rather, the point being stressed is that the occasionality, defeasibility and negotiability of understandings, of the 'sense' of utterances and actions, are ignored in methodological procedures predicated upon seeing strict equivalences between such utterances and actions (e.g. questionnaires, interview schedules) and in theoretical models postulating causal explanations of social conduct. Any questionnaire or interview format encodes responses and enables them to be extracted from their occasions for purposes of summary codification and tabulation. The imposition of measures presupposing the equivalence of sense and closure between answers to questions is achieved by *fiat*.[31] There is no room for logical modalities and indeterminacies here. Cicourel's discussion of the many difficulties and unfounded claims for such conventional methodologies remains unanswered by their users, except for attempts to remedy the situation, as in Goldthorpe's recent comment upon the need for 'pilot' studies to check for the 'degree of indexicality' of utterances coded in questionnaires.[32] To what extent such studies could be undertaken (and how), remains unresolved. And the vexed question about the sort of inferences that could be made on the basis of questionnaires constructed with such caveats has not even been raised.

Perhaps I should anticipate some objections at this point. It will doubtless be noted that there is no clear consensus on these matters within the practice of ethnomethodology (even though I believe that one is emerging), and that a school of such heterogeneity cannot constitute an alternative 'paradigm' for sociological work. I do not find these objections interesting, if only because they do not confront the epistemological issues raised but seek to deflect them onto concerns for the social-organizational structure of ethnomethodological practices. A more serious objection will relate to the question of verification or falsification of whatever analytical propositions are made within studies of the reasoned structures of action. It is not at all clear what 'correctness' or 'refutation' means in an ethnomethodological context (just as in the context of transformational-generative linguistics). I take it that there cannot be any decontextualized rules of adequacy here, and it is in this sense that we speak of an 'art' (perhaps an exact art). The work of explicating conventional presuppositions and reasoning structures in interpersonal communication appears to proceed quite well without our worrying too much about the applicability of these concepts to the enterprize. A sound piece of analysis seems to be one that renders transparent some aspects of reasoning and communication in a logically coherent and parsimonious manner for some materials. Discerning connections and conventions hitherto known-but-unnoticed, oriented-to but inexplicit, is a matter of observational acuity and conceptual skill, neither of which can be made available in formulaic terms.

Normative Depiction and Analytical Explication: An Example of the Contrast

In order to illustrate concretely the sort of analytical level being proposed here by way of contrast to the substantive and normative description usually found in ethnographic work, let us consider some data and its analysis. The following transcription was made from a recording *in situ* of the opening and development of an attempt by a mental health social worker to effect an admission order on a man of about 40 years:

1 *Mental Welfare Officer* (hence: MWO)—opening the conversation: Dr ... Dr K. asked us to call ... to take you to hospital

2 *Prospective Patient* (hence: PP): Err ... I'm all right as I am.

3 *MWO*: You know Dr K. and Dr S. that saw you last night—

4 *Patient's Wife* (hence: PW): —Yes—

5 *MWO*: —they want you to go up this afternoon, and they've asked us to call... we've got the car with us, you know—

6 *PP*: —Aah, I, I'll make it in me own time// if you don't mind

7 *PW*: //ya can't make it in yer own time

8 *PP*: Course I can. (Pause of 1.5 secs.)

9 *MWO*: Err, well, you know, I mean Dr K.'s quite busy and he's made an appointment for you this afternoon at the hospital// ( )

10 *PW*: //no harm to go and see him is there?// ( )

11 *PP*: //no, I-I'd rather go on me own I ... I

12 *MWO*: Won't take us long down the motorway in the car ... go up the M55. Be there in no time.

13 *PP*: Nah I'll remain as I am (Pause of 2.0 secs.)

14 *PW*: Ya can't remain as y'are ya gotta see the doctor ...

(*Transcription conventions*: (i) ... indicates pause in talk of no more than 0.5 secs. (ii) — indicates point of interruption. (iii) // indicates point at which an overlap commences. (iv) ( ) indicates word, phrase or other vocable not recoverable for transcription due to inaudibility on the tape.)

At first, it seemed possible to gloss this data as it stood by invoking Goffman's notion of the 'betrayal funnel' to describe the typical course of the pre-patient phase of the career of someone subjected to mental-hospitalization procedures. Goffman elucidated this conception as follows:

Passage from person to patient may be effected through a series of linked stages, each managed by a different agent. While each stage tends to bring a sharp decrease in adult free status, each agent may try to maintain the fiction that no further decrease will occur. ... Further, through words, cues, and gestures, the pre-patient is implicitly asked by the current agent to join with him in sustaining a running line of polite small talk that tactfully avoids the administrative facts of the situation, becoming, with each stage, progressively more at odds with these facts. ...[33]

A cursory inspection of the data presented above would enable a reader to locate collusion on the part of the pre-patient's wife with the mental welfare officer, an avoidance of the actual facts of the situation on the part of them both facilitated by euphemisms such as 'he's made an appointment for you this afternoon', and the wife's 'no harm to go and see him is there?', and the cumulative effect of such euphemistic deceptions in assuring the patient that no further decrease in his adult free status will occur on keeping the appointment. Goffman's notion of the 'betrayal funnel' seems to work reasonably well in covering this case. Notice, however, that it works only if we presuppose a normative commitment to the assumed perspective of the pre-patient here. *He* may be thought of as the one being 'betrayed' by his wife and the mental welfare officer, whereas to the wife there is no betrayal, perhaps, but only kindness and tact, and for the officer there is only deceptive persuasion used to avoid forcible admission under the auspices of the preference to secure an *informal* admission wherever possible. To see in the interaction the operation of a betrayal of the pre-patient is to commit oneself to a way of looking which is differentially sensitive to one possible perspective of the participants to the exclusion of others. It is an ironic formulation, rather than a methodologically controlled attempt to explicate the organizational structure and reasoning conventions that inform the conduct of the encounter.

Let us attempt to provide a normatively uncommitted or disinterested analysis of this material. It will be immediately obvious that we are at once shifting the focus away from the substantive appraisal of the situation and towards more abstract concerns.

Initially, we can observe that such a sequence of communicative interaction operates at more than one level of member-orientation. Speaker-hearers are not only necessarily engaged in grasping the meanings of the words spoken, but in orienting to each other's word-strings as utterances that constitute discourse slots or 'turns at talk'. Moreover, the interlocutors orient to the perceived illocutionary force of each other's utterances;[34] that is, they analyze them into *actions* and monitor those actions for their discourse-sequential implicativeness.[35]

A basic sort of sequential implicativeness of illocutionary utterances that has been described in the literature on conversational organization is that of 'adjacency positioning'.[36] Various utterances that can be analyzed into actions (e.g. questions, complaints, invitations, warnings, requests, etc.) occasion, or make appropriate, immediately subsequent utterances on the part of the hearer (thus selected as next-speaker) that are analyzeable as belonging to some group of alternative classes of next-utterance. For example, if speaker A makes an offer, then speaker B, the intended recipient/hearer of the offer, can do an acceptance or rejection in the immediately ensuing 'turn at talk', where the acceptance or rejection is hearable as such by tying to the offer just heard as made. Further, the absence of a standardized next-utterance-type as an appropriate second-part to the first-part of an adjacency-pair can be found to constitute a 'noticeable absence' (as when a question gets no answer in the immediately subsequent slot, or, more strongly, when a greeting gets no return-greeting in circumstances entitling both). Sometimes, a sub-sequence may be inserted or 'embedded' into an adjacency pair that preserves the pairing organization, as in a structure like:

A: Want to go to the movies? — Q¹
B: What time? — Q²
A: Starts at eight. — A²
B: Sure, let's go. — A¹

Such 'insertion sequences' are familiar enough;[37] but note that the structure is extendable according to constraints upon patience and memory. Further, we noted that the second-part of an adjacency-pair might be drawn (preferredly) from some group of alternative classes of relevant next-utterance. This is because an offer, say, or an invitation, can occasion *either* acceptance *or* rejection, and a complaint can occasion *either* a negative response *or* a positive one (e.g. denial, or excuse or apology).

With this simple apparatus in mind, let us turn back to the data presented on p. 26. Notice that utterance 1 could be considered, from the standpoint of an exclusive concern with form, or with the propositional functions of talk, as an informational statement or simple declarative. As such, it might be thought to occasion as its return-utterance something like an acknowledgement or a question about it. It gets, however, utterance 2 which might, also taken purely in terms of form, appear to be an unsolicited personal-state disclosure. Seen in these ways, utterances 1 and 2 might start to look quite bizarre conceived as a pair: informational-declarative/personal-state disclosure. We should not, I take it, be content with that way of hearing these two utterances and their possible relationship to each other. And I would argue that our discontent is not purely a function of our prior knowledge of the category-auspices of the speakers (that the first speaker is a mental welfare officer and the second speaker is a prospective patient). In fact, it may be claimed that the utterances-in-sequence themselves, detached from such category-knowledge, constitute sufficient grounds for dismissing the purely formal hearing as totally inadequate. For it is surely implausible to maintain that wherever an informational statement is made and no personal-state disclosure is subsequently offered by the hearer, *that* could be a noticeable absence? We should at least try to see whether or not we can assimilate these utterances-in-sequence to some more reasoned adjacency-pair formulation before we give up on that structural description.

It seems clear that utterances 1 and 2 might more defensibly be thought of as instantiating the adjacency-pair of offer/rejection. The pre-patient's 'Err . . . I'm all right as I am' can be heard to reject the offer of the lift to the hospital, where it seems to *constitute* the first utterance as having been an offer. The pre-patient's rejection in utterance 2 is formulated in such a way as to supply within itself a possible reason for rejecting the offer just heard as made. It seems to be a feature of rejections-of-offers that they can take the form of informational disclosures (assertions) that work to reject the offer at the level of *presupposition*. Take the following case:

A: Need a lift home?
B: My car's right outside.

Rejections-of-offers that work at the level of presupposition, then, can qualify as *candidate pre-closings* of either a topic or a whole conversation.[38] Rejections of offers that work at the level of assertion, by contrast, can leave open the possibility for the initiator of the offer to inquire about the reason(s) for the rejection, thus continuing the topic of the offer by binding the one rejecting it to furnish his grounds. So, we have in utterance 2 an adjacency-pair second-part operating, due to its topic-sensitivity, as a candidate pre-closing of the conversation, or as minimally some kind of *unit-closure device*.

Utterances 3 and 5 (interrupted by utterance 4, the wife's 'Yes') together constitute a partial-repetition tying back to utterance 1, with some expansion after a possible turn-transition point with 'we've got the car with us, you know—'. I shall treat utterances 3 and 5 as one turn-at-talk by the MWO, and as constituting a repeat of the original offer. It is significant that, when the second utterance produced after what can be heard as the first-part of an adjacency-pair somehow fails in its acceptability or appropriateness, the producer of the first-pair-part is faced with a conventionally restricted set of alternatives for repairing the situation. He can choose to treat the second utterance as the product of *error* (e.g.

mishearing, not hearing, misunderstanding, not understanding) or as itself an *intentional action* (e.g. joking, ignoring, snubbing, being facetious, being pompous, etc.). In the case of full and partial repetition, the producer of the repetition of his first utterances *can make out that* the second speaker did not hear properly what had been said, or misunderstood it in some way, even though the producer of the repetition may suspect that the return utterance was in fact produced quite intentionally as a tied next-action. Take the following instance:

A: Hi! How *are* you?
B (pompously): *Pardon?*
A: How are ya doing these days?

We can deal with return-insults to our opening utterances by treating them as the product of mishearing, misunderstanding, etc., trading upon this systematic possibility for dealing with unacceptable returns. And, as the above fragment shows, when the second utterance cannot be heard to fit in any sense as an appropriate or acceptable second-pair-part, the repair preference may be to repeat the first-pair-part (here, the greeting) with some expansion or reformulation.

Utterance 5 in our transcription, then, completes utterance 3 as a single turn-at-talk which works to expand and partly reformulate utterance 1 to which it thereby ties. We can characterize it as something like a repeat-offer, occasioned by the unacceptability of the pre-patient's rejection but avoiding any direct challenge to that unacceptable rejection. As a repeat-offer, utterance 3–5 again occasions acceptance or rejection as an appropriate next-action on the part of its intended recipient, the pre-patient. In this way, it works to *recycle* the opening of the conversation which, from the standpoint of the MWO, failed to generate an acceptable return from the pre-patient. (Although it cannot be determined from this data alone, nor from ordinary intuitions, it should be noted that MWOs operate with a preference for converting an involuntary admission to mental hospital into a voluntary (or informal) self-admission by the pre-patient wherever possible. In this light, we can discern some discourse-independent grounds for the MWO's recycling of his offer, since he treats it as an offer that cannot ultimately be refused, but as one which nevertheless should be couched *as* an offer rather than, e.g., an order. Nonetheless, we cannot derive analytical propositions of an abstract order by importing such uncontrolled contextual information into the analysis; hence the parentheses around this comment.)

The pre-patient's utterance 6 again seems to reject the (reformulated) offer of utterance 5, but this rejection is a rather different sort of object from the one produced in his utterance 2. Here, it seems to have a *concessionary* character. ('Aah, I, I'll make it in me own time// if you don't mind'.) In this way, although declining the offer made by the officer to take him in the car, the patient orients to the *point* of the offer—his going to 'hospital'— in a positive way (although this is not taken seriously by his wife as a genuine alternative possibility, as she contradicts it with utterance 7). The patient, now orienting to his wife's remark in utterance 7, reaffirms his intention to go in utterance 8. Let us, however, focus upon the pre-patient's utterance 6.

Utterance 6, looked at as a sequential object, is an adjacency-pair second-part. It is also part of a second whole adjacency-pair of the same type as the first. Utterances 1 and 2 could be seen to comprise an adjacency-pair of offer/rejection, and utterances 3–5 and 6 as comprising another, tandem, adjacency-pair of offer/rejection. We argued that utterance 2 could also be characterized as a *unit-closing device* which, instead of accomplishing closure, provided for a recycling of the adjacency-pair it had sought to foreclose. (We indicated how this could be achieved in terms of the repair preference for repetition-tying.) Utterance 3–5 (considered as one turn-at-talk) reiterated the offer in a way provided for by the repair preference, and utterance 6 once more rejected the offer. We noted that this second rejection was concessionary.

Consider this structurally similar instance taken from a recording of parent-child conversation:

1 *Parent*: Aren't you going to take that medicine the doctor gave you?
2 *Child*: Mmm. Maybe.
3 *Parent*: You better take it, you know. (Pause of 1.5 secs.)
4 *Child*: Yeah ... when I need it.
5 *Parent*: You'll swallow it *right now*!

The child's utterance 4 here is also something like a concessionary rejection. It is also placed as a return to a recycled urging or request, and works strongly to effect closure.

Note that in the analysis so far we can see how sequential-object characterizations may be supplemented with topic-organizational characterizations (that is, notions like 'adjacency-pair part' work together with notions like 'unit-closure device'). We cannot be content purely with illocutionary concepts such as offering and warning, etc., because by themselves they do not handle the *turn-allocational component* of discourse-organization. The notion of an adjacency-pair and recycled adjacency-pair, as employed in this analysis, enable us to see how turn-allocations could have been organized. Given

that there are two structural possibilities for turn-allocation organization in multi-party conversation, namely, speaker self-selects and
current speaker selects next, it is relevant to consider how the
construction of a turn-at-talk provides for turn-allocation, and the
adjacency-pair structure does this by showing how a current speaker
can select the next.

Let us now take a different analytical perspective on the data,
still sustaining our interest in the abstract, disinterested analysis
of reasoning and member-orientation. Utterance 1 initiates some
talk, but it does so without employing either of the routine formats
for initiating a conversation—namely, the adjacency-pair of greeting/
return-greeting and the adjacency-pair of summons/answer. Sacks
has suggested that 'beginnings' which unacquainted persons initiate
and which dispense with greetings conventionally signal that the
initiating speaker does not seek to engage in a conversation as
such, but perhaps to pursue some limited practical purpose; e.g.[39]

A: D'ya have the time?
B: Sure, it's . . . ten after six.
A: Thanks. (Departs.)

It might be argued that salesmen, amongst others, *do* conventionally
initiate encounters with greetings (sometimes quite profusely!), but
note that such initial greetings typically betoken lengthy courses
of idle, preparatory conversation.[40]

The MWO's opening utterance has some additional properties.
Note that the offer takes the form of a task-announcement featuring
reference to a person (Dr K.) who is not co-present. (The full
name of the psychiatrist was, in fact, given.) It is on behalf of
this absent person that the prospective task is to be performed
by the MWO, as is clear from what he says. It is, therefore,
available that the task itself (taking the guy to the mental hospital)
has been initiated by someone *other than* the speaker (the MWO)
and that the MWO is doing someone a professional service by
performing it, or is doing a favor for the doctor, or is in some
other way *personally disinterested* in its performance as such. The
MWO's intended action is not intendedly assignable to him as
its initiating agent, and his invocation of 'Dr K.' serves to identify
himself *without direct self-reference*. Further, it may be used to achieve
a sense of *obligation* for the patient (along with the reference to
the doctor's being 'quite busy' and having 'made an appointment'
nonetheless) independent of any such orientation to the present
speaker (the MWO). Consider the MWO as a task-disclosure agent.
There are certain preferences for the disclosure of those tasks which
are believed by the disclosure agent to be courses of action that

recipients will not appreciate, desire, be interested in, or orient to in any positive way, but which nonetheless are felt by their agents to be compulsory. One preference is to seek to deceive the recipient about the nature of the task, whilst another is to introduce it in a hearably 'direct' way. The success or failure of a deception is contingent upon the adequacy of the deceiver's situated analysis of the presumed knowledge, belief and state of awareness of the recipient. Where the recipient knows, is aware of, or believes that *ABC* is the case and it is *ABC* that is to be concealed from him, then the success of the execution of the task becomes contingent upon the extent to which the recipient is prepared to 'play along'. Here, to play along with a perceived deception can be a way of initiating one's own *counter*-deception, or just to allow that the perceived deception is *legitimate* (because it avoids unpleasantness, etc.). In dealings with persons whose mental capacities are diffusely called into question and considered problematic by the disclosure-and-task-performing agent, their unpredictability and abnormality of awareness might be considered to complicate the problem, but such abnormality is typically considered incalculable. However, notice that the deception-strategy employed by the MWO in the data trades upon the reasonableness of the practice of keeping appointments (with a busy doctor), presupposing that there could be a 'reasonable response' on the part of the pre-patient. *If* we hear the MWO's invocation of 'an appointment' as euphemistic and deceptive (given the assumption that the *real* task is to effect a hospitalization order), it is nonetheless a device whose use orients to the presumed reasonableness of the hearer whose purportedly 'unreasonable' orientation to the world has prompted the hospitalization order in the first place. One cannot, therefore, argue that such a strategy is merely a 'substitute' for strategies whose effectiveness depends upon their recipients' having a sane orientation to the world, since such a device as the one employed in our data relies for its rationality upon *exactly that kind of orientation*, given that the patient is thought not to know or be aware of the real situation as the MWO conceives of it.[41]

More could be said about the data, and a different mode of individuating the illocutionary actions would naturally require a different analytic focus. But each analytical proposition entertained in the above discussion should, if adequate, illuminate *further* materials, since every particular convention or reasoning-procedure analyzed out is claimed to be available to any competent cultural member of the natural-language community and does not constitute a set of resources peculiar or unique to the MWO nor to the other participants. It is perhaps strange that 'symbolic interactionism', especially in its approaches to 'deviant behavior', has not taken seriously the problem of the tacit articulation of a standpoint involved in *any* substantive ethnographic description, and this is perhaps why the debate about whose side to take (that of the deviant or of the deviant-controller) in such ethnographic work has been so resistant to resolution within the terms of substantive ethnography. If the arguments of this chapter are sound, then such a resolution within substantive, descriptive sociology cannot be on other than a normative basis. The aim of the sort of analysis provided above is to reformulate the analytical problems in such a way that, although still tied to the concrete particulars of social interaction, they do not confuse social problems with sociological problems and they are not restricted to position-taking within the commonsense world of normative affairs.

I do not believe that there is anything in this style of work that could be thought of as committing the fallacy of psychologism, nor of idealism. The interactive orientations and reasoning-procedures analyzed out are intersubjective, socially-available resources furnished by the culture, not mentalistic elements or psychological constructions of the individual. And at no point are we being culturally 'conservative' in specifying what the culture makes available in these respects. Some of the conventional orientations located here may be transient or malleable, others less so, and some (e.g. the basic turn-allocational possibilities for conversational interaction) may be analytic to the very concept of social interaction.

In the ensuing chapters, I shall be concentrating, as noted in the Introduction, upon the analysis of the use of mental predicates as constitutive of what mind could be, seeking to demonstrate in detail that so-called 'subjective phenomena' are constituted for us by intersubjectively-shared reasoning-procedures and modalities of situated language-use (especially avowals and ascriptions). What I have sought to achieve in this chapter is a clearing of the ground, by showing that the real problems of description and explanation of human action and interaction are not psychological or mentalistic in nature, but arise due to the occasionality, defeasibility and normative negotiability of substantive descriptions of actions *and* substantive explanations of those actions. Having recognized this, and switched levels accordingly, we can now proceed to show how the mental categories (thought, understanding, intention and so on) can themselves be treated in terms of the mechanisms of social-reality production and sense-assembly in everyday, practical, commonsense affairs. At least, that is the promise of what follows.

2 Transparency of Mind: The Availability of Subjective Phenomena

'Colloquial language is a part of the human organism, and not less complicated than it.'—Wittgenstein, *Tractatus*, 4.002.

One of the prevailing tendencies in the Anglo-American philosophy of mind holds that any elucidation of mental concepts requires attention to the public conventions and social contexts of their proper use. Conceptual analysts have sought to show how the sense of such concepts must be connected to the ways in which they can be acquired by a speaker of a public language and used routinely in communicative situations. In displaying the logical grammar of our mental concepts (the occasions and modalities of their employment), analysts typically furnish examples of mundane social situations from which such concepts obtain their various senses and (which is the same thing) within which they have a part to play. When considered in abstraction from specific circumstances and forms of conduct, the so-called 'psychological phenomena' of understanding, intending, thinking, believing, hoping, expecting and others can so easily be pictured in theoretic reflection as purely inner states or processes.

Early behaviorism constituted an over-reaction to the frightening idea of a psychology programmatically committed to the formulation of laws putatively governing these 'inner mental states and processes', these intangible, private activities and states of mind. That mentalist presuppositions were being tacitly shared was evident from the

35

ways in which the behaviorist 'rejection' of mentalism was articulated. In the early proposals of the behaviorist program, the focus was restricted to the physical behavior of organisms on the grounds that mental phenomena are 'unobservable', except perhaps by individuals introspecting them in uncontrolled ways. More recently, the position adopted by behaviorists depicts the mental states and processes postulated by mentalists as the unscientific, pseudo-explanatory fictions of the layman. Neither position laid mentalism to rest. The attempt to describe and explain human conduct without recourse to mental concepts was, of course, eroded in practice even earlier than in policy, and successive 'operationalizations' of such allegedly 'inner processes' as intending, understanding, and the rest, were entertained in various ways in psychology, testifying to the persistence of a basic adherence to mentalist versions of mental concepts on the part of many psychologists and social psychologists.

The history of psychological theory in terms of its various orientations to the mental life has still to be written, and this is not the occasion to attempt it. However, the contemporary psychological scene is replete with approaches to cognition. The various perspectives within which work is being done—subjective behaviorism (e.g. Miller, Galanter and Pribram), representational-mediation theory (e.g. Osgood, Mowrer), humanistic psychology (e.g. Maslow, Rogers, MacLeod, Giorgi), mentalist linguistics (e.g. Chomsky, Katz and Fodor), computer simulationism (e.g. Schank, Colby, Abelson, Winograd) and phenomenological psychology (e.g. the work of the contributors to the *Journal of Phenomenological Psychology*)—all exhibit a considerable diversity in their concerns with, and models of, mental functionings, and newer approaches are burgeoning to compete with them.

What interests me about this theoretical ferment is the scant attention being paid to the contributions of the conceptual analysts in the philosophy of mind, which, if correct, would point to some rather different directions for empirical research into the 'psychological' and the 'subjective' than are currently dominating the field. The radical critique of both mentalist *and* behaviorist conceptions of 'psychological phenomena' offered by linguistic philosophers seems to me to lay the foundations for a *sociological* inquiry into subjectivity which would take quite distinctive directions on the basis of that critique.

First, then, I want to sketch some of the elements of the contemporary, Wittgensteinian philosophy of mind with reference to two key concepts: understanding and intending. Then, I shall proceed to examine some of the problems which have arisen when the understanding of natural-language use is conceptualized in terms of mental operations. Next, I shall indicate a more appropriate style of work for the investigation of some 'psychological phenomena', drawing upon the work of ethnomethodologists. Finally, I shall outline some work which deals with mental predicates as publicly avowable and ascribable categories and category-phrases, in which the problem being posed is not mentalistic in form (e.g. how can we check the phenomenological validity of avowals, and ensure the correctness of our ascriptions, of mental predicates?) but social-organizational (e.g. how—on the basis of what culturally available reasonings and presuppositions—do members actually avow and ascribe mental predicates to one another?).

1 Telling from Conduct-and-Context: The 'Private' Becomes Public

The success enjoyed by the linguistic philosophy of mind in its demystification of mental concepts has been facilitated by a systematic attention to the logic-in-use of such concepts; i.e. to the range of permissible tasks in practical discourse which such concepts can be used to perform. Let us consider two examples of this process of demystification in operation.

Firstly, and for present purposes, most centrally, consider 'understanding'. Taken in isolation from contexts in which the word becomes applicable for practical, communicative purposes, it might easily appear to mean (or to have as its referent) some private, inner mental activity. Ryle, however, effectively demonstrated that understanding cannot be an activity (and *a fortiori* not an activity of 'the mind') because to understand, to have understanding, are *achievements*. 'Understand' is not a process-verb like 'play', but an achievement- or terminus-verb like 'win': to say of oneself, 'I understand', or of others, 'You (he, she, they) understand(s)' is generally to mark out a success-claim, and never to be describing a temporally-extended course of action. Whilst *trying to* understand is such a course of action, understanding itself is an achievement. Whilst Brown[1] and others[2] in cognitive psychology have tended to reduce understanding to the experience of a 'click of comprehension', 'it should be noticed', observed Ryle,

that there is no single nuclear performance, overt or in your head, which would determine that you had understood the argument. Even if you claimed that you had experienced a flash or click of comprehension and had actually done so, you would still withdraw your other claim to have understood the argument if you found that you could not paraphrase it, illustrate, expand, or recast it; and you would allow someone else to have understood it who could meet all examination-questions about it, but reported no click of comprehension.[3]

Ryle goes on to note that there are public, contextually-furnished *criteria* (which need not proliferate beyond what is situatedly practical and 'sufficient') which inform the *rational* avowal and ascription of understanding, and no experiential or mental process can in itself fully constitute understanding nor count as a determinate criterion.

Ryle's *Concept of Mind* was published four years earlier than Wittgenstein's revolutionary work, *Philosophical Investigations* (1953), but both men were engaged in a very similar enterprize. It is not surprising, then, to find in Wittgenstein's analysis a similar stress upon the crucial conceptual connection between 'understanding' and 'correct public display or application'. (It might be noted here that the use of 'understanding' as a term for 'sympathy' is not at issue.) For Wittgenstein, understanding was neither an action nor a process. One cannot, for instance, be given an order such as: Understand! and proceed to perform the 'activity', and one cannot locate any separate activity of understanding when one is doing something with understanding:

Say a sentence and think it; say it with understanding.—And now do not say it, and just do what you accompanied it with when you said it with understanding![4]

In Wittgenstein's analysis, whatever experiences may *accompany* a person's performances in puzzle-solving, translating, arguing etc., none of them could constitute the understanding that may be achieved:

Try not to think of understanding as a 'mental process' at all.—For *that* is the expression which confuses you . . . In the sense in which there are processes (including mental processes) which are characteristic of understanding, understanding is not itself a mental process . . .
Thus what I wanted to say was: when he suddenly knew how to go on [completing a number-series puzzle—JC], when he understood the principle, then possibly he had a special experience—and if he is asked: 'What was it? What took place when you suddenly grasped the principle?' perhaps he will describe it . . .—but for us it is *the circumstances* under which he had such an experience that justify him in saying in such a case that he understands.[5]

'Understanding', then, can mean knowing how to proceed, knowing how to use a word, instrument, map or any contextually relevant item, knowing how to behave, knowing what is to happen, and any of a vast variety of things. Wittgenstein proposes that it would be quite misleading to call someone's utterance of 'I understand' a 'description of a mental state': 'One might rather call it a "signal"; and we can judge whether it was rightly employed by what he goes on to do'.[6] The criteria for understanding, for having understood, cannot be private, inner mental or experiential states or processes, but must be *scenic*; if theorists try to contemplate the 'meaning' or fix a 'referent' for the word 'understanding' out of contexts instead of examining it, along with its other participles, as a tool or signalling device in avowals and ascriptions in common-sense discourse, they will tend to conjure up quite inappropriate and metaphysical positions about it; it will appear esoteric if disengaged from its conventional tolerances for use in public communication.

We distinguish not only between trying to understand (process) and actually understanding (achievement), but also between *thinking that* one understands and actually understanding. Since I can say, 'I understand X' and then discover that I was wrong for some particular X, my saying it cannot be *performative* in Austin's sense.[7] One cannot understand by saying 'I understand' as one can promise by saying 'I promise'. Consequently, this 'signal' may flag only a *claim* which cannot in itself suffice to *establish* that I have understood. The basic tie between actually understanding and being able to perform scenically in some way is exemplified by Malcolm:

> That a child says 'red' when a red thing and 'blue' when a blue thing is put before him is indicative of a mastery of those words *only* in conjunction with the other activities of looking, pointing, trying to get, fetching and carrying. Try to suppose that he says the right words but looks at and reaches for the wrong things. Should we be tempted to say that he has mastered the use of those words? No, indeed. The disparity between words and behavior would make us say that he does not *understand* the words . . .[8]

For some feats of understanding, more words will not suffice to justify the ascription; for other undertakings, a person's past history of successes will often be enough for us to bear in mind when appraising his claims to understand. But in *no* case would an *experiential self-description* suffice *on its own* as a proper justification of an avowal or ascription of understanding, no matter how many times such a self-description had been previously associated with one's actually having understood other things. Although we may, in our everyday affairs, relax this constraint, allowing someone's expression of a 'click of comprehension' to count as grounds for attributing understanding to him, we usually do so where we have other, independent reasons for believing that he has understood.

Understanding actions and utterances in most practical contexts of social interaction is not organized so as to permit the constant declaration of understanding and its incessant checking and testing, but is in various ways contextually provided for or displayed for practical purposes *in* conduct. We shall return to this point further on. Understanding, then, has no experiential essence, and as such cannot be treated as a noetic act of consciousness in Husserlian terms. The idea that the essence of 'understanding' can be determined by some reflective method of free variation of its constituent 'mental elements' is a wholly misguided enterprise. In contradistinction to Husserl, Wittgenstein remarks that '*Essence* is expressed by grammar'[9]—not by decontextualized speculation.

Let us consider another mental concept, again schematically. The concept of 'intention', like that of 'understanding', appears to refer simply to an inner, mental act or process prior to or accompanying an action, if it is considered in isolation from questions of logical grammar—its range of reasoned applications in commonsense discourse. Considered as a mental occurrence or as a mental act, any intention may be thought of as the exclusive province of the person who owns it, who is therefore sovereign with respect to its correct articulation. On this model, a person could intelligibly and appropriately avow any sort of intention, irrespective of the observable facts of his situation deemed relevant by others, and expect to be accorded the sole rights of disclosure. There could be no sustaining of another person's challenge such as 'You could *not* have had such an intention', since on the purely mentalist model, only the individual avowing the intention is said to have access to it. It is apparent that such a model cannot be defended. To learn the expression 'I intend' is not to learn, miraculously, to assign a label to some introspected experience—for how could one be trained to make the correct identification of his introspected percept?—but consists, rather, in learning how to perform what Austin termed a 'commissive'.[10] To declare one's intention is to perform a specific sort of illocutionary act which, like all such acts, requires appropriate 'felicity' conditions. Thus, there is a clear and crucial connection between particular sorts of intentions and particular sorts of circumstances. As Louch has noted succinctly, an avowal or denial of some intention cannot by itself defeat a situationally warrantable ascription of an intention:

We tell the man who has driven his car over a curb, up a steep bank, and down the sidewalk, thus running down a man who is blackmailing him, that his car was not out of control. Such cases lead very readily to think of intentions as 'imbedded in human customs and situations' (Wittgenstein, *Investigations*, para. 337)[11]

A description of an intention is a description of an action (an *envisaged* action), not of an experience. Avowals and ascriptions of intentions, then, are organized by, and gain their intelligibility from, not some mental divinations but from the particulars of public states of affairs. This does not amount to denying that a person can sometimes keep his intention to himself, but it *does* establish that what he is keeping to himself is only accurately describable *as* an intention (rather than, say, a yearning) on the basis of relevant facts about his situation. To refrain from disclosing one's intentions does not mean that one has tucked them away in one's mental storehouse (a metaphor sadly taken too literally by mentalism) where no-one else can ever find them, since it will often make perfect sense to say that someone *did* find out what another's undisclosed intentions were, purely on the basis of his scrutiny of relevant circumstantial detail. (Think of the husband's discovery of poisons hidden away and diary entries detailing his wife's secret preparations for the attempt on his life—all of which could amount to discovering her intention to commit murder.) And yet, what of such cases where someone appears to 'discover' his or her *real* intention; would that qualify as evidence in favor of the mentalistic model? Louch has another relevant comment which illuminates this issue:

> Of course, a person might say of himself, 'I did intend to, after all' and thus seemingly describe himself in some peculiar way. So the wife whose husband continually brings home a lady friend for coffee manages to spill coffee all over the lady's elegant dress. 'I didn't mean to', she cries in alarm, excusing her conduct. But later, especially after it happens for the third time, honest attention to circumstances might lead her to say, 'I suppose I meant to after all'.[12]

Declaring one's intention is not to engage in an incorrigible description of one's mental state, but is to commit oneself to or admit some course of action; imputing an intention (even in the face of a first-person declaration to the contrary) is not to guess at the inner workings of someone's mind but to appraise (often enough correctly) the circumstantial facts which can reveal the person's actual commitment(s). Such avowals and ascriptions are bound up with varying situations, and especially with the social allocation of responsibility and praise or blame. It therefore makes no sense to seek some general, *psychological theory* of human intentions. Theorists who treat intentions as distinguishing features of *all* human actions tend to forget that only for some actions in some contexts is it intelligible to describe them as intentional. The rational avowal and ascription of intentions have, we might say, their own *occasionality*.

There is some discussion in the work of Weber, and more extensively in the work of Schutz, of the 'intended meaning' of action. Schutz was concerned to criticize Weber's apparent disregard for the 'problems' involved in grasping the intended meaning of an action for the actor, problems which he grouped together under the heading of 'subjective' vis-a-vis 'objective' meaning. Schutz's was a peculiar confusion about the role of intentional action, and as such deserves to be unravelled separately. In his terms,

> . . . observational or direct understanding is simply the understanding we exercise in daily life in our direct relations with other people. Precisely for that reason, however, the inference from the overt behaviour to the intended meaning lying behind it is anything but a cut-and-dried matter . . . external behaviour is merely an 'indication' of the existence of subjective meaning . . .[13]

It is strange to find a phenomenologist embracing such a behavioristic conception of observational understanding. Behaviorists have notoriously tended to treat 'observation' of people's conduct as if it were merely the observation of physical movements or 'external behavior', to which something 'mental' must be/is 'added'. Such a conception naturally leads one to think of the world of human conduct dualistically, in which there are observable 'behaviors' and essentially non-observable addenda such as 'meanings', 'intentions' and the like. The passage from the observations of physical behaviors to these 'mental' elements 'lying behind' is then thought of as an *inferential* passage.

Clearly, several important notions are being misused; those of 'observation', 'intended meaning' and 'inference'. Taking observation first, there is no reason to believe that we ordinarily observe *only* physical behaviors such as bodily movements and vocal noises— we observe, rather, a whole gamut of intentional (and other kinds of) activities and discourse in daily life 'in our direct relations with other people'.[14] We do not observe some body movements or external behavior and then *infer* the sense of such occurrences; we simply see meaningful conduct in its context. And seeing meaningful conduct in its context does not entail grasping the 'intended meaning' it may have for the participants in that conduct, although where ambiguities arise we may sometimes wish to know what someone thinks he is up to where context cannot supply such information for our purposes. Indeed, there is no reason to think that people go about cognitively equipped, as it were, with the 'intended meanings' of their actions which observers must somehow infer as a precondition for the adequate description or explanation of their conduct. Usually, conventional knowledge and situational data will suffice, though there are no guarantees beyond those practically available to any ordinary observer.

There are occasions when determining only an actor's 'intended meaning' of his action will be positively misleading in terms of providing a proper account of his action. Suppose, to take the usual example in this discussion, that a man were chopping wood, intending his action to be thought of by an observer as 'gathering winter stocks for his fire', whilst actually he was letting off steam following a row with his wife. Taking the man's action as a case of stocking up for his winter fire (its 'intended meaning') would be a case of being *deceived* about its nature. It can be seen from this that we often contrast an 'intended meaning' with a genuine one in cases where to have grasped *only* the intended meaning has led us astray, has resulted in an *inaccurate* description or explanation of an action. And yet, again, very often the intended meaning of an action, as the phrase is used by Weber and Schutz, is identical with the way in which it is identified by ordinary observational procedure.

The 'problem' of subjective meaning seems to arise from the mistaken idea that the social scientific observer must somehow attain incorrigible descriptions of empirical conduct if he is to be 'objective', and this consideration has led to the further erroneous assumption, actually articulated by Schutz elsewhere, that 'strictly speaking, the actor and he alone knows what he does, why he does it, and when and where his action starts and ends'.[15] Thus, to be objective is correctly to depict the member's self-description. Yet this presupposes that the member is sovereign with respect to his avowals of intention and descriptions of his activity, whereas it is apparent that in both cases he must *live up to* the public standards and public circumstances in his self-descriptions if they are to be thought intelligible and appropriate. The world of action-description is a world of contestable assertion, defeasible claim and situated appraisal, not one of monads labelling a bare matrix of motions and noises.

It might still be argued from here that we surely must seek to know the 'intended meanings' of people's utterances in order to understand them. However, in most ordinary communicative situations, the *sense* of what I say (and do) is determinable quite independently of any of my possible intentions in saying it; if it were not, communicative interaction could not proceed in the orderly way it usually does, since we would continually be ascribing and/or avowing our communicative intentions in order to make elementary sense of another's words or speech acts and to ensure that he has grasped the sense of ours. But how could the words with which the communicative intentions are articulated themselves be understood without still *further* intention-determinations, etc. *per impossibile*? It seems necessary to postulate *con*ventions as the bases for our mutual understanding of talk and action. Even on those occasions where we (intelligibly) intend to mean one thing rather than another, we are still relying on a conventional meaning that is independent of our intention on that occasion (unless what we are doing is *giving* the word or phrase a special meaning *for* that occasion).[16]

No doubt such talk of conventions and contexts, ascriptions and avowals and scenic operations will be thought of as quasi-behavioristic. Yet classical and most contemporary behaviorism can derive no comfort from our account of 'psychological' concepts and subjectivity. This is because the observability of intentions and understanding is not reducible to the observability of special constellations of organismic behaviors *per se*. As noted earlier, the concept of observation does not need to be narrowed like this. After all, there are only rare occasions when looking at persons all I see are physical behaviors in the behaviorist's sense; for instance, when I am observing the reflex of a patient's leg on being tapped below the knee (although even this is a cultural and not a purely natural event). Rather, when I observe someone's *conduct* I do so in context, and it is *both* his conduct and the context in which it is performed that enable me to say of him that he has such-and-such an intention or that he has understood what has been said or argued about, etc.

The public criteria for 'understanding' and 'intending' are circumstantially bound and not restricted to some codified set of associated behaviors *or* experiences, as if these could be listed as a fixed set of 'conditions'; members of a culture must exercise situated judgments, must *analyze* contexts for what could *count as* criteria for proper ascription or for the ratification of an avowal in those specific cases. I emphasized this because, for Chihara and Fodor, Wittgenstein was supposed to have espoused a fundamentally behavioristic version of mental predicates: they assert, '(in learning them we learn) criterial connexions which map these terms severally onto characteristic patterns of behavior'.[17] This would presuppose an operationalistic view of the meaning of such predicates. Wittgenstein, however, held a very different view of meaning, one in which there are rules, 'but they do not form a system, and only experienced people can apply them right. Unlike calculation rules'.[18] Thus for Wittgenstein, a 'criterion' is never understood as a strict meaning-rule, but rather, as Cook has remarked, 'such details of particular cases that we would find it relevant to take notice of in our everyday life'[19] in properly ascribing mental and other predicates and in ratifying their avowal by others. Such details cannot be restricted to Chihara and Fodor's 'characteristic patterns of behavior', for, as we have indicated, the surroundings or contexts of activities will be relevantly co-criterial.

In the light of this discussion, I want to turn to consider some contemporary ideas about understanding as these emerge through work addressed to questions about natural-language understanding, and to focus upon the modern attempts to extend the Kantian idea that understanding is 'the faculty of rules'.[20]

2 Understanding Language as Rule-Following 'Mental Operations'

It is possible to contrast the prevailing assumptions of a good deal of recent thinking in psycholinguistics and cognitive psychology with the explications of subjectivity and human language-understanding to be found in philosophical discussions of the subject deriving from the thought of the later Wittgenstein. Hunter has expressed the view that Wittgenstein espoused what could be called a 'self-sufficiency' conception of the operation of natural languages, which proposes that:

> Whether in saying things meaningfully, or in understanding what other people say, or what we read, we do not need, and do not generally use, any logical or psychological paraphernalia of any kind: the words themselves are quite sufficient. We do not need to imagine a room to understand a description of a room; we do not need a sample of pain or yellowness to understand what 'pain' or 'yellow' means; we do not need to translate an expression into another expression, and we do not need to guess, or interpret, or apply rules: we understand language just as it stands.[21]

Hunter is arguing that, for Wittgenstein, requiring mental images, object samples, paraphrases, interpretations and rules is not *constitutive* of our ordinary use of, and comprehension of, language, but only occasionally (or exceptionally) appropriate or relevant to it. We are not taught language purely by explicit semantic and grammatical instructions (how could we be?), nor by strict rules, nor by anything as simple and restricted as association-conditioning, but through complex and very varied forms of training, molding, shaping, drilling, correction and so on in which the learner is active in trying things out, taking up cues, responding to his own needs and purposes by groping for linguistic articulations, and in many other ways attuning himself to produce and understand novel utterances.

By contrast, work in post-Chomskian psycholinguistics and in the artificial-intelligence approach to cognition seems to presuppose that human language-understanding is made possible—is constituted—by following rules of decoding, by employing 'inner' representations or maps, by inferential algorithms, decision procedures or other forms of what Hunter calls 'psychological paraphernalia'. This disjunction arises between the approaches largely because modern theorists in the behavioral sciences are impressed with a fact which they believe requires some formal explanation; namely, that persons learn to produce and understand well-formed utterances which they have never before encountered, an ability referred to as 'generative' or 'projective', which cannot be accounted for in the mechanical terms of behavioristic learning theory. (The same projective ability is pointed to in the area of what is called 'human pattern-recognition competence', where a finite exposure to a finite set of objects provides for the 'recognition' of a potentially infinite number of new and varied objects as all being of a certain kind.[22]) Fodor and Katz, representing this recent preoccupation with the 'projection problem', have sought to criticize the Wittgensteinian conceptions of language and meaning on the grounds that such conceptions are essentially unhelpful in coming to grips with the problem of characterizing the compositional 'mechanisms' that enable people to handle novel utterances.[23] Wittgenstein and others in his tradition focussed upon the piecemeal elucidation of the meanings of various words by looking for their situations of ordinary use and some of their combinatorial tolerances, and eschewed any attempt to formulate semantic structures or precise rules for their definition and use in the formation of possible sentences. The latter, argue Fodor and Katz, are pre-requisites for the solution of the 'novel-utterance' problem. They argue that speaker-hearers are equipped with encoding and decoding rules of a recursive sort which enable them to produce and comprehend *every* well-formed utterance. These rules are followed out of awareness throughout our discourse and comprehension; they are operative unconsciously.

No reasonable response to the Fodor-Katz argument was forthcoming from the philosophers which dealt with the 'projection problem' until Hunter outlined a variety of objections in his chapter, 'On How We Talk'.[24] Hunter argued that human speaker-hearers are not endowed with any 'system' for constructing and understanding utterances; such a 'system' explanation might work for a talking-machine, but when applied to people it gives a very misleading impression of ordinary speaking and ordinary understanding and results in the incoherent misassimilation of important conceptual distinctions. Hunter's attack centers upon the strange and abstract sense in which the question, 'How do we produce and understand new utterances?' is being asked, and he proposes that the oddness of the question is in part responsible for the inappropriateness of the explanation offered in terms of a system of encoding and decoding rules.

The question, how do we talk creatively, does not have a clear context, since where we ask how something is done we are usually *unable* to do it ourselves, and yet here the question is not asking for instruction about something we do not know how to do, since most of us can, of course, speak and understand utterances creatively. On the other hand, if the question means: how do we construct utterances that adequately express what we have to say, then it is a misleading question because 'it is never the case that there is something definite there, whose meaning is transparent to me, but which I do not know how to express, and could use advice about expressing'.[25]

The basic difficulty begins here because Fodor and Katz (and others) are not asking, how do we talk in certain specific ways, or for certain specific occasions, but how do we talk creatively at all? They answer by postulating a mental apparatus consisting of a generative system of rules. The rules are of an encoding and decoding sort. Yet clearly the notions of 'encoding' and 'decoding' are, like the initial question, not being used in their ordinary senses—we do not speak and understand by any process like encoding and decoding, as these are ordinarily understood, in our mundane social intercourse. Indeed, it is only where someone's words are wholly *unfamiliar* or immediately incomprehensible that I might seek some code by means of which to decipher their 'words' or noises.

Further, in my own case, I do not produce utterances by first having some pre-verbal thought and then consciously sift my encoding apparatus to select the appropriate word combinations for its verbal articulation. Katz, in another discussion along the same lines,[26] addresses himself to this, and so speaks of the encoding and decoding operations as 'tacit' or 'unconscious'. And yet what is tacit knowledge, other than Ryle's familiar category of 'knowing how', practical knowledge of a *non*-propositional sort? This is clearly not what Katz has in mind, since the tacit knowledge he is ascribing to speaker-hearers has propositional content—they know a system of

rules and can operate with them. Apparently, some esoteric criteria
for propositional-knowledge ascription are at work in Katz's account,
since the sort of knowledge being ascribed is neither knowledge-how-to
(skills, capacities)*nor* ordinary propositional knowledge (knowledge-of)
because no-one can articulate such knowledge of encoding and
decoding rules nor answer questions nor pass tests concerning such
'knowledge'. All they can do is talk, a slender basis for Katz
to ascribe to them this mysterious sort of 'knowledge'. Nothing
thereby could rule out any other sort of ascription to speaker-hearers;
it has no warrant, other than the purely negative (and hence
insufficient) one of claiming that all *other* competing formal accounts
of how we talk creatively seem to fail.

Katz sometimes writes as if his 'rule system' operates in the
nervous system. Confronted with the incoherence of the Chomskian
construction, 'unconscious propositional knowledge', we witness a
retreat to biology or neurophysiology. Now it becomes the central
nervous system that is burdened with the application of, or the
following of, the encoding and decoding rules postulated in the
theory. To this, Hunter objects cogently that it falsely universalizes
what is in fact an occasional process, namely, 'arriving at what
we shall say', and falsely biologizes it as an *occurrence* in the nervous
system rather than an occasional, conscious and constructive undertaking on the part of persons. Moreover, whilst it makes sense
to say of persons that they can sometimes misapply rules, fail
to notice things, forget the relevant rule, apply it carelessly and
the like, it makes no sense whatever to predicate such errors of
the nervous system:

> The nervous system does not fail to notice things, forget to
> take certain steps, or to make certain allowances, and does not
> misapply rules: it just malfunctions.[27]

Nervous systems, like machines, may operate in regular ways;
but why, apart from metaphorical convenience, anthropomorphize
them by suggesting that they follow rules? The peculiar unintelligibil-
ity of this piece of personification is the result of ascribing the
properties of computer-like talking machines to human speaker-
hearers and then taking oneself literally. Gunderson, commenting
upon a similar ascriptive propensity within artificial-intelligence cir-
cles, has this to say:

> If I observe a design in the sand formed by the wind and
> tides it may be possible to describe the design in such a way
> that instructions in the form of a programme for a computer
> can be based on my description so that the machine will etch

a design in the sand. This does not show that the wind and tides were programmed to make a design on the sand.[28]

A recent example of a semantic theory of a natural language designed to represent speaker-hearers' actual 'underlying rules' is that of Harrison.[29] Although seeking to avoid the Katzian idealization which separated meaning from situated, practical discourse (which restricted the focus to lexical entries and selection-restriction and projection rules for the disambiguation of novel word-strings), Harrison nonetheless continued to work with a tacit-rule-following model of discourse and understanding:

> . . . the production by a learner of utterances of a given sort (statements about the presence and bodily location of pains, say) is governed by a sequentially ordered set of rules such that by following the rules in the correct sequence the learner can, when he finds himself in a situation to which this particular set of rules is applicable (that is, when he is in pain), generate an utterance appropriate to that situation, even though the utterance which is generated by following the rules on this occasion may not be one that he has ever heard uttered before . . .[30]

Harrison's cognitive 'machinery' consists in sets of instruction-sequences capable of being embedded in larger sequences that enable speaker-hearers to slot vocal noises into phases of interactional conduct in ranges of situations, where the noises are capable of serving given interests, needs or purposes.[31] Although for the most part concentrating upon the concept 'bring', Harrison encounters difficulties in keeping his machinery of 'linguistic devices' (the instruction-sequences) reasonably parsimonious, and of providing some principled grounds for distinguishing between worldly information of contextual and pragmatic sorts which he wishes to separate out, and worldly information properly included within the scope of his devices. His approach, however, is technically impressive and attempts to avoid the Chomskian narrowing of our notion of 'knowing a language'.

Nonetheless, it remains difficult to discern what *empirical* constraints enable Harrison to ascribe his linguistic devices to actual speaker-hearers or first-language learners, as if they were a part of their stock of knowledge. Harrison's instruction-sequences look like descriptions of rather mechanical steps in, e.g., looking at objects for purposes of matching, performing deletions and substitutions on standardized questions and commands, and choosing which of an array of possible words one is to articulate. We do not need to be said to *know* Harrison's descriptions in order to know how to do the things which they are (mechanical) descriptions of. He does at one point consider his sequences of instructions to be analytic descriptions of language-involving 'habits' and 'dispositions' (features of Ryle's 'knowing *how*') and not explications of a speaker-hearer's propositional knowledge (his 'knowing that . . . '), but then goes on to state that his instruction-sequences or devices are 'the rules by adherence to which he (the speaker-hearer) *produces* his linguistic performances'.[32] Learning the meaning of a word is asserted to be learning to 'operate a series of devices' for using it.[33]

Again, we can ask in what sense do we, as language-users going about our normal routines, adhere to these (or any) rules or use these devices? And again we encounter the difficulty pointed to by Gunderson—that of treating behavioral protocols as themselves constituting 'underlying knowledge'. Such protocols may be formulated as rules that *fit* observed conduct, but, as Quine has remarked,[34] there is a difference between a rule that fits and a rule that actually *guides* some behavior. Quine's distinction between fitting and guiding is the same as Wittgenstein's distinction between being in accord with and actually following (a rule, an instruction). Warnock observes:

> One could no more, I think, follow a rule of which one was unaware, than one could follow a route marked on a map which one has never seen. Of course, as I travel from Oxford to Aberystwyth, it may happen that I take the route marked, unknown to me, on your map; but in doing so I do not follow your map, nor fail to do so.[35]

It becomes hard to see how any *cognitive* claims can be made about a rule-system formulated solely as behavioral protocols and constrained by criteria of parsimony, elegance, generality, etc., which arise and vary independently of the determinable or actual state of knowledge of those to whom the rules are being imputed.

Perhaps we are dangerously close to committing the reproductive fallacy, as Pylyshyn has recently argued against Dreyfus's critique of work in artificial intelligence,[36] in which the critic asks for more than an analytic version of the phenomena, insisting that he must be provided the phenomena *themselves*. This is not what is being asked for here; the cognitive psychologist or psycholinguist is not being urged to *duplicate* the human speaker-hearer's cognitive apparatus of rules and functions. Rather, the whole notion of a cognitive apparatus of propositional rules of language and perception is being called into question. Of course, it can function adequately as a metaphor in some contexts, but our recurrent problems with the 'cognitive rule-following' model of language-use and understanding lead us back to Wittgenstein's 'ordinary linguistic self-sufficiency' conception of the functioning of talk and understanding. The *general* question, 'how is language understood by human speaker-hearers?' appears misguided and the source of epistemological confusion. Katz's mentalistic linguistics was described as a product of just such confusion.

Is there, then, any way forward for empirical studies into 'psychological' and 'subjective' phenomena that does not turn on reductionist or mentalist presuppositions? I believe that we need to reassess the analytical level at which we are working, and that we should begin by particularizing some of our problems with cognitive concepts. We should cease, as analysts, to ascribe underlying rules and other propositional knowledge to members in order to solve our substantively formulated problems. Instead, we should, as Wittgenstein remarked, take stock of the fact that members of a culture mundanely traffic in cognitive categories and predicates amongst each other, and have practical ways of making subjectivity-determinations. Can we produce formal, sociological descriptions of the orderliness of these practices?

3 Conventionally Assignable Presuppositions and Cognitive Determinations

Any master of a natural-language and common culture (any 'member') can find it possible (and can claim entitlements) to infer *more* about someone's beliefs, knowledge, intentions and understandings from his assertions than he says in them. That is, ordinary cultural members are both context-analysts and presupposition-analysts as an integral feature of their membership. As hearers, they can infer (with commonsense warrants) a great deal about another's subjective state or knowledge from what his utterances are treatable as presupposing. We rely upon presuppositional information for the adequate understanding of much ordinary talk. On occasion, it is not only what is said but where, when and by whom it is said which provides members with the basic data for presupposition-analysis as hearers in mundane situations.

Linguists have considered semantic presupposition for some time,[37] although not in terms of the present concern of this chapter. Sociologists have access, through the writings of Schutz, to the idea that social conduct is predicated upon a presupposed stock of knowledge, but again the notion has not been exploited for its relevance to the problem of subjectivity and mental states. Before showing how the notion of 'conventionally assignable presupposition' may be put to work in a sociology of cognitive phenomena, it will be necessary to illustrate it with some elementary examples.

The mutually-monitored sequencing system of conversational turn-taking is a major element furnishing the base environment of a 'context' of speaking and listening.[38] Sometimes we go wrong when we fail to *tie* or connect an utterance with what has preceded it in terms relevant to the analysis of what it hearably presupposes. Labov has a nice example of such an occasion:[39]

> *Linus*: Do you want to play with me, Violet?
> *Violet*: You're younger than me. (*Shuts the door*).
> *Linus*: (*Puzzled*): She didn't answer my question.

Linus could hear Violet's utterance as an appropriate sort of answer to his question (or request) by determining the cultural convention (that of playing only with one's peers or elders when a child) that we might grasp as presupposed by Violet's utterance. Violet's utterance can be heard *conventionally* to presuppose that children do not or should not play with those younger than themselves; that is a conventionally assignable presupposition in this instance. Moreover, Violet, in having uttered 'You're younger than me' in a response-to-question slot, can be heard *pragmatically* to have presupposed Linus' familiarity with that convention. Linus' ascribable misunderstanding could be thought of in terms of a failure in the analysis of conventional presupposition. If we wish to hold Violet in some way responsible for Linus' misunderstanding, we can speak of her pragmatic presupposition as unwarranted. Another instance of tied utterances (this time forming an adjacency-pair[40] of offer-rejection) in which the understanding of the second utterance turns upon a presupposition-analysis by the hearer would be the following:

> A: Would you like to go with me to the party at Al's place?
> B: I'm finishing my assignment.

Sequential organization, as well as speaker's assignable membership category and the occasion of speaking, constitutes a basic constraint upon assignable presuppositions. Our present interest in presuppositions, however, is not so much discourse-organizational but cognitive: they are mundanely available as sources of revelation about members' subjective states and beliefs/knowledge. Members' 'subjectivities' are not observable only through warranted avowals, but via what their utterances (their illocutionary activities) are warrantably and conventionally treatable as presupposing. A clear formulation of one aspect of this insight is provided by Sacks, who notes that:

> . . . the fact that they (members) assert **a statem**ent, and assert

it in the doing of some activity, can be informative for us (as hearers) of the status of the item they assert in their corpus of knowledge.[41]

For example, where a speaker makes some assertion as part of the doing of a complaint or an excuse, his hearer could claim that he presupposes the *truth* of that assertion. For the speaker, the very utterance of the assertion as part of performing the act of complaining or excusing may be thought of as turning (in part) on its intended truth. More narrowly, the use by a speaker of what the Kiparskys[42] have termed 'factive verbs' (e.g. 'know', 'regret', 'ignore', 'forget', 'understand', and others), along with an object-complement in a simple declarative utterance, conventionally signals his belief in the facticity of that object-complement. (E.g. under normal circumstances of sincere communication, if I say: 'He regretted having insulted her', I presuppose the belief that he did in fact insult her.) Similarly, my selection of 'who' or 'which' to characterize an animal can signal for you my belief about its humanlike qualities or lack of them.[43] In such ways, members' 'minds' become mundanely transparent to us. We are still at the beginnings of the enterprize of providing a formal description of the variety of ways in which presupposition-determinations can be made and of their relevance to commonsense, cognitive revelation.

Members can discover instances of imitation, improved competence in some area of knowledge, ideological or religious conversion and even insanity by discerning a *disjunction* (or series of disjunctions) between what is seeable as presupposed by what a member says and the state of knowledge/belief normally assignable to him or claimed by him on prior occasions. Discrepancies between avowals of attitudes and intentions etc. and what is presupposed in other utterances may also be determined. We need, as analysts, to locate the orderly bases of these achievements.

It is rather significant, I think, that we tend to treat assignable presuppositions as superior to avowals in many cases where our interest is in the disclosing of people's attitudes and beliefs. Ryle's remarks on what he terms 'disclosure by unstudied talk'[44] are pertinent here; we do not usually think of a person's (or his utterances') presuppositions as continually and consciously self-monitored, and so tend to think of them as less subject to deceptive manipulation than the contents of avowals, and thence as more likely to reveal his *real* states of mind.

Members' ways of finding out what another 'has in mind' are not usually propositionally known. Whatever these methods consist of, in any ordinary and organized practices, they will be found to have an intersubjective, cultural and conventional form, because we are dealing with *common* practices. Even where members merely consult each other as to their knowledge, beliefs, intentions, and so on, such consultations will be specifically occasioned and will constitute their own interrogative structure(s) of asking and listening in culturally-available ways. And where idiosyncracies become apparent, it should be remembered that we must employ our cultural resources to *find* some practice to be idiosyncratic. The argument here, however, emphasizes that simple consultation or avowals are not the privileged, exclusive nor even most commonplace method employed by members to determine some aspect of another's subjectivity.

Of course, members' practical determinations of other members' subjectivities have the property of defeasibility.[45] That is, they are not immune from being contested, rebutted, argued against or falsified in circumstantial ways; since they have the logical status of *ascriptions*, they likewise result in defeasible products. However, in situatedly warrantable ways, members can be 'correct' in their determinations, and so the property of defeasibility is not an *omnipresent* concern.

Nonetheless, since warrants for subjectivity-determinations are essentially situated and for-practical-purposes, analysts can have no interest in merely reproducing them as *their* findings, results, claims or technical specifications. On the contrary: analysts are not in the business of using members' ascriptive work to substitute for their analytical work; they are no more members' mouthpieces than they are telepaths. Rather, their properly sociological focus upon psychological and subjective phenomena must consist in the technical specification of the culturally available modes of inquiry which ordinary members employ to make whatever subjectivity-determinations they do make in the plethora of organizationally located occasions in which they make them. This reformulation of the problem derives from and is consistent with the ethnomethodological reformulation of the problem of social order,[46] and the Wittgensteinian insistence upon the primacy of the public world in matters of psychology.

Since relevant work on psychological-disclosure-by-presupposition (semantic, pragmatic) is undeveloped, I want to turn to consider a fully cognate area in which more work is available: the study of the conventional practices for ascribing (and avowing) mental predicates in conversation.

4   Structures in the Use of Mental Predicates

By 'mental predicates', I mean to include such categories and phrases as: motive, (mis)understanding, hallucinating, recognizing, remembering and forgetting. There is a host of others,[47] but these will suffice for purposes of summary demonstration of the way of thinking being propounded in this chapter. As we have argued, some such predicates (e.g. 'believes', 'knows') may be formulated by members on the basis of conventionally-available presupposition assignations. (Of course, such predicate-ascriptions may not actually be verbalized wherever relevantly usable.) At this point, our interest is wider than the study of disclosure-by-presupposition. Already published work (and work in progress) has dealt with other practices for making subjectivity-determinations in terms of their production procedures.

Blum and McHugh have worked out some observations on motive-talk with special reference to motive-ascription,[48] but tended to restrict themselves to logical elucidations of the permissible uses of the concept of motive in the absence of relevant data. (Data for such work would consist in transcriptions of naturally occurring, practical communicative activities.) They concentrated upon motives as one class of reasoning devices for 'making a social environment orderly and sensible',[49] insisting that motives do not operate as causes for actions nor as psychic mainsprings. In this way, they sought to elucidate what they termed the sociological 'deep structure of motives'.[50] However, a large part of their elucidation consisted in a discussion of aspects of what philosophers before them have called the 'logical grammar' of the concept—the *a priori* conditions for the intelligible applicability of the category. These include: (i) that the action being talked of in terms of its 'motive' is presupposed to be in some way 'fishy', 'odd' or deviant;[51] (ii) that the action being thought of as having some motive be one also thought of as performed by acting with theoretic awareness or with some reasoning; (iii) that a motive is a (potentially) public phenomenon such as an action, circumstance(s) and/or displayed feelings; (iv) that a motive may be cited in entitling an agent to (have) perform(ed) some specific action; (v) that a motive may be attributed to someone concretely unknown on the basis of specific sorts of scenic evidences, and so on. However, a loose way of talking occasionally leads Blum and McHugh to confuse 'motive' *per se* with 'motive-talk' and also with the grounds for motive-ascriptions, as when, for example, they state that 'motives are observers' rules'[52] where they presumably mean that motives are ascribable by observers in everyday life according to rules; and again, when they assert that 'motive is a procedure'[53] where they presumably mean that a motive-ascription is (ordinarily) based upon some situated investigatory procedure. *Articulating* a motive may be a procedure for, e.g., justifying or showing claimable entitlement(s) to have engaged in, or to be about to engage in, some course of action.

Now, knowledge of some of the standardized features of those occasions in which the concept of 'motive' is logically applicable is relevant. Yet the empirical researchers' problem can obviously only *begin* with such logical-grammatical elucidations. Their task consists, amongst other things, in specifying some of the *pre*-logical conventions of reasoning and conventions of usage informing ordinary motive-talk, including motive-ascribing and avowing. Blum and McHugh furnish only one example of such a pre-logical feature of the use of 'motive', but it is an important one. They claim that

> . . . motives depict for us how the event shows or displays a biography. Insofar as the biography and the event can be seen to be membership, this is done through the ascription of motive . . . It is through motive as a culturally available designation that the observer recovers alter's membership out of observed temporal phenomena, because motives delineate the biographical auspices of acts in situations.[54]

Motive-ascription is seen in part as a categorization problem solved for practical purposes of assembling (from a universe of possibilities) some order in the environment of acts and persons. To find that a person with a unique biography has a certain motive for a completed action can be implicitly or explicitly to bring that biography under the auspices of a particular membership-category and typification whose sense and relevance is furnished by the motive being ascribed:

> Thus, when users formulate the biography called 'husband', the relevance of which to the event 'murdered wife' is decided through a formulation of circumstances and characteristics such as jealousy, they are formulating the biography (husband) as the type of person whose jealousy could produce the event of a murdered wife.[55]

Of course, to find that the corpse is relevantly categorized as a 'wife' is to find that a consideration of possible motives can enter into the description of the event in question, since to invoke 'wife' is to make programmatically relevant the standardized relational pair-part 'husband' at the outset.[56] In selecting descriptors for events for which a motive is relevant, members may use their conceptions of ascribable motives and their linkages to ascribable biographies as preferred resources. For example, to say of a corpse that it is a 'slain gangster' rather than a 'murdered father of two' is already to invoke motive-ascription possibilities in a programmatic way. Further specifications of members' preferences in dealing with motives await detailed empirical work. Let us move on to consider another 'cognitive' category.

We have already said something about the use of the category 'understand'; little is usually said about 'misunderstandings' as potentially orderly occurrences. Sacks, in a brief consideration of the ways in which misunderstandings can arise and be attended to in conversation,[57] has proposed that one structural basis for them may lie in the inaccurate or inappropriate extraction of a hearing-rule for some utterance-in-sequence, where the sequential organization itself within which the utterance is located may be thought by participants to have generated the possibility of the misunderstanding.

Sacks gives an example of a list being developed in a conversation where the formative hearing-rule[58] which collects up its components fails to cover the last item on that list: '... I went to hear Pete Seeger, the next weekend I went to hear Joan Baez and the next weekend I went to hear Wayne Morse'. He reports that the next speaker queried who Wayne Morse could be, and, when told of his identity as a U.S. Senator, acknowledged that as obvious information and thereby displayed that his difficulty with the reference was not incurred on the basis of ignorance of the person named, but on the basis of its location at that point in the sequence of talk. The formative hearing-rule for the list's components was something like 'folk-singers' or 'entertainers', but this failed to handle the unprefaced culmination of the list with a member not identifiable as a rule-furnished list-member. Sacks proposes that other, less rigid sequential formats than lists, occurring as part of the ordinary exchange of talk, may provide for regular sorts of misunderstandings and non-understandings and specific sorts of repair-work designed to accommodate to their occurrence.

Much of Sacks' work on the organization of conversation demonstrates the relevance to co-conversationalists of *tying procedures* of various sorts, e.g., by pronomial transformations on substantives in just-prior utterances, by the adjacency-positioning of speech-acts conventionally paired together (e.g. question-answer, greeting/return-greeting, summons-answer, offer-acceptance/rejection, etc.), by utterance-completion and elaboration techniques, by precise positioning of overlaps,[59] and many other phenomena. These tying procedures enable co-conversationalists to monitor, over the course of their interaction, the ongoing understandings that are displayed and detected therein, as well as enabling them to achieve topical coherence.[60] Instead of (mis)conceiving ordinary conversational understandings as psychological acts, Sacks and his colleagues treat them as socially-produced and monitored achievements displayed through identifiable structures of linguistic performance. A member's orientation to such structures provides him with grounds for locating/ascribing *both* understandings and misunderstandings accordingly. A simple but succinct example may show how members are attentive to the sequential location of utterances as bases for understanding them, and that such a claim is not merely the analyst's stipulation.

There is a class of utterances which Schegloff and Sacks call 'misplacement markers', including such phrases as 'By the way', 'Incidentally', and the like. Of these markers, the following properties may be noted:

> (they) display an orientation by their user to the proper sequential-organizational character of a particular place in a conversation, and a recognition that an utterance that is thereby prefaced may not fit, and that recipient should not attempt to use this placement in understanding their occurrence. The display of such orientation and recognition apparently entitles the user to place an item outside its proper place.[61]

Members may inspect the sequential organization of speaking and the presence or otherwise of misplacement and other reparative devices when locating the basis for a misunderstanding. We do not immediately jump to the conclusion that a man's mind is not working properly until we can find no grounds in the public domain of talk and conduct for his failure to understand such talk and conduct.

When we *do* conclude that a man's mind is not working properly, we do not thereby necessarily conclude that he is mentally ill. I have examined elsewhere[62] some of the properties of insanity-ascriptions, and, in a recent paper,[63] I tried to show how hallucination- and delusion-ascriptions can operate as methods for dealing with unacceptable perceptual accounts. Both analyses employed data of ordinary communicative exchanges as occasions for explicating some of the conventional structures of reasoning that inform the ascription of such 'mental' predicates to persons in our culture. (Mental illnesses are not, where seriously ratified, first-person avowable states; in fact, it is customary to find them being ardently *dis*avowed.) One of the striking features of psychiatric diagnosis, in cases where a prospective patient exhibits what for the clinician are delusions, is the three-way ambiguity which arises with respect to determining whether or not hallucinations are present. Where someone articulates claims about the world as he experiences it, and such claims are hearably delusional, it can be quite unclear as to whether his perceptual account is an account of (i) an hallucinatory experience, (ii) his delusional fiction or (iii) a delusional interpretation of a genuine percept. Generally, the clinician expediently settles for an amalgam of 'delusion-and-hallucination', unless the character of the account suggests to him the possibility of (iii), in which case some minimal definitional collaboration with the patient may be possible. The categories of the functional mental illnesses and 'symptoms' operate as pragmatic accounting-schemes employed in practical affairs; they are not labels for mental entities.[64]

In concluding this schematic overview of sociological approaches to psychological phenomena, I want to show briefly how one might handle *memory*, considered now in terms of the socially organized character of recollection and forgetting.[65] It is not doubted that members can remember things by themselves (just as they can understand things when alone). However, remembering is a defeasible achievement and not purely a mental process, and certainly not reducible to 'having images of the past before the mind's eye', for this describes reverie or day-dreaming. On occasion, some image *may* be present to consciousness when one remembers something or someone, but in itself such an experience cannot be the sole criterion for remembering. To have remembered is to be *correct* about the past event, person or situation; we distinguish between actually having remembered and merely thinking that we have remembered, between remembering and being mistaken about one's images. Moreover, much remembering is achieved without any images at all (just as much understanding is achieved without any 'click of comprehension' at all). To remember is not to engage in a course of action; one can be ordered to *try* to remember, but not to remember. A person's memory can deceive him, but this does not involve remembering *incorrectly*! Note also that when we are asked, 'Do you remember . . . ?' we can often answer straightaway without any notable mental or experiential occurrence; as Ryle has remarked, a major use of 'remember' is simply to express that one has learned something and not forgotten it.[66]

Members are routinely involved in producing recollections as part of their conversational activity. Anything topicalized in discourse which requires some display of memory, some recollection, will conventionally provide for its appropriate amount of detail relative to the assignable interests and state of knowledge of speaker(s) and hearer(s). For example, a general inquiry positioned as a topic-opener such as, 'What's been happening back home?' will ordinarily not be heard as a request for a minute-by-minute report encompassing every encountered event, extending even beyond the point in time at which the questioner was himself 'back home', but will be heard instead as a request for some selective and hearer-relevant account of events. Since utterances are ordinarily constructed by orientation to the assignable state of knowledge and relevance of their prospective hearer(s)—a principle termed 'recipient design' by Sacks[67]—recollections will be found to be subject to control by such a principle. For members interacting within the practical attitude, 'selectivity' of recall cannot have the sense of merely editing from a stream of images, but takes the form of a charge or negative ascription based upon a consideration of presumed topical and known-in-common relevances. These form the seen-but-unnoticed baseline for *appropriate* editing and selection of whatever 'comes to mind'.

An articulated recollection of some kind may be informative for hearers as to what sort of knowledge the speaker is assigning to them as a basis for producing his memory-display; members operate with some broad ideas about the *kind* of detail relevant to classes of events being displayed as recalled or remembered. Disclosures of memory may be elicited as well as 'touched off' by some passing remark, and where they are elicited, various possible consequentialities of disclosure may be self-monitored more closely than in cases where they are 'touched off'.

The ties between socially appropriate recall and the ascription of knowledge and ignorance are complex: some item belonging to a (claimed) corpus of knowledge may be forgotten without impugning a claim to possession of that corpus, whilst forgetting some different item might impugn or weaken not only a specific knowledge-claim or knowledge-ascription, but one's more general status as a competent member also. Psychiatrists trade upon the conventions controlling socially competent memory when they require of incoming, referred persons that they recall what day it was yesterday, the age of the next of kin and the name of the President (amongst many other recurrent items of this sort). Conversely, recalling some item belonging to a corpus of knowledge might be heard to entitle the person to claim possession of the entire corpus, where another such item might be thought of as an isolated item. However, members appear to orient to the production of some recollected item from a corpus as a potential first-item, and operate with a conception of memory as containing networks of investigable item-connections such that the disclosure of one item of a certain kind implicates the availability of disclosures of further items. For some remembered and articulated items, it proves difficult for the recaller to disavow various 'connectable' items about which his hearers may enquire, using as their warrant commonsense knowledge of typical courses of action or event progressions. Take the following interchange:[68]

A: Do you remember the time the police chased you in your

car 'round town?

B: Yeah . . . for an hour till I hit that (　　　) wall.

A: What'd they say when they caught ya?

B: (Pause) Don't remember . . .

A: Aw, *c'mon*!

There are certain things which members are normatively expected to be able to remember, whilst there are things which members are normatively entitled to claim to have forgotten. One could refer to the latter events and experiences in terms of 'privileged forgettings'. Whereas to forget an appointment, anniversary and such events may be thought of as a moral rather than cognitive failure, a case of a trauma, psychotic episode or other grievous life circumstance can be permissibly, even preferredly, 'forgotten' irrespective of its *actually* being forgotten. Indeed, there is some evidence that sustaining a claim to have forgotten one's mental illness is conventionally treated by peers as evidence of more complete recovery from it.[69]

These observations about the socially organized character of recollection and forgetting are preliminary and intended as suggestions for further looking and more detailed specification or correction. They do show, however, that a particularly *sociological* treatment of memory may be possible. To reiterate an earlier point, our interest need not be in 'underlying' rules or structures putatively 'in the mind', but in public displays of psychological phenomena and subjectivity-determinations as socially-organized accomplishments. It would be a retrograde step to attribute the properties of such social phenomena to individuals' minds; the reorientation proposed here involves attributing the properties of mental-predicate ascriptions and avowals to the culture, not to minds. If it is argued that cultural knowledge is stored in minds, that should be treated as a harmless metaphor *unless* it is taken to mean that we cannot have researchable access to it, or that such knowledge is 'stored' in some propositional form, or that all members have equivalent cultural competences.

Conclusion

This chapter has sought to characterize, and expand upon, the promise of some contemporary thinking in the philosophy of mind. In the first section, two problematic concepts were examined—'understanding' and 'intention'—from which it was argued that neither can intelligibly be construed as having simple, 'mental referents' (either as states or processes) and that neither can be construed in purely behavioristic terms. Problems in the conceptualization of 'intended meaning' in interpretive sociology and in the conceptualization of natural-language understanding in cognitive psychology and psycholinguistics were unravelled and subjected to scrutiny. It was suggested that the attempt to specify a 'psychologically real' cognitive machinery of underlying rules and functions is misconceived as a serious research enterprise. (This is not at all the same as asserting that attempts to formulate a set of rules to cover some corpus of sentences or forms of conduct might prove unworkable as a technical undertaking for some purpose.) The second section dealt with some work by Fodor, Katz and Harrison accordingly.

In the third section, some different directions for the analysis of human subjectivity were sketched, and a tentative programmatic statement was advanced consistent with the explicated logic of mental concepts and with the critique of neo-mentalism in linguistic theory and cognitive psychology. This statement called for the investigation and careful description of the culturally available procedures for commonsense subjectivity-determinations and mental-predicate avowals and ascriptions in interactional situations. In the final section, some examples from current work were outlined relevant to such a perspective.

Speaking from a rather different vantage-point, G. H. Mead wrote:

> If mind is socially constituted, then the field or locus of any given individual mind must extend as far as the social activity or apparatus of social relations which constitutes it extends; and hence that field cannot be bounded by the skin of the individual organism to which it belongs.[70]

Members' practical employment of mental categories in their routine affairs testifies to the transparency of mind in the only terms that preserve the integrity and intelligibility of our reasoning—intersubjective and conventional terms. We lose our bearings when we detach our questioning about psychological phenomena from their anchorings in the mundane world of everyday interaction and its organization.

3 Deleting the Subject

The claim that human beings are endowed with *innate* knowledge of one kind or another is an ancient one. Although for many philosophers the thesis of innate knowledge was laid to rest by Locke's critique in this regard, in recent years attention has shifted to a consideration of Noam Chomsky's neo-Cartesian rationalism in cognitive psychology, arising out of his investigations into syntax.[1]

For Chomsky, 'a child is born with perfect knowledge of universal grammar, that is, with a fixed schematism that he uses . . . in acquiring languages'.[2] He adopts this position because of what he regards as discoveries in linguistics of properties of language that 'can reasonably be supposed not to have been learned'[3] in the course of normal language-acquisition on the part of children. Chomsky stresses the absence of direct grammatical instruction in childhood language-acquisition and the rapidity of its achievement, arguing that children learn by inductive procedures governed in their scope and functioning by innate principles. The most oft-quoted example which he gives to show that at least some linguistic principles are not learned, but are innate structuring principles governing what *is* learned, is the following.

Take the case of simple, interrogative transformation: 'The man is tall: is the man tall? The book is on the table: is the book on the table?' Chomsky states that children learn to effect such transformations, and can proceed to make them on longer, previously unheard sentences. However, if the children were proceeding by induction alone, then they would probably extrapolate the *wrong* general principle for such transformations. If, for instance, the child were to discern a principle of transposition in the above instances, requiring that a declarative sentence be analyzed for the first occurrence of 'is', which may then, to form a question, be shifted to the front of the sentence, such a principle would indeed handle the examples given. However, extrapolation and generalization of such a simple transposition procedure would give rise to ungrammatical constructions for various other cases. Consider the longer declarative: 'The man who is tall is in the room'. Were the child to search for the first occurrence of 'is' and transpose it to the front of the sentence, he would generate the ungrammatical construction: 'Is the man who tall is in the room?' instead of the correct interrogative: 'Is the man who is tall in the room?' Chomsky claims that *all* children (barring perhaps those with brain-damage, etc.) manage to effect the *correct* transformation on such longer strings. He argues that this must mean that the children are governed in their acquisition of linguistic knowledge in this sphere (as in many others) by a highly abstract, innate principle structuring their induction of rules. This principle, which he terms 'structure-dependence', runs as follows (for this case): Scan the simple declarative sentence and analyze it into abstract phrases; locate the first occurrence of 'is' after the first noun-phrase and then shift it to the front of the sentence. Given that all known languages contain structure-dependent operations, Chomsky argues that it could count as an innate principle governing our acquisition of linguistic knowledge (or grammatical 'competence').[4]

Chomsky's innatism is not simply a neurophysiological one; he is not just saying that children are born with a certain neurological circuitry (on the same lines as a fixed computer wiring arrangement) that delimits their possibilities of concept-formation, learning skills, perceptual potentialities and so on. He is saying also that the child is 'born with perfect knowledge of universal grammar'. (op. cit.) It is this claim which enables him to argue for an affinity with Descartes and Leibniz, and makes his position more radical and interesting than would have been the case had he remained content with a neurological-constraint thesis. For Chomsky's position is self-avowedly mentalistic.[5]

It seems at first rather strange to attribute to first-language learners such abstract knowledge and such intellectual capacities as rule-induction and hypothesis-formation. But before we unpack some of these problems, we should reconsider the examples just given purportedly favoring an innatist interpretation of language-acquisition and an innatist interpretation of the basis of human languages (at least in their deep, grammatical dimension). Searle, in a brilliant re-analysis of the declarative/interrogative transformation case just discussed, has suggested that the innatist inference derived from it is an artifact of seeing the transformation in purely syntactical terms. Searle has proposed that a more functionally-oriented communication scientist might proceed as follows. He will observe that both statement-making and question-asking are speech-acts containing subsidiary speech-acts of reference and predication, and that the same reference and predication can occur in both statements and questions.[6] From here, the functionally-oriented analyst will hypothesize that the rule *in best accord with* the child's transformational procedure in moving from 'the man is tall' to 'is the man tall?' will be: in asking a yes-no question Q corresponding to a statement S, one predicates interrogatively in Q what was predicated assertively in S, while keeping the reference constant in both Q and S. From here, the explanation of why the longer sentence 'is the man who tall is in the room?' sounds anomalous, and would be rejected, can be phrased in functionalist terms, *entirely bypassing the issue of innateness*. Given the injunction to hold the reference constant, it is clear that 'the man who tall is' cannot be a possible referring expression. The referring expression, 'the man who is tall', which appeared intact in the longer declarative sentence, *must be kept intact in the interrogative one*, and it is this which more parsimoniously accounts for the commonality of success in effecting the transformation. The same rule will handle both of Chomsky's examples, and is clearly derivable by induction alone.

Chomsky tends to understate the actual communicative functions of structured forms of talk when analyzing those structures into syntactical rules of transformational-generative grammar. He depicts the language-acquisition process as a matter of solitary data-processing and hypothesis-formation on the part of the child:

> A theory of linguistic structure ... attributes tacit knowledge of these (linguistic) universals [e.g. structure-dependence—JC] to the child. It proposes, then, that the child approaches the data with the presumption that they are drawn from a language of a certain antecedently well-defined type, his problem being to determine which of the (humanly) possible languages is that of the community in which he is placed. Language learning would be impossible unless this were the case.[7]

I have said enough already about Chomskian versions of 'tacit knowledge' in connection with the earlier discussion of the Katz-Fodor model of natural-language understanding. Suffice to say here that knowledge of something like the structure-dependence principle would have to be propositional (given that it is a *principle*), and that the notion of tacit propositional knowledge is incoherent. But consider further how Chomsky scientizes the child; he is endowed with a highly intellectual 'presumption' even before he has mastered his first language, and he is set to work on an intellectual problem of the first magnitude in selecting from all humanly *possible* languages (—is he supposed to know them all—tacitly?) the one belonging to those trying to teach him! A genuinely precocious infant, the Chomskian child is much more akin to a well-trained anthropologist at work than young Tommy down the street learning to speak. As soon as we start to conceive of children as active participants in communication situations with adults who normally encourage appropriate responses and novel, well-formed strings of words, we cease to over-intellectualize the achievement of language-acquisition. Ryle has remarked on the absence from Chomsky's accounts of this achievement any reference to terms such as 'showing, stimulating, correcting, guiding, leading, emulating' and others.[8] There is clearly a tendency in Chomsky's work to unify the manifold character of *learning*, and to see it as occurring in a single, well-defined way, rather than as consisting of families of practices and interactions occurring in very diverse contexts and for very diverse purposes (of adult *and* child).

Expressing a functionalist view consistent with that of Searle, Toulmin has argued against the current formulations of linguistic innatism.[9] Acknowledging the very stable and complex end-product that we call 'capacity to speak grammatically', Toulmin nonetheless argues that complex behavioral end-products do not require for their explanation any postulation of innate mechanisms of the same 'form' as the behavioral end-product. For example, honey-bees construct combs with cells of hexagonal cross-section, a complex behavioral end-product originally thought to require explanation in terms of some innate programming of hexagonal 'forms' into their central nervous systems. However, it transpires that the hexagonal property is a result of the bees' activities *and* the environmental energetics of their *task situation*, one that involves them in packing cells into the narrowest space which in turn assures that they will take on a hexagonal structure (due to the physics of compression in this case).[10] The conjoint structuring properties of activities and task situations must be investigated also in the case of language-acquisition and usage. Toulmin argues that grammatically-structured talk might, on the honey-bee analogy, be thought of as the expression of more general capacities 'only when set to work on appropriate external tasks'.[11] Recall Searle's re-analysis of the interrogative transformational procedure in terms of the *tasks* of questioning and preserving constant reference.

Toulmin himself remarks that a language that lacked any symbolic device to mark the *functional* distinction between what he calls 'indexical terms' (for use in drawing attention to what is being talked about) and 'descriptive terms' (for use in saying something about the subjects so indicated) would be inefficient, confusing and needlessly ambiguous. It can be argued on such grounds that we could expect to find a universal grammatical distinction between noun-phrases and verb-phrases without drawing upon evolutionary speculations about neurological inscriptions or innate mental contents.[12]

Goodman's remarks on Chomsky's notion of a mental schematism, subsisting in the mind but out of awareness, are especially trenchant. He complains: 'just what Chomsky means by "idea" is hard to determine', and asks what a 'schematism' could be, apart from systems of linguistic or other symbols used for organizing experience and which would, if 'in the mind', be propositionally known to the user. Are the universal-grammatical principles anything more than descriptions, by an observer, of the organization of speaker-output?

Chomsky's answer may be that what is in question is much more than one among alternative sets of descriptions; it is a theory that by its explanatory and predictive power may vanquish competitors and shine forth as the one and only truth about the mind. Yet even so, the theory need no more be in the minds in question than the theory of gravitation need be in bodies. And since a theory may be embodied in one language or in many languages, but can hardly exist apart from languages, how could it be in the mind prior to language?[13]

Chomsky is here depicted as in the grip of a panlogistic fallacy, similar to the one described by Karl Popper in which the question 'how can English describe the world?' is answered by, 'because the world is intrinsically British.'[14] There is no basis for ascribing the components of a theory of (speech) acquisition and behavior to the persons whose conduct forms the data base itself. What, then, could be the point of having any such theory? Now the answer would have to be, not 'to understand how the mind works' but rather, 'to understand the structures and functions of language-use'. Note that such a reformulation of the project deletes the subject and decenters the locus of inquiry, shifting it to an idealized version of 'grammatical and semantically intelligible language-use' quite independent of minds or brains. We are now dealing with an abstract structure in terms of its postulated intrinsic organization, for whose characterization we shall indeed have to draw upon our reasoned intuitions but for whose analytical description we shall no longer need to propose the existence of disembodied mental schemata. This is likely to be more readily appreciated as the 'autonomy' of syntax from semantical and pragmatical concepts (e.g. 'presupposition', 'felicity conditions', 'sequential object', etc.) is eroded, and, along with it, the distinction between 'competence' (purely linguistic knowledge) and 'performance' (features of actual language-use, including knowledge of the culture, world, situation and memory). This does not presage a return to that form of behaviorism against which Chomsky's account was developed.[15] For we need make no predications of either an S–R-reinforcement sort or of an 'unconscious' competence. We do not need to restrict ourselves to either form of conceptual stipulation. The vocabulary of dispositions, capacities, conventions and functions (understood without their customary behavioristic reductions) will suffice. The work of Searle, and Sacks, indicates this very well.

The idea of a stored-up, unsullied grammatical competence, extracted by innately rule-governed induction from a corpus of adult sentences, presupposes a model (or, as Wittgenstein would say, a 'picture') of human intelligence which does not fit well with the logical grammar of the concept of intelligence. Louch has argued that:

Intelligence is not something of which the behavior is symptomatic, something inferred from behavior, but is exhibited in the behavior, providing that one is looking at the given action, whether it be problem solving, similarity noting, inference making, or block building, from the point of view of paradigms of that kind of behavior. These are paradigms of what it is to do something well or properly. To speak of a man as intelligent is thus to describe much of his behavior as matching canons of correct procedure. *It is at once to describe and assess an agent's performance.*[16]

Intelligence, then, is not the name of a mental space or store-house, but a concept with an appraising function. It is the psychologist's fiction that construes intelligence (along with 'mind' and 'consciousness') as measurable and objectified properties of persons. To speak of 'the intelligence' as if it were a discrete mental faculty, or, in newer jargon, 'cognitive structure', is to reify into a phenomenon a concept belonging to the ordinary-language region of polymorphous categories. This takes its toll in the quite misleading claims subsequently made about the nature of mind in rationalist linguistics. I do not know what to make of assertions such as: '. . . language is both used and learned in accordance with strict principles of mental organization, largely inaccessible to introspection, but in principle, at least, open to investigation in more indirect ways'.[17] Phrases such as 'mental organization' and 'cognitive structure' seem to have been used referentially, but upon closer examination they turn out to be either metaphors for hitherto unexplicated phenomena or else just empty phrases. They do not literally describe anything physical or cultural.

Chomsky has, more recently, been quite explicit about *extending* the 'innateness hypothesis' beyond the domain of linguistic (specifically syntactic) skills (the 'language faculty', as he terms it) to include within its scope 'principles that bear on the place and role of people in a social world, the nature and conditions of work, the structure of human action, will and choice, and so on.'[18] This extension of the innateness thesis finds concrete expression during the course of a discussion of Wittgenstein's approach to the problem of mental phenomena.[19] Chomsky argues that, contrary to the view espoused in Wittgenstein's later writings, people could be said to be applying 'a tacit theory of human action' to guide their assessments and judgments about what other people are doing.[20] Taking the case of reading as an activity ascribable to people, Chomsky claims that it is possible that:

I have a (no doubt in part unconscious) theory involving the postulated mental states of humans performing certain acts such as reading, etc., which is related to my (also unconscious) system of linguistic rules in such a way that I assert that A is reading when I believe him to be in such a mental state, and my assertion is correct if my belief is correct.[21]

Leaving aside our persistent difficulties in making literal sense of the notions of 'unconscious theory' and 'unconscious system of linguistic rules', let us focus on the claim that when I say of A correctly that he is reading, then my belief about his mental state is correct. The first point to raise is that reading could hardly constitute a 'state' at all (and hence not a mental state) because it is a process. Thus, when Chomsky goes on to argue that the important question is whether or not we ascribe a 'criterial mental state' to persons when we say of them that they are reading,[22] it would have to be rephrased as a question about ascribing a 'criterial mental process'. Let us assume that this substitution is granted to us. Does the argument still make sense?

To understand the problems involved, we must recapitulate Chomsky's arguments against Wittgenstein's discussion of reading. I believe that much of the confusion arises from attempting to arrive at a short, summary version of what Wittgenstein was saying, instead of appreciating the largely negative and ramifying form of his 'therapeutic' remarks. However, since Chomsky has sought to concretize his claims for the existence of an unconscious theory of human action as guiding our action-ascriptions in the case of reading, it is necessary to outline Wittgenstein's actual sketch of the concept of reading.

Chomsky focusses on Wittgenstein's treatment in the *Blue and Brown Books*, although these were preliminary notes for the more fully developed passages in the *Philosophical Investigations*, paras. 156–71. We shall consider both, but concentrate upon the latter.

Wittgenstein takes up the question of the nature of reading as part of a larger concern with the expression 'to be guided' by something,[23] especially 'mental mechanisms'. What happens, asks Wittgenstein, when a child reads a newspaper article? His eyes glide along the printed words, he pronounces them aloud or to himself, 'but he pronounces certain words just taking their pattern in as a whole, other words he pronounces after having seen their first few letters only, others again he reads out letter by letter'.[24] We should also predicate the act of reading of this child if he had said nothing aloud or to himself whilst letting his eyes glide along the sentence(s), as long as directly afterwards he could reproduce the sentence(s) or articulate some moderately paraphrased version of them. Of course, in some circumstances, we might have evidence of his having previously read the sentence(s) in question and of his having committed them to memory. Then we might ask ourselves whether or not in the case at hand he has actually read them or just *pretended* to read them. Here, we shall perhaps be inclined to say that only the person himself knows whether he was actually reading or not, and we shall be tempted to locate the difference between the two possibilities (reading and pretending to read) in the presence of a 'conscious mental act'. However,

> . . . we must admit that as far as the reading of a particular word goes, exactly the same thing might have happened in the beginner's mind when he 'pretended' to read as what happened in the mind of the fluent reader when he read the word . . . (if the difference cannot lie) in their conscious states, then (it lies) in the unconscious regions of their minds, or in their brains. We here imagine two mechanisms, the internal working of which we can see, and this internal working is the real criterion for a person's reading or not reading. *But in fact no such mechanisms are known to us in these cases.*[25] [my italics].

Having located the source of our 'great temptation . . . to regard the conscious mental act as the only real criterion distinguishing reading from not reading',[26] Wittgenstein proceeds to undermine this temptation in a series of astute observations. He gets us to imagine the following cases:

We give someone who can read fluently a text that he never saw before. He reads it to us—but with the sensation of saying something he has learnt by heart (this might be the effect of some drug). Should we say in such a case that he was not really reading the passage? Should we here allow his sensations to count as the criterion for his reading or not reading?

Or again: Suppose that a man who is under the influence of a certain drug is presented with a series of characters (which need not belong to any existing alphabet). He utters words corresponding to the number of characters, as if they were letters, and does so with all the outward signs, and with the sensations, of reading. . . . In such a case some people would be inclined to say the man was *reading* those marks. Others, that he was not . . .[27]

Wittgenstein goes to great lengths to show that there is no necessary uniformity to cases of reading, in terms of subjective experiences or mental states. If his arguments are sound, then Chomsky's claim, that my assertion that someone is reading is correct if my belief that he is in a certain mental state is correct, must be abandoned. Let us consider some further examples, designed to back the claim that we use the word 'read' for a family of cases, employing *different* criteria for a person's reading in *different* circumstances. Wittgenstein notes that on some occasions of reading we might see printed words and say them out loud. 'But, of course, that is not all, for I might see printed words and say words out loud and still not be reading. Even if the words which I say are those which, going by an existing alphabet, are *supposed* to be read off from the printed ones.—And if you say that reading is a particular experience, then it becomes quite unimportant whether or not you read something according to some generally recognized alphabetical rule.'[28] Again, suppose that I at one time read a sentence in print and at another read it in Morse code—is the mental process really the same?[29] Can we postulate *one* particular mental process for all cases of reading? Don't we have to particularize the subjective experiences or processes according to the occasions of reading under consideration? There are transitional cases in reading in which one may repeat all or part of a text from memory, glance at a few words and take in the rest of the sentence with great attention, guess some words from context, pay attention to one's mental images in some cases and not in others, say words to oneself for some passages but not others, and so on.

. . . now just read a few sentences in print as you usually do when you are not thinking about the concept of reading; and ask yourself whether you had such experiences of unity, of being influenced and the rest, as you read.—Don't say you had them unconsciously! Nor should we be misled by the picture which suggests that these phenomena came in sight 'on closer inspection'. *If I am supposed to describe how an object looks from far off, I don't make the description more accurate by saying what can be noticed about the object on closer inspection.*[30] [my italics]

When we consider our 'ordinary' experiences of something, we should resist the temptation to build into our consideration those constituents that arise only from an extra-ordinary focus upon them. Moreover, we should resist the temptation to impute any *special* experiential element to all cases and say that, since it isn't always present to 'consciousness', then it 'must' be there *unconsciously*. This temptation only arises when we are in the grip of the fallacy that there *has* to be some common ingredient present in each case of our use of a word to refer to some activity. Feyerabend, noting the way in which Wittgenstein's arguments are incompatible with phenomenological assumptions, remarks:

How do they (the phenomenologists) know which (mental) phenomenon is the 'right' one [in their search for the 'essence' of mental concepts—JC]? They proceed from the assumption that the essence is not open to general inspection but must be discovered by some kind of analysis which proceeds from an everyday appearance. In the course of this analysis several phenomena appear. How are we to know which one of them is the phenomenon that we are looking for? And if we know the answer to this question, why then is it necessary to analyze at all?'[31]

If all that were relevant or criterial to reading were some sort of mental process, then how could we make any distinction between someone's actually reading and his merely believing that he was reading—or, how could we bar a person from making the inference that he is actually reading from his simply attending to something going on inside him? Certainly, we *may* have all sorts of experiences, mental images, 'inner' voices, and various other subjective processes taking place whilst we read (and in some cases none of these things will be present), but clearly a 'special mental process' is not what gives the concept of 'reading' its uses in ascriptions and avowals for every case. Feyerabend puts the case succinctly in the following:

It is possible that a person who is supposed to find the Mental Reading Process by introspection, being tired, should experience and describe quite unusual things while thinking all the time that the task which was set him by the psychologist is being performed by giving these descriptions. No psychologist will welcome such a result. Instead of thinking that new and illuminating facts about reading have been discovered, he will doubt the reliability of the guinea pig.[32]

If I state that I am now having the mental experiences of reading but am actually standing and staring into space, no one is going to believe that I am really engaged in a new form of reading. Rather, they will start to question the postulated mental essence of reading (or perhaps simply question my honesty). All of this goes to show that nothing mental or experiential can be *criterial* for the act of reading to be acknowledged as having occurred. (Exactly the same line of argument can be given to undermine the physiological-reductionist account of reading.) Chomsky seems to have been totally unaware of the extensive discussion (and approval) of Wittgenstein's case against mentalistic accounts of reading (and other activities and achievements, like understanding and expecting). He apparently sees no conceptual difficulties in claiming that it is an intelligible hypothesis to propose a mental state as criterial to the proper avowal and ascription of 'reading'. Let us return to take up Chomsky's argument. He says:

> ... the criteria that Wittgenstein actually discusses, both here and elsewhere, are not in fact 'criteria for correct assertion' in this sense, but rather 'criteria for justified assertion', that is, conditions under which a rational person would be justified in stating, possibly erroneously, that so and so is reading, and so on. These are criteria in the sense in which having a certain visual image might serve as a criterion that justifies my asserting that there is an oasis over there while walking through the desert, although my perfectly justified assertion might still be incorrect.[33]

For Chomsky, it is 'the unconscious mental state attributed to A as the criterion for correct (not justified) assertion of the statement that A is reading'[34] which counts to determine the meaning of the word 'reading'. In a footnote, he adds: 'We might say that in "normal cases' criteria for justified usage do serve as criteria for correct assertion as well, but this is empty unless "normal cases" are something other than cases in which justified assertions are, furthermore, correct'.[35] The sense in which Chomsky speaks of criteria for correct (true) assertion is that in which the criteria in question relating to the meaning of a word are empirical conditions conceptually related to *actually correct assertion*.[36]

Chomsky's hard and fast distinction between justified and correct assertion, and his demand for some specification of 'normal cases' independent of those cases in which justified assertions happen to be true, both indicate that he has not appreciated the role of the concept of 'criterion' in Wittgenstein's thinking. For Wittgenstein, the notion of a 'criterion' *replaces* the notion of truth conditions in semantics. A criterial relationship between an assertion and its evidences is weaker than classical entailment but stronger than inductive evidence.[37] If *q* is a criterion for *p*, then it is part of the meaning of *p* that *q* is a conventionally fixed evidence for the truth of *p*. *However*, a criterion is not decisive evidence in itself, for additional circumstantial evidences can defeat the criterial support for an assertion. And yet, *undefeated criterial evidence constitutes the correctness of an assertion*. There is no *further* meaning to be given to the notion of 'correct assertion' than this. Chomsky is right to point out that my having a certain visual image may entitle me to assert that there is an oasis a few miles across the sand, but that such an assertion may turn out not to be correct. However, when we investigate such an example further, it turns out that the sort of evidences we use to decide upon the correctness of the assertion that there is an oasis (e.g. that trees and water can be seen and touched) are of exactly the same sort that justify such an assertion. Merely having a visual image will not count as a *sufficient* criterion at all. (We have heard of mirages.) But a correct assertion in such cases will simply be *an assertion justified by criterial evidences that are deemed sufficient by convention and are not defeated in the circumstances of asserting*. (It should be remembered that, for Wittgenstein, *avowals* in the first-person present-tense of *psychological* concepts are done without criteria of any kind; the above argument holds for second- and third-person assertions about someone's wanting, or expecting something to happen, etc.) All such correct assertions obtain their correctness from no other source and without any other guarantee: it should be borne in mind that many of our assertions considered correct are also considered defeasible.

Chomsky wants to claim that the difference between cases of justified assertion that A is reading, and cases of correct assertion that A is reading, lies in the presence of an unconscious mental state in the latter cases. I think that enough has been said to show that this notion is incoherent, and that, even if we substitute 'conscious mental process or experience', we still cannot use this as a criterion for someone's actually reading: if someone were to avow such a state sincerely whilst staring at the ceiling, we should not say of him that he *is* reading but that he must be under the influence of some hypnotic suggestion or drug, etc. He may *think* that he is reading, but clearly we can see that he isn't. Only by decontextualizing and distorting the concept of reading as it is *used* (and that is what is at issue here, not the fabrication of some *different* concept), could we imagine that inner processes are in any sense at all definitive of someone's being engaged in reading something, and that all else (behavioral and circumstantial particulars) is epiphenomenal. If this conclusion makes a *theory* (especially a mentalistic theory) of reading impossible, then so much for theorizing here.[38]

Chomsky's notion of a tacit theory of action guiding our correct ascriptions of actions to people hinges upon just such a mentalistic reduction of the concepts of reading, expecting, understanding and so on. His major contribution to the psychological literature was to have shown how Skinner's mechanistic reduction of creative language-use to 'verbal behavior' and S–R-reinforcement behaviorism could not work and preserve the integrity of the concept of language-use. It is paradoxical that someone so successful in his anti-reductionist argumentation should now be proposing an equally illicit form of reductionism on the other side of the hackneyed behaviorism/mentalism dichotomy. All of which, of course, is wholly independent of Chomsky's outstanding technical achievement in the study of grammar which should, I believe, be appraised apart from his misunderstanding of its status as a contribution to cognitive psychology.

4 Basic Experiential Expressions

The study of subjective experience (long the province of phenomenology) has often failed to transcend the established terms of the behaviorism/mentalism duality, in spite of the availability of much relevant work in the contemporary philosophy of mind. In what follows, I seek to reaffirm the relevance to the study of basic human experiences of the pragmatics of ordinary-language use and of experiential expressions in particular.

We acquire a public, experiential vocabulary and a practical knowledge of its employment in our ordinary activities as part of acquiring a natural language. We acquire this experiential 'sub-language' (family of language-game features) through various processes of public training in its use. This training is made possible only by virtue of the existence of what Pears has called 'teaching links'[1] or *socially-relevant criteria* of the basic experiences we have or undergo or suffer. I shall begin by discussing perceptual introspectionism and then shall take up some issues connected with the use of the concepts of 'pain', 'sounds', 'looks', and 'appears'. A sociology of experience based upon the project of investigating the parameters of experiential language-use in social interaction will be proposed.

Perceptual Introspectionism

How do we learn to describe our basic experiences? One proposal, to be referred to here as the doctrine of perceptual introspectionism, holds that we acquire the capacity correctly to employ basic experiential concepts (e.g. 'pain') in our own case by inspecting our own inner, experiential state, identifying it and then learning to match it with the appropriate linguistic category or expression as if we possessed the experiential equivalent of a bottle somewhere inside our skin for which we are selecting the correct label. The linguistic category that we employ, derived indeed (it is conceded) from our social training in a natural language, is then supposedly put to work to refer to our own private experience.[2] This is, I believe, a fundamentally mistaken conception of experiential knowledge, but it is deep and pervasive and requires to be exposed piecemeal. The argument that will be defended here is that human experiences are available to us as objects of possible knowledge solely in virtue of the social procedures of linguistic training, and that, whilst of course we may all *have* experiences before we acquire any language at all, a training in the conceptual resources of a natural language is a pre-requisite for our *knowledge of* subjective experiences. Consequently, the notion of a purely 'private' experience as a possible object of knowledge is incoherent.

Consider the perceptual introspection model of experiential language-acquisition. Such introspection itself cannot furnish us with any concepts for our experiences. Wittgenstein spent many paragraphs on this issue:

Experience does not direct us to derive anything from experience.[3]

and, elsewhere,

Do not believe that you have the concept of color within you because you look at a colored object—however you look. (Any more than you possess the concept of a negative number by having debts.)[4]

The very idea of introspection presupposes observation, but in the case of basic experiences such as pain, I do not observe but simply *have* a pain; I do not 'pick out' my pain, I feel it where it is to be felt. (So strong is this intrinsic connection that were I to claim that I am feeling a pain in my leg which has just recently been amputated, my claim is not ridiculed, and instead the idea of a 'phantom limb' is constructed to accommodate my claim.) I cannot make a mistake in 'observing' my pain, and, where no mistake is logically possible, then the concept of observation falls away. I can, of course, avow and report my pain, and describe it in various ways, but I am not doing this by observing anything.

Perceptual introspection of something could not provide us with any account of the *meaning* of an experiential expression. We might say 'this' is what we mean, refer to, when we use the word 'pain' of ourselves, but such mental gesturing inwards (if that is really what is happening) cannot provide an explanation of the sense of the word, for it provides no criteria for its proper use, and allows of no teaching links for language-training. The idle mental gesturing would be utterly useless in instructing someone in the proper employment of a concept like pain in syntactical contexts and as a feature of possible speech-acts like pleas for mercy, entreaties, threats, warnings, expressions of pity and sympathy, etc. If the 'this' cannot be expanded into an account of the meaning of the term pain, then it cannot be what the term pain actually means. Wittgenstein gives us an excellent example to underscore this point. Imagine a community in which each member had a box with something inside it. Everyone calls the object in the box a 'beetle', but no one can look in anyone else's box and can only determine the nature of 'beetle' by looking into his *own* box. Wittgenstein proposes that, *if* 'beetle' has a use in the public language, then the object in the box must be irrelevant to its meaning. If this private object *does* play a part in the understanding of 'beetle', then intersubjective communication would be impossible.[5] Now, suppose that you undertake to teach a child the meaning of 'tickling'; you tickle him in the ribs, and he laughs and jerks away. You say to him: 'Now you know what "tickling" feels like'. And you may repeat such a scenario with certain variations, ensuring that the reaction of the child is such as to enable you to ascribe to him the experience of being tickled. But suppose that the child felt something you cannot know anything about: will that be relevant to your deciding from his subsequent use of the word 'tickle' whether he understands it?[6] Wittgenstein concludes that:

> If we construe the grammar of the expression of sensation on the model of 'object and name', the object drops out of consideration as irrelevant.[7]

The 'object' is irrelevant to the teaching and meaning of the sensation-concept. Perceptual introspection cannot facilitate its being learned.

> How do words *refer* to sensations?—There doesn't seem to be any problem here; don't we talk about sensations every day, and give them names? But how is the connection between the name and the thing set up? This question is the same as: how does a human being learn the meaning of the names of sensations?—of the word 'pain' for example. Here is one possibility:

words are connected with the primitive, the natural, expressions of the sensation and used in their place. A child has hurt himself and he cries; and then adults talk to him and teach him exclamations and, later, sentences. They teach the child new pain-behavior. 'So you are saying that the word " pain" really means crying?'—On the contrary: the verbal expression of pain replaces crying and does not describe it.[8]

We can see that the 'experience itself', whilst assuredly the phenomenon for which the appropriate concept can function as a name, is not a part of the language-acquisition process in the way in which, e.g., chairs themselves may be pointed to and used in various ways as a part of teaching the neophyte the use of the concept of 'chair'. This is not because the 'experience' is 'beyond the language' (except in the trivial sense, surely not at issue, in which any empirical phenomenon is distinct from the word[s] used to describe or name it). Rather, the experiences themselves are conceptualized in and through the language in distinctive ways that do not depend upon some mysterious form of inner ostension. However, we do not only learn to say: 'I'm in pain' or its equivalents; we learn to employ a variety of descriptive categories in connection with our pain-avowals. Although Wittgenstein clearly states that he is nowhere arguing that pain is simply pain-behavior, his claim that first-person avowals are *substitutions* for naturally expressive pain-reactions tends to elicit the following sort of objection:

> ... one is not only able to give a criterionless avowal of pain and its location, but also a criterionless description of its phenomenological features, e.g., that it is dull or sharp, throbbing or nagging, searing or stinging, etc. Indeed we have a rich, if under-employed, vocabulary for the phenomenology of sensation. These descriptions, even though not descriptions of an *observation*, are informative and supply important diagnostic data. They are ordinarily conceived of as true or false. Moreover there is, by and large, no natural expressive behavior which manifests those phenomenological features, and our descriptions of them do not replace any primitive behavior.[9]

Hacker, who puts the above objection to what he terms Wittgenstein's 'non-cognitive thesis of avowals', goes on to note that we say, in the first-person present-tense, that we are *not* in pain, but this can hardly be said to be a learned substitute for a natural form of 'absence-of-pain-behavior'.[10] Hunter, however, has remarked that the concept of 'pain' does not serve to denote something 'that is distinguishable from what is denoted by the adjectives that describe it.'[11] We could scarcely notice a change in our pain from mild to sharp and still call it the 'same' pain, any more than we could speak of a change of location of a head-ache from the head to the stomach. In this sense, Hacker is perhaps ill-advised to speak of a 'phenomenology' of pain, and of the description of its 'phenomenological features', since pains do not qualify as phenomena *independent from* what are referred to by the use of descriptive categories. Pains have no 'identity-sustaining properties' apart from those accorded to them by descriptors such as 'sharp', 'dull', etc. The use of the word 'pain', then, should be thought of not in terms of material-object nouns but as a signal that a certain range of issues are relevant such as location, intensity, sympathy, admiration, calling for a doctor, fetching bandages or aspirins, and so on. If we misassimilate the use of the concept to the use of concepts of material objects, we will become rapidly confused as to how we could acquire the capacity to describe our pains by using a *public* language. In Ryle's terms,

> Epistemologists are fond of using words like 'pains', 'itches', 'stabs', 'glows', and 'dazzles' as if they were 'neat' sensation names. But this practice is doubly misleading. Not only do most of these words draw their significance from situations involving common objects like fleas, daggers, and radiators, but they also connote that the person who has the sensations, likes, or dislikes, or might well like or dislike, having them. A pain in my knee is a sensation that I mind having; so 'unnoticed pain' is an absurd expression. . . .[12]

Ryle notes that when someone claims that his pain is stabbing, grinding or burning, although he does not necessarily think that his pain is given to him by a stiletto, a drill or a hot poker, still he is saying what sort of pain it is by likening it to the sort of pain that would be given to anyone by such items. In this sense, the descriptive categories used with the concept of 'pain' are not in some sense 'pure' phenomenological descriptors posing a problem for Wittgenstein as to how they could be said to substitute for ordinary pain-behavior; rather, they are sensation-descriptors *in terms of what common objects are regularly used to do* (or look or sound like) in ordinary cases, and their proper use can only be mastered by extensive training and experience *after* the initial concepts of basic sensations are available in the way Wittgenstein suggests.

Hunter has also shown some other ways in which the concept of 'pain' does not function like an ordinary material-object concept, or a concept of a discrete sort. If there were, for instance, a pain-reaction-killing drug which, when taken, would leave the sensation unchanged but render the sufferer perfectly indifferent to it:

> ... we would certainly not say that the erstwhile sufferer was now *in pain*, and it would at the very least be unclear whether we should say that he now *has a pain*. We say that a person is in pain when he has a sensation from which he recoils; and we are simply not prepared for the case in which he has only the sensation, without the least inclination to recoil.[13]

This shows how closely related is our use of the concept of 'pain' and the presence of some observable behavior that contextually constitutes a reaction to or recoiling from some inner sensation. Given that pains *are* tied to reactions, it can hardly be argued that pains are wholly private phenomena. Although we may sometimes be misled by stoicism or pretence, it is the absence of any *natural* expression that can distinguish these exceptional cases. Furthermore, in a perfectly ordinary sense of 'same', we all have the 'same' pains—sharp ones, dull ones, pains in the stomach and head, etc. We may not all suffer simultaneously, and *some* of us may never have experienced *certain* pains at all (think of a gun-shot wound), but no one's pain can be uniquely his own when he is *capable of acknowledging it in others* when the need arises.

First-person present-tense avowals of pain, then, originate as substitutions for or expansions of our natural, *pre*-linguistic behavior (wincing, moaning, crying, etc.). To say, initially, 'I'm in pain' is, as Wittgenstein argued, to have acquired a new form of pain-behavior, a linguistic form of pain reaction. Later acquaintance with, and training with, common objects and their functions (as well as unpleasant encounters with some of them) provides the basis for our expansion of such bare linguistic reactions as 'I've a pain in my leg' (when clutching one's leg) to more sophisticated reports such as 'I've a dull, throbbing pain in my leg'. The *referential force* of the expression 'I'm in pain' is not given either by perceptual introspection nor by observation of (and conclusion from observation of) one's conduct, but is a function of its occasioned place in a series of circumstances of action and reaction in some real situation. By this I mean the following: an intelligible self-ascription (avowal) of pain requires of the self-ascriber that his conduct *and* its circumstances live up to the standards required by others for its appropriateness and intelligibility. If I disclaim joking, pretence and stoicism, but ascribe pain to myself whilst behaving in ways quite at odds with my self-ascribed state, then either my disclaimers will be disbelieved or I will be thought by others not to have mastered the concept of *pain* at all.

Behaviorists are perfectly right to insist that the concept of 'pain', and various other experiential and mental-conduct concepts, cannot be wholly severed from observable conduct; where they go wrong is in thinking that the concept has a unitary meaning *in terms of* such conduct alone. This illegitimate form of reductionism gave rise to the equally illegitimate phenomenological fallacy in which the referent of 'pain' is some putatively private and ultimately inscrutable inner experience. We cannot, of course, give a unitary definition for 'pain'. We can only show how it can be used to make sense in expressions and on occasions of real, practical use. Searching for a 'referent' for the concept is a very misleading method for untangling its complexity; the notions of 'application' and 'reference' may mislead us because we often work with an inappropriate paradigm for 'applying a word'. Malcolm hit on this when he remarked:

Do I have a model of what it would be to apply the name 'directly'? No. I have this picture—that learning the meaning of 'pain' is applying the sign 'pain' to pain itself. I have that picture, to be sure, but what does it teach me, what is its 'application'? When shall I say that what it pictures has taken place, i.e., that someone has learned the meaning of 'pain'? It doesn't tell me; it is *only* a picture.[14]

For some behaviorists, the word is supposed to be applied 'directly' to the pain-behavior; for some phenomenologists, the word is supposed to be applied 'directly' to the lived pain-experience itself. But if these are essentially idle formulations, disengaged 'pictures' arising due to our being beguiled by a unitary model of the working of our language, we need to take a synoptic view of the operation of our experiential concepts and their acquisition.

When I say, in the first-person present-tense: 'I've a pain in my leg', I am referring to my pain, but not by applying a word to an object like paint to a wall; I am *manifesting*, or expressing, my pain—the expression itself is a part of my reaction to the pain. That is how it gets taught. When I say, in the first-person perfect-tense: 'I had a pain in my leg, but it's all right now', I am not referring to anything private (unless I had not disclosed that particular pain before), nor am I referring to my memory of the pain as it passes through my mind. (The word 'pain' in my utterance referred to the pain in my leg and not to the memory-image of it!) But what does this retrospective referring consist in? The ordinary use of 'to refer to' here involves 'saying (X) *when* ...' and not fixing a label to an object. Thus, when I say that I am referring to the pain I had yesterday, I am saying this (appropriately and intelligibly) *when* I have had such a pain. There is nothing mysterious about this sort of 'referring';

what leads us astray is ungrounded reflection upon the isolated assertion that 'the word pain refers to an experience or sensation'. Detached from its mundane sense, this assertion is extremely misleading for it conjures for us a picture of 'referring' which has no place in our grasp of the way we live our lives. Words in themselves do not attach or apply to anything; people use them in signalling in all sorts of ways, and when they are referring they are not doing just one unitary and invariant sort of thing (such as verbal pointing), and certainly not 'attaching a word to a phenomenon'.[15]

In learning the ascriptive use of the category 'pain' for second- and third-person expressions ('He's in pain', 'You're in pain', etc.), we are trained in quite diverse ways to identify socially-relevant criteria in conduct *and* its circumstances until we can demonstrate a (non-propositional) mastery of how to ascribe these categories and expressions consistently and appropriately according to our trainers and others in actual instances. We learn to monitor other people's avowals and/or reactions, and also to monitor the surrounding circumstances. The latter procedure does not consist in learning a *set* of such circumstances; as Malcolm has observed, contextual particulars are non-enumerable.[16] Rather, we are trained to make judgments in the light of surrounding circumstances, and our successful response to such training is not reducible to mastery of a set of contextual particulars that we could list.[17] If our training consisted only in the inculcation of the ability to discern *behavioral* criteria for someone's being in pain, then of course we should not be able to distinguish between genuine cases of pain in other people and cases where avowals and/or conduct formally resembled such genuine pain-behavior but which were actually, manifestly, cases of pretence, joking, play-acting etc. Clearly, we have to learn this as a part of learning about life's ways; we have to learn to be sensitive to the contexts of actions and utterances, since they are required for the successful disambiguation of certain kinds of cases. The idea that we learn words in circumstances of use, but then are able to use them without being able to state a definite set of appropriate circumstances for use, is one that baffles some people. (I believe that it forms the basis of the construction of a 'projection problem' in theoretical linguistics and cognitive psychology generally, as already noted.) However, Wittgenstein draws our attention to the following analogy:

'No one thought of *that* case'—we may say. Indeed, I cannot enumerate the conditions under which the word 'to think' is to be used—but if a circumstance makes the use doubtful, I can say so, and also say *how* the situation is deviant from the usual ones.

If I have learned to carry out a particular activity in a particular room (putting the room in order, say) and am master of this technique, it does not follow that I must be ready to describe the arrangement of the room; even if I should at once notice, and could also describe, any alteration in it.[18]

We do not, then, learn to ascribe pains according to fixed rules of context, although we can certainly identify cases whose features are apt to lead us to abandon an ascription, or to change it. This is a proto-phenomenon—a fact of our human form of life—which is assumed in all training and language-acquisition. It is not itself a *part of* language-acquisition, except in the sense that as a capacity it is drawn upon.

Sounds and Sights

When we hear sounds, we do not perceive an internal echo of the sounds; we simply hear sounds. However, what Ryle has called 'the language of originals and copies'[19] is typically introduced into metaphysical discussions of what it is to hear and see, from which of course we derive the cinematic model of the mind. Ryle's strategy in undermining the relevance of the language of originals and copies consisted in part in drawing our attention to the obvious inapplicability of such a conceptualization to the exercise of the sense of smell. If we do not 'smell with the mind's nose', then seeing with the mind's eye and hearing with the mind's ear become transparent as the metaphorical constructions they are. When we report upon a sound we have heard, we are not describing some phenomenal experience pertaining to a private, inner realm, but describing the objectively heard sound. If no one else heard it, then we could either fault their hearing or claim that we 'thought' that we heard it, that it 'seemed' to us that we heard it, where what we are now doing is not describing thoughts or seemings but justifying our previous reportage. (Note that the use of 'thought' and 'seemed' in connection with perception accounts usually guarantees no further questioning of us; we cannot sensibly be asked how we know that we seemed to have heard a sound; there is no such construction as 'seeming to seem to hear something'.)

It should not be thought that there is something essentially enigmatic and 'subjective' about our use of descriptive expressions relating to sounds. Take the expressions 'twice as loud' and 'half again as loud'. In most usual contexts of utterance, these expressions function well enough for practical purposes: we may, for instance, where asked to turn down our stereo 'half again as loud', take action by reducing the volume by half as measured by the relevant dial on the set, or we may simply estimate half-volume. Clearly, however, not all of an environment's hearable sounds can be calibrated *in situ*, and for some claims about pitch and loudness, only further personal testimony is available. There is no independent calibration to which we appeal to settle many of our routine discrepancies of judgment about sounds. But notice that, whilst judgmental discrepancies are found to arise which may only be resolved, if at all, by independent instrumentation as an authoritative standard, we do not ordinarily think of experiential expressions such as: 'It's twice as loud as it was before' as enigmatic either for us or for the person saying them. As hearers, we may find that such expressions cannot themselves be used to settle the matter for some *special* purpose, but we do not ordinarily consider that the very same person who is using them faces a problem of correspondence between his actual experience and his employment of linguistic resources to express or describe it. Indeed, if we pressed people using such expressions to be more and more 'precise', they would soon run out of satisfactory analogues, descriptors and metaphors on their own. Theoretically, however, one can continue to calibrate an instrument in finer and finer ways, to discriminate more and more precisely, and this fact sometimes encourages us to think of experiential expressions as somehow altogether 'inaccurate' or 'misleading' by comparison. One such example is provided for us by the psychophysical research of Smith Stevens on subjective accoustics.[20] Let me quote the following comment on this research from W. V. Quine:

> For years he [Smith Stevens] gathered subjective testimony of the pitch and loudness of sounds: whether this was twice as high as that, or half again as loud as that. He plotted these findings against the physical frequencies and volumes and came out with significant correlations—not linear, but logarithmic. Significant, but of what? Was it uniformity of error in his subjects' effort to estimate physical frequency and volume? Or was it uniformity of subjective experience, coupled with uniformity of meaning attached to enigmatically subjective expressions like 'twice as high' and 'half again as loud'? Or did the subjective experiences vary from subject to subject, while the meaning attached to the subjective expressions varied in a compensatory way? The uniformities surprise me and I am prepared to find them instructive, but I am at a loss to sort them out.[21]

Firstly, Quine asks: do the correlations show uniformity of error in our accoustical judgments (or at least in those of Smith Stevens' subjects)? If we treat experiential expressions like 'twice as high' as expressions of measurement, then according to the testimony of the calibrated instruments measuring decibels, and so on, our hearing apparatus might be thought of as defective. However, in what sense could *we* be thought of as 'measuring' sounds in order to produce descriptive expressions like 'twice as high'? If we treat an experiential expression like 'twice as high' or 'half as loud again' as produced by us on the basis of some esoterically subjective measuring system, then we will naturally think of these expressions as poor ways of saying '*n* decibels more' or '*n* decibels less', *ignoring the very different language-games that we play with these different expressions.* It is only by virtue of such a misassimilation that we could come to believe that our experiential expressions are essentially faulted rather than occasionally so. Quine treats such expressions as 'enigmatic', but for many of the practical purposes for which we employ them (e.g. complaining about stereos) they do their job perfectly well and are not at all treatable as enigmatic. Quine seems to be thinking of our ordinary experiential protocols as enigmatic by contrast to the supposedly clear-cut and precise protocols generated by consulting the pointer-readings on an instrument. But he forgets that, for many occasions, to speak of decibel readings would be heard as 'enigmatic', where 'half as loud again' would suffice very well. In this sense, *generalized* comparisons of normally-situated experiential expressions with physical measures can prove troublesome in terms of making inferences like those of Smith Stevens. The undecidability occurs because we are tacitly assigning some of the properties of pointer-readings to experiential expressions and then taking stock of the ways in which they differ from pointer-readings. This is like faulting a move in football by using the rules of chess. It is not that we have two distinct 'realms', the phenomenal and the objective, in cases of sounds. We do not have, on the one hand, 'sounds-as-subjectively-measured' and 'sounds-as-objectively-measured', because we simply cannot attach any sense to the claim that we inwardly 'measure' sounds. Our judgments about sounds are not bad measurements because they are not measurements. To understand the nature of such expressions of experience, we have to look outward, not inward. We have to look at the sorts of circumstances in which such expressions have a practical life. They do not have any practical life in games where judgments are being set against other forms of measurement; they are merely idling.

The idea of a phenomenal realm of appearances co-existing alongside an objective world of actualities gains a certain initial plausibility from a consideration of the perception of colors. On closer inspection, however, it turns out that here as well the idea of two 'realms'

is the product of conceptual confusion about the functioning use
of color categories. In order to master a color vocabulary, speakers
must agree, in a given communication community, about the broad
range of applicability of color concepts to items in the world.
We are not taught 'the looks of things', but the *actual* colors
of things for the communication community. The availability of
the concept of how colors 'seem' or 'look' or 'appear' (e.g. 'This
seems, looks, appears red to me') does not imply that this is
the basis for all inferences, or that appearances are the tacit objects
of all descriptions, because to be able to describe the appearance
of a color presupposes a conceptual grasp enabling one to describe
an actual color. Hacker articulates what is at issue:

> Learning what 'red' means is learning, e.g. to call out 'red'
> on seeing something red, to bring a red thing on demand, to
> arrange objects according to color. Only then can the distinction
> between red and appearing red be taught, not because it is
> a subtle distinction, like that between scarlet and crimson, but
> because the concept of seeming thus and so is parasitic upon
> the concept of being thus and so. The red visual impression,
> Wittgenstein emphasizes, is *a new concept*[22]

When we have learned to guard our declaratives about colors,
e.g., by saying 'This *looks* red', we have not learned a way of
describing something in a phenomenal, inner realm, but a way
of *limiting our responsibilities* for our perceptual judgments, a way
of justifying or excusing our perceptual claims when confronted
with disagreement. Notwithstanding the familiar (Husserlian) hypos-
tatizations, there is no phenomenal realm of pure appearances;
only guarded, qualifying forms of descriptions of a shared world.
If we are barred from presupposing a shared world of basic experiences, then we are deprived of any means of accounting for the
possibilities of mutual understanding of color categories (and a
host of other concepts!). Shared perceptual agreement comes first,
then disagreements and disparate claims about *specific* 'appearances'
enter into our use of language.

Appearances

The way things 'appear' is often taken to be the paradigmatic
consideration entertained when proposals in favor of some form
of 'subjectivist' account of perception and experience are made.
And yet, we use the concept of 'appears' independently of the
employment of any of the senses in particular. We can say, 'it

appears to be a counterfeit', where all sorts of tests, requiring all sorts of evidence and the exercise of various perceptual and judgmental abilities may be involved in making such a determination, albeit a guarded one, about the coin, painting or whatever.

Constructions such as: 'It appears as a spot in the sky', or 'She appears to enjoy difficult problems in logic' are open to invalidation by others in the light of appropriate circumstantial data. *Inter*subjective issues are throughout bound up with so-called 'subjective' claims about appearances. In Austin's terms:

> It is perhaps even clearer that the way things look is, in general, just as much a fact about the world, just as open to public confirmation or challenge, as the way things are. I am not disclosing a fact about *myself*, but about petrol, when I say that petrol looks like water.[23]

The same argument holds for 'appears'. However, notice that we will often find that someone's claims about the way the world appears to him *can* tell us something about himself rather than the world in cases where the report of the appearance is totally unacceptable in terms of group culture and its interpretive procedures. For instance, if you were to tell me that the ordinary scene we have both observed outside your window now appears to you like a nightmare from one of Dali's surrealist paintings, this would tell me something about *you*: viz. that you are hallucinating, or joking, lying, the victim of an illusion, etc. Your scene from the window could not have appeared to *anyone* like that, so there is something wrong with you or the circumstances of your looking.

If I were to say: 'He appears to be guilty', I am not committing myself thereby to any perceptual claim; I might add that he *looks* quite innocent.[24] If I were to say: 'It appears that they've all gone', I shall not ordinarily be taken to be describing some subjective 'reality', but taking stock of the objective situation, perhaps complaining about it or expressing surprise at 'their' absence. Often, we use 'appears' contrastively, as in: 'She appears on the surface to be very friendly, but try making real friends with her and you'll soon see that it's all a façade'. Sometimes, though, we employ the term non-contrastively when we haven't really enough evidence to make a firm determination about something but enough for a good guess: 'He appears to be Chinese', or 'It appears to be a kind of spider'. And we can speak of appearances when confronted with *known* cases of illusion: 'It appears to be much longer than the line below, but of course it isn't when measured with a ruler', or: 'He appeared to have cut her in half' said describing a magician's act.

We must be extremely cautious when we speak of 'subjective reality' on the basis of a *general* distinction between appearance and reality. In a strong sense, appearances are often just as 'real' as other kinds of perceptual claims. And it can be very misleading to propose that what is reality for one is appearance for another. In general, this simply could not be the case, given the existence of a shared language and inter-translatable languages. A shared language, as already stressed, presupposes agreements in basic judgments about things in the world.

Finally, consider how often guarding or qualifying protocols become reified into features of a subjective, inner space: we say, 'I think that X', where 'I think' is used in an *opinion-prefatory* fashion; we say, 'I believe that X', when we are articulating a *guarded propositional claim*; we say, 'It appears to me to be X', where we are *hesitant about our perceptual claim*, making ourselves available for refutation or confirmation by further evidence(s), and yet each of these protocols ('think', 'believe', 'appears') has at one time or another been projected into our 'minds' as peculiar sorts of mental operations or subjective representations. Instead of making such projectional errors, sociologists should be alert to the pragmatics of use of such expressions. In this way, as the scope of subjectivist theorizing is reduced, the scope for sociological explication can be extended.

5 Some Thoughts on Thinking

I

It can be argued that 'thoughts' of various kinds are already sociological data and topics of inquiry, for people's 'attitudes', 'beliefs' and 'opinions' have long been probed and correlated with other things by social scientists. Leaving questions of methodological adequacy to one side, it is clear that *some* corpus of social-scientific knowledge-claims contains reference to the thoughts that people are supposed to have entertained about a host of matters, from the most locally specific item to the most global, historical course of events. The actual *data* of thoughts collected sociologically consist of spoken or written answers to questions; meaningful utterances constitute the 'thoughts' themselves for purposes of inquiry. Of course, the perennial question is: do these utterances represent respondents' *real* thoughts about the issue at hand? Although this question sometimes takes on a metaphysical tinge, it is usually resolvable by reference to (commonsense) observation of respondents' relevant courses of action. (Not that such connections are routinely made as a matter of empirical procedure, of course; too often we are expected to swallow claims about people's thoughts on the basis of evidence gathered through a questionnaire or interview schedule which, if gathered without such trappings, would hardly convince an intelligent layman who knows that deeds can belie words.) Note, however, that neither in our ordinary interactions nor in systematic inquiries do we usually say that in order to determine what a person's thoughts are we must always have access to something other than what he says and does and the circumstances of those sayings and doings, or trustworthy reports of those things. We can be misled, lied to or deceived about a person's thoughts *and* actions, but being misled, lied to or deceived in these ways cannot be an invariant feature of our social world in these respects, for in order to possess the concept of 'thought' (and the concept of 'action') in the first place, we must have publicly available standards of appropriate use and reference for them, which presupposes some agreement on actual cases.

Similarly, in our ordinary affairs, when we are judging what someone's thoughts are about something, we do not normally feel any need to introduce into our considerations any reference to hidden or unobservable 'acts' on the part of that person. To claim that a thought is an 'act of consciousness' is *eo ipso* to commit oneself to a range of utterly inappropriate uses of the word 'thought', and to deny to oneself a range of intelligible and conventional locutions. For if thoughts were acts of consciousness, then no-one could claim to know another's thoughts unless he had witnessed the acts in question or had been reliably informed about them. But descriptions of thoughts are not necessarily descriptions of actions at all, unless the thoughts were *about* actions. In this latter case, they may be about all sorts of actions which could hardly qualify as pertaining to the hidden recesses of consciousness; I may have a thought about playing chess tomorrow, but playing chess is hardly an act of consciousness available only to my introspective gaze. A thought may (sometimes) be the result of thinking, but is not itself any kind of 'act'. If I am asked about my thoughts on some matter, I do not then proceed to describe a series of (mental) activities, but to articulate my opinions, judgments, conclusions or assessments. Having thoughts is not invariantly to be identified with thinking. Occasionally, we may say, perhaps by way of correcting ourselves or someone's account of what we meant, that we 'thought of X when we said S'; here, it looks as though we are reporting upon something we *did*, or, minimally, upon something mental that occurred along with the saying itself. However, what we thought of when saying something is shown, not by describing some occult act which we performed at the time, but by articulating a preferred interpretation of what we said at that time, or by how we react (in words and/or actions) to subsequent responses or events, or by what consequences we were prepared for and unprepared for. It was, of course, Locke who believed that the meanings of words were thoughts in our heads, and that to understand someone's words involved grasping his thoughts in a kind of 'synchronous act' paralleling the physical uttering and hearing.[1] Against this view, several arguments have been levelled and, in my view, successfully.

Bennett, for example, has this to say of Locke's inner-act theory of meaning:

> (He) could not comfortably explain how he knows that 'parrots make articulate sounds yet by no means are capable of language'. According to his kind of theory, the parrot's cries are 'insignificant noise' rather than meaningful language because a requisite inner activity or process is not going on in the parrot—but how does Locke know that it isn't going on? . . . For years now Smith's use of English has been normal and socially acceptable; but we have not checked on what has been happening inside Smith's body or 'inside' his mind; and so we do not—according to Locke's theory—know that he has ever understood or meant anything.[2]

Wittgenstein attacks the Lockean approach (although not by name) in a series of remarks on the relationship between meaning and language. He observes:

> When I think in language, there aren't 'meanings' going through my mind in addition to the verbal expressions: the language is itself the vehicle of thought.[3]

In fact, the whole thrust of Wittgenstein's many observations about meaning is to refute the contention that meaning is a kind of thinking and that meanings are thoughts. (Indeed, he argues that meaning in language-use is in many critical ways independent of mental acts, states, processes or experiences of any kind.) He notes that 'mere explanation of a word does not refer to an occurrence at the moment of speaking',[4] and strives to replace mentalistic meaning theories with an account of meaning in terms of conventional use, of occasions, and of contexts of speaking and hearing. For example, his emphasis upon the public conventionality of language-use as the grounds of sense is to be found in various comments, such as:

> Can I say 'bububu' and mean 'If it doesn't rain I shall go for a walk'?—It is only in a language that I can mean something by something. This shews clearly that the grammar of 'to mean' is not like that of the expression 'to imagine' and the like.[5]

For Wittgenstein, meaning cannot be a process or mental event accompanying the utterance or understanding of a word, (phrase or expression) but is rather given by its technique(s) of application in linguistic practices. Wittgenstein provides some pertinent cases:

> Someone says to me: 'Shew the children a game'. I teach them gaming with dice, and the other says 'I didn't mean that sort of game'. Must the exclusion of the game with dice have come before his mind when he gave me the order?[6]

and, in order to buttress his claim that statements about what is meant by a word are employed differently from those about 'an affection of the mind',[7] he asks:

> Does one say, for example: 'I didn't really mean my pain just now; my mind wasn't on it long enough for that'? Do I ask myself, say, 'What did I mean by this word just now? My attention was divided between my pain and the noise—'?[8]

Clearly, we do not determine the sense of a word or expression by introspecting our thoughts, unless it is unfamiliar to us or arises in an unfamiliar context, requiring us to think hard about it (where, obviously, we can conclude *wrongly* that it means such-and-such). Another distinction to be noted here is succinctly stated by Wittgenstein:

> The language-game 'I mean (or meant) *this*' (subsequent explanation of a word) is quite different from this one: 'I thought of . . . as I said it.' The latter is akin to 'It reminded me of . . .'[9]

Consistently stressing the connection between the sense of a word or expression and the means by which its use is acquired by a language-learner, Wittgenstein gets us to face the absurd consequences of the meanings-equal-thoughts doctrine. He also exposes the conceptual connections (grammar) of the word 'meaning', demonstrating that they are ramified in largely different directions from those of the words 'thinking' and 'thought'. My thoughts can be interrupted, but the meanings of my words can hardly be interrupted. I can say something thoughtlessly, but this does not entail that what I say is thereby devoid of meaning. Moreover, we distinguish between *thinking* that we know the meaning of a word and *actually* knowing it, a distinction which would be hard to sustain under the Lockean thesis.

Thoughts, then, are neither acts of consciousness nor the means by which we understand one another, although on occasion we may have to think *before* we understand.[10] Perhaps thoughts are to be identified with specific mental words and images themselves?

Whilst there may be no 'meanings' going through the mind when we think in language, as Wittgenstein noted, there are often words, whole sentences, images and the like 'going through the mind'. Are *these* our thoughts? It is possible to overlook Wittgenstein's use of the word 'vehicle' in the remark 'the language is itself the vehicle of thought',[11] and to construe him as arguing for this thoughts-equal-words-or-sentences account. The means whereby something may be achieved, however, are not identical to the achievement.

The idea that thoughts are identical to words or images which may appear to one's mind or which may be conjured up especially is very pervasive, and probably stems from over-extrapolation from instances such as the following: you are asked to 'think of any number from one to ten' and you picture either the word 'four' (or some other number) or the image '4' to yourself. This sort of case is then made to stand for, becomes a paradigm for, every case of having thoughts or of thinking. It also encourages the view that 'thoughts' have a mysterious, non-physical realization in the mind. To correct this account of thought and thinking, we have to remember that in the particular case just mentioned what we have done is to 'picture' something, and picturing and thinking or having a thought are not everywhere interchangeable; White shows the conceptual nature of the error we tend to commit in the following remarks:

> The words and images that accompany my thought are not themselves the thought, but the form that the occurrence of the thought took. How does the mere appearance of an image of a cluster of diamonds constitute thinking of my diamonds rather than thinking of my wife's diamonds? Why should the utterance of the word 'diamond' be counted as thinking of diamonds, rather than thinking of the word 'diamond'? It is how I take the image or word that constitutes it as my thinking of it as so and so. And how I take it is shown in what I am now disposed to do, not in what happened at the moment of my becoming disposed. ... I might think of the same thing three times in one single day and have a different experience each time.[12]

There is nothing in the occurrence of word *w* or image *i per se* which makes of it the thought *that X*; the particular occurrence has to be related to, or actually express, my coming to a conclusion, for the same occurrence might elsewhere be totally unconnected with my thinking about a problem or trying to reach some conclusion, or I may reach that conclusion without picturing those words or images.

The opposite error consists in the claim that thoughts are essentially inscrutable phenomena which lie behind words, images, sentences and the other apparatus of representation. Although most of the arguments so far presented militate against this notion, it will help to consider how such a notion might have arisen in what Wittgenstein termed a 'grammatical misassimilation', or an uncontrolled grammatical analogy. We take such overt activities as speaking and writing and try to find some activity corresponding to the word 'thinking' and some location for the results of thinking, for the thoughts themselves. We seek to sustain an analogy whose details we have not worked out clearly; thus, we say that the thought is not the same as its sentential expression (since the same thought can be expressed in different ways and in different languages), and then ask, since the sentential expressions are somewhere, *where are the thoughts*? Since we can find a location for the activity of speaking, *where is the activity of thinking located*? The prime candidate for both is inside our skulls. Wittgenstein comments that this search is like looking for 'the place of the king of which the rules of chess treat, as opposed to the places of the various bits of wood, the kings of various sets'.[13] What is systematically overlooked is that when we say that different words express the same thought we are saying (when speaking in the ordinary way) that different words are accomplishing the same task and *not* that they are differentially clothing the same naked mental entity.

Although we say, metaphorically, 'use your head!' to someone who does not seem to us to be thinking about what he is doing (because of poor performance, etc.) we are not instructing him to go about exercising some hidden cranial capacity, but rather to begin attending more diligently or intelligently to the task at hand; to suppose that our command implicitly instructs someone to undertake some cranial action is as peculiar as supposing that when someone says that he has a word at the 'tip of his tongue' he could actually reach into his mouth and pull it out. But isn't thinking at least *some* sort of activity? This brings us to the crux of the conceptual discussion.

II

There is no *uniform* series of endogenous or exogenous events which together differentiate thinking, which make of thinking that which it is. For 'the phenomena of thinking are widely scattered' and the concept 'widely ramified'.[14] For example, I may say that I think that so-and-so, and be reporting my guarded claim about a factual or moral matter without in the least making reference to a chain of mental events. I may be told by someone to 'think it over', but if I obey this order by talking to myself, am I then carrying out two activities, the talking to myself *and* the thinking?[15] Ryle has gone a long way toward clarifying the nature of the concept of 'thinking' by treating it as a category with properties similar to those of categories like 'trying', 'hurrying' and 'repeating'.[16] These 'adverbial verbs' are incapable of specification in terms of one or more concrete ingredients, by contrast to verbs such as walking, hitting, eating and speaking for which specific sorts of concrete specifications are available. Such 'adverbial' verbs have no 'autonomous' content; they operate *as* verbs, but do the job of *adverbial qualification of other verbs.* 'Thinking', then, can mean 'with thought' as 'hurrying' means 'with speed', and clearly, on this account, both are predatory upon some other (verb of) action. This analysis of thinking has the following consequence: it makes inappropriate the attempt to understand thinking by close behavioral or introspective study just as it is inappropriate to seek to understand the nature of 'trying' by observing what we do when we try to do something. In White's terms:

> It is not the movements, external or internal, that I make, or the ways in which I make them, when I bang the table that allows us to call what I am doing 'trying to attract attention'; it is the fact that these, or some entirely different, movements are made in certain circumstances—namely, for the purpose of making people attend to me.[17]

By the same token, 'thinking' does not name some specific behavioral and/or mental manifestation (activity or state) but rather characterizes any such manifestation by relating it in certain ways to its context. There is no contradiction between this account of what it is to think and the fact that thinking has, at least on some occasions, genuine duration. I can be thinking for an hour about a problem, and my thinking can be disturbed or interrupted. This makes it look as if thinking were genuinely a processual activity. However, I can be hurrying to work, and I can be interrupted as I am hurrying (or trying to do something, or repeating something), without this entailing that hurrying (or trying or repeating) is a processual activity of the same logical status as walking, speaking, drinking or smoking. If you ask me what I am doing and I tell you that I am thinking, my answer remains just as vague as when I tell you that I am hurrying. This is because 'thinking' is a relational concept. It is, in fact, a polymorph. In other words, thinking can take various forms, none of which is *necessary* to it.

For when I tell you that I am thinking I might be doing any
of a number of different things; puzzling over a problem in logic,
working out my budget, musing over a story I've just finished
reading, considering the racing odds or trying to remember where
I left my pipe. To say only that I am 'thinking' is either to
offer a prolegomenon to information about what I am doing, or
is a way of cutting the question short, so to speak. For the fuller
descriptions of what I am doing to be appropriate, to make sense
as descriptions of my activities *in context*, then of course they
have to be at least consistent with what is relevantly known about
me and my circumstances. However, given minimal consistency
(i.e. the absence of perceivedly defeating circumstances) what I
claim about such things as musing, pondering and considering etc.
have to suffice. Provided that my conduct and relevant circumstance
(including, perhaps, your knowledge of me) do not belie my claim,
it can hold without your needing to peer into my skull: my self-ascription is 'correct' where it is rendered sincerely and remains situationally undefeated as such. Hacker, discussing Wittgenstein's position
on first-person, present-tense psychological self-ascriptions of this sort,
summarizes cogently:

> . . . those psychological terms which we ascribe to ourselves, with
> every right but without justificatory evidence, depend for their
> sense upon the existence of natural manifestations of inner states.
> These natural expressions of psychological states constitute part
> of the criterial evidence which justifies others ascribing the relevant
> psychological predicates to us. Our self-ascriptions are not made
> on the basis of criteria, but they only make sense because there
> are such criteria.[18]

The sense of cognitive predicates, criterionlessly self-ascribed, is
given by the criteria that justify ascribing them to others; were
there no behavioral and circumstantial manifestations to operate
as 'teaching links' for the cognitive predicates, they could not
have a sense and could not enter into a functioning, public language.
This clearly does not entail that pondering, musing, considering
and so on are *reducible* to patterns of behavior, only that some
characteristic (sequences of) conduct must be taken as expressing
the pondering, musing and considering in various circumstances
(although not in all). The ascription of 'thinking' to someone
takes various forms, depending upon whether the case at issue
is one of 'thinking that X is the case', 'thinking something over',
'thinking about X', 'thinking of X', 'thinking something out' or
'thinking it through'. It is with *these* connections that we acquire
the concept of thinking and our ability to ascribe (and avow)

it intelligibly. We know, if we have grasped what it is to say of someone that he thinks such-and-such, that we are not predicating of him some continuous mental ratiocination but the opinion or judgment that such-and-such is or may be the case (which in turn is a matter of his conduct, including usually his preparedness to assent to certain sorts of propositional claims). We know that, where we are allowing of someone that he 'thought it out', or 'thought it up', we are entitled (indeed, obliged) to require of him that he can express his thought in an appropriate way:

> If someone claims to have just composed a couplet silently and we ask him to recite it, we would not allow him to pause till he had *also* found the words, even if he claimed to have done his thinking wordlessly.[19]

A synoptic consideration of the various ascriptions and avowals involving the use of the concept of 'thinking' reveals that the 'disclosure problem'—the special practical problem of not knowing what another is thinking of or about—is indeed a very restricted sort of problem, and open to investigation for its occasionalities. Synoptic investigations of the mundane uses of 'think' and its participles also show how spurious is that metaphysics which insists upon locating (or trying to locate) a single, general referent for the noun 'thought' or for the verb 'think'; as Wittgenstein has warned us so often, we should not make the mistake of looking for a 'thing corresponding to a substantive' in all instances;[20] the words 'thought' and 'thinking' have their practical *uses* (which alone give them their life, their sense) and we ignore these only at the expense of substituting unintelligible ones in their place. We soon discover that, in our grammar, we do not identify thoughts with ethereal objects, nor thinking with a chain of mental images (even though images of all sorts may be found, in specific cases of avowal or ascription, to be bound up with thinking). We have only to compare and contrast thoughts-with-images with daydreams-with-images to realize that images in themselves cannot *constitute* thoughts or episodes properly describable as thinking. 'Thinking cannot consist in any procession of items or changes, since any such sequence could occur in mindless reverie.'[21] Having a succession of mental images or manipulating imagined symbols, diagrams etc. cannot count as constitutive *criteria* for thinking.

There is, however, no doubt that the having of mental images or subvocal symbol manipulation are genuinely mysterious; we may still ask, how are such phenomena possible at all? The problem here is that we may believe that answers to such questions *must* be scientific (e.g. neurophysiological, causal) and also that we are not entitled to claim any knowledge of thinking at all until such questions have been addressed by some (unknown) mode of controlled inquiry into our brain functioning. The development and exploitation of the computer metaphor in much contemporary psychology has encouraged the proliferation of quite spurious analyses of what it is to think or to have a thought,[22] and sociologists are usually content to let the matter rest with their sister discipline. Yet once it is seen that these concepts are actively and delicately employed in conventional ways in socially organized discourse, which employment alone gives them their meaning, it becomes clear that social, communicative relations are of the first importance when considering the nature of such phenomena as thought and thinking. 'Technical' operationalizations of these concepts (e.g. the identification of all thinking with 'problem-solving') are unilateral extrapolations or idle redefinitions in this area; if the concept of 'thinking' is logically polymorphous, then attempts to unitize or reify its meaning are bound to obscure inquiry.

III

So far, nothing has been said about the rules which are claimed to govern our thinking. These rules are identified with the rules of logic (and, by extension, the *a priori* conceptual conventions of natural languages). Wittgenstein, writing in his *Remarks on the Foundations of Mathematics*, seems to ignore his caveats in *Zettel* (where he warned us not to treat the concept of thinking in a unitary way), and he asserts:

> The laws of logic are indeed the expression of 'thinking habits' but also of the habits of *thinking*. That is to say they can be said to shew: how human beings think, and also *what* human beings call 'thinking' . . .

> The propositions of logic are 'laws of thought', 'because they bring out the essence of human thinking'—to put it more correctly: because they bring out, or shew, the essence, the technique, of thinking. They shew what thinking is and also shew kinds of thinking.[23]

Wittgenstein is concerned to combat the illusion that rules of logic inhere in the organization of the physical world (including our brains); he wants to argue that rules of logic are not laws of nature, but humanly constructed conventions integral to the meaning of thinking itself. As Pears has remarked:

It is Wittgenstein's later doctrine that outside human thought and speech there are no independent, objective points of support, and meaning and necessity are preserved only in the linguistic practices which embody them.[24]

Considering a view (unfairly attributed to Peter Winch) in which logicality is reduced to a matter of arbitrary conventions, Lukes argues for an *a priori* conceptual relationship between what it is to think and the basic rules of logic:

> Does this (Winch's position) imply that the concept of negation and the laws of identity and non-contradiction need not operate in (some) language? If so, then it must be mistaken, for if the members of (a society) do not possess even these, how could we ever understand their thought, their inferences and arguments? Could they even be credited with the possibility of inferring, arguing or even thinking? If, for example they were unable to see that the truth of *p* excludes the truth of its denial, how could they ever communicate truths to one another and reason from them to other truths?[25]

Now, clearly we have to admit that people are not, ordinarily, accredited with powers of discursive thinking unless they exhibit the capacity to speak rationally, and this will involve being able to differentiate up from down, backwards from forwards, absence from presence, sameness from difference and the contradictory from the non-contradictory, etc. But we must resist the temptation to infer from all this that rules of logic 'show what thinking is'. We must take note of the fact that our linguistic conventions permit us to ascribe 'thinking' to someone *in the absence* of logicality on his part. We should not conflate 'thinking' with 'reasoning', even though much thinking involves reasoning, and reasoning involves accord with the rules of logic. Consider the following:[26]

A: I'm finding it difficult to follow your train of thought.
B: I know; I'm not thinking very clearly today . . .

Such an interchange would, I take it, be unintelligible to us if we invariably appealed to rules of logic as *criteria* for the ascription of thinking or having a train of thought. Yet there is nothing self-contradictory about speaking of persons as having thought about something in an illogical or confused way. Although we sometimes charge a person with not having thought something out at all in virtue of the kind of thing he claims as the product of his thinking, we also allow that a person has been thinking about something, or thinking something over, when what he tells us contains violations of logical rules (of inference, say, or of concept-combination). We may also say of someone that he has been thinking of his brother or of his summer vacation, and we may avow such thoughts ourselves, where the issue of accord with rules of logic is irrelevant; for how could I think of my brother either logically or illogically? And yet surely this is a case of thinking just as much (albeit in a different way) as lengthy propositional reasoning or doing mental arithmetic. Wittgenstein and Lukes implicitly identify all thinking with these latter sorts of thinking in their remarks quoted above.

When we *focus* upon those cases in which the ascription of thinking amounts to an ascription of reasoning, we find that there is more involved than the tacit (or explicit) appeal to rules of logic as criteria. In our ordinary affairs, the ascription of logicality to someone's reasoning is more than a matter of the discernment of logical form; even the most perfectly ordered syllogistic structure requires something other than its form for it to be taken as constituting a logical piece of reasoning. McHugh, drawing on the work of Perelman, claims:

> . . . a syllogism requires backing, for there is nothing in the universal that can be said to necessitate agreement by a reading of the statement. It is always possible that even a syllogism will be argued. The existence of this possibility is a feature of syllogistic logic. It obviates a self-evident logic. What a syllogism would require to be 'self-evident' is the following: (1) a before-hand knowledge of the grammar of its terms; (2) a language structure which conforms to that of reality; (3) a perfectly known reality; and (4) immediate knowledge of reality by all users of the language . . . Furthermore, a before-hand knowledge of terms means that it (a syllogism) cannot be self-evident, for such knowledge would comprise a mediating factor between the syllogistic sentences on the page, or utterance in the air, and some reader or hearer. Thus, something else must be 'established' before the syllogism.[27]

McHugh is arguing that the premisses themselves, and the conclusion relating to them, have to be acknowledged (if indeed they are) by readers or hearers on the basis of certain sorts of orientation and background knowledge and/or belief. To accept that some reasoning has been 'logical' involves the acceptance of some interpolated, strategically relevant contextualization. (Such contextualizations may encompass considerations as diverse as object-constancy and speaker's authority.) Psychiatrists and others often invoke strategic contextualization explicitly in trying to furnish possible logical connections for cases of 'thought-disordered' assertion; e.g.[28]

Patient: Not feeling well today, but yesterday I was fine.
Mental Welfare Officer: What made you feel all right yesterday?
Patient: I was Atlas!
Mental Welfare Officer: Oh ... you – you were ... on top of the world, eh?

Ordinarily, however, when we are listening to the assertions of a person whom we already consider crazy, our readiness to supply strategic contextualization diminishes. The work of psychologists like Cameron and existential psychiatrists like Binswanger and Laing is permeated with attempts to reinstate strategic contextualization for such cases, and their success or failure in explicating a 'hidden rationality' or a 'hidden logicality' in the outpourings of their patients depends upon the extent to which their readership is prepared to invoke the device of strategic contextualization along the lines suggested to them. An example from Cameron's studies of asyndetic thinking and metonymic distortion shows the kind of work which has to be done to render a patient's assertion to show its fundamental logical connections:

Case 16 says he is alive 'because you really live physically because you have menu three times a day; that's the physical.' (What else is there besides the physical?) 'Then you are alive mostly to serve a work from the standpoint of methodical business.' The first sentence obviously means that on the physical side you live because you eat (have menu) three times a day. '*You really live physically because*' conveys the sense of 'on the physical side you live because', but the actual phraseology is distinctly metonymic and until translated into a more conventional logical structure, leaves one with an uncomfortable sense of uncertainty as to the exact intention of the speaker. In the second sentence, '*to serve a work*' represents an inadequate fusion of *to serve* and *to work*, in which the normal elimination of one phrase or the other is wanting. The remainder, '*from the standpoint of methodical business*', is the patient's idiom for daily routine.[29]

If Cameron's analysis seems at once reasonable but labored, it is perhaps because we operate routinely with what we could call an *economy convention* for the use of strategic contextualization in logicality ascriptions. This convention circumscribes the expectable effort to be expended by a hearer in strategically contextualizing someone's assertions. (There may be a wider latitude permissible when the reasoning being considered is written down.) Competent members of a culture are taken to acquiesce in this convention in the sense that they are normatively enjoined by the culture to produce utterances which require minimal supplementation for their logical coherence and connectedness to be perceived. Reasoning from unspoken premisses (i.e. reasoning *enthymematically*) is permissible as long as the suppressed premisses can reasonably be thought of as forming part of a presumed shared corpus of knowledge or belief. To display, orient to, accomplish or sustain the *sense* that someone's utterances, reasonings or inferences are *logical*, one must provide for their being self-evidently so. This is a general constraint upon the degree to which the provision of strategic contextualization ought to be economical—the more the work of supplementation, the less the appearance of transparency or self-evidence. Moreover, by orienting to the 'self-evidence' of a member's assertion (where such self-evidence provides for its 'logical character') one can provide contextualization through which one reflexively displays that 'self-evidence' and thereby finds that it was there all along.[30] It should be clear, however, that 'self-evidence' in its members' sense does not mean 'already said in so-many-words', since the logicality of an assertion may be predicated upon its hearer grasping its presupposition and tacitly assenting to it.

Assertions analyzeable as self-contradictory when accorded one kind of contextualization can be analyzed by hearers as non-contradictory if they accord to it a different kind of contextualization. In this we may begin to discern the dependence of logicality-ascriptions upon modes of hearer-orientation quite distinct from appeals to rules of logic alone. As an example, consider the following assertion recorded during a mother's description of her daughter's post-hospital behavior to a mental welfare officer:[31]

> She wants us to think she's not hearing those voices any more, but she'll still talk to herself when we're in the room with her.

This remark could be taken intelligibly as a self-contradictory claim—the initial ascription to the daughter of an intention to conceal her hallucinating behavior could be heard as *contradicted* by the subsequent clause ('but she'll still talk to herself when we're in the room with her'). After all, a condition for being concerned to conceal something is that one does not produce that thing (in this case, a form of behavior) in the presence of those from whom one wishes to conceal it. How can someone be reported as wanting to conceal something from someone when she is also reported as producing that thing in the presence of that person?

Is there a method for hearing such conjoined reports as *other than* self-contradictory and thereby unwarranted? There is, and the method consists in shifting the 'illogic' or 'self-contradictoriness' from the account (and the account-producer) to the *subject* of the account. Now, we can start to find the daughter hallucinating in front of her parents one moment and denying it the next, or hallucinating and forgetting who else is present at the time. The internal consistency—the self-evident logicality—of the mother's account is upheld only at the cost of making out that the daughter's behavior is particularly irrational; we contextualize the mother's account strategically by invoking a scheme of background understandings that features various possible notions about her daughter—that she lies pointlessly to her parents and cannot control the occurrence of her hallucinations or some other variant upon the theme of mental disorder. If we do not make this shift in the ascription of illogicality, we may start to doubt whether the account-producer (the mother) understands what is logically involved in ascribing the desire to conceal something from someone, or we may simply charge fabrication on the basis of an inconsistency in the account. Not only, then, do we seem to employ contextualizing resources economically, but also under the constraint that they accord with *locally* ascribable knowledge.

Finding that someone's thinking is logical, then, is a judgmental accomplishment not pre-determinable in its entirety by rules of logic. Finding that someone's thoughts are disorganized—even clinically disordered—is similarly not reducible to pure considerations of violations of logical form. Any such practical determinations are warranted and structured by the social distribution of knowledge and belief, the situated analysis of the case at hand, and the use of devices like strategic contextualization and its attendant economy convention.

IV

Social psychologists have tended to treat thinking solely in terms of discursive reasoning, asking questions about its strategies (e.g. Bruner's inquiry into 'scanning' and 'focussing').[32] In everyday life, the concept is not so restricted. Actions and utterances are often taken to be *expressions* of thoughts in a wider sense than 'outcomes of discursive reasoning', and in ordinary use we employ various devices and judgmental procedures in ascribing thoughts and thinking to each other. What is sociologically relevant about thought and thinking is their communicative invocation as categories of avowal and ascription, along with the whole range of publicly used 'mental-conduct concepts',[33] and the conventionalities exhibited in our ways of handling them, as competent communicators. The models of thought and thinking propagated in mentalistic psychology simply obscure the logic-in-use of these categories for us. Moreover, the misassimilation of all thinking to discursive reasoning governed by rules of logic prevents us from appreciating the polymorphous nature of the concept; its irreducibility to any *one* fixed ingredient over all cases. The further false general identification of the meanings of our words and actions with the 'corresponding thoughts' putatively in our heads has also been an unfortunate legacy of psychologism.

Plotting the 'life-space' of these concepts takes us beyond the prophylactic functions of much logico-grammatical analysis. There are interactional issues bound up with uses of 'think' and 'thought'. Consider, for example, the issue of having 'the right to think (that) ...' as it mundanely arises in ordinary affairs. Take the following fragment:

(*A*)

1 A: I thought he was inviting us to dinner ...
2 B: How come?
3 A: 'Cos he asked us if we were doing anything tonight.
4 B: Well it didn't seem to *me* he wuz inviting anybody.

Characteristically, the use of 'I thought' in utterance 1 constitutes its predicate as less than rigidly espoused at the moment of speaking, although it is consistent with more than one hearing. A could be expressing a guarded conclusion still held, or retrospectively reconstituting an originally firm impression as now in doubt. B undertakes to question A's 'right to think/have thought' that A and B (and perhaps some others) were being invited to dinner. However, A produces a basis for his right in utterance 3 which turns on what Sacks has called the 'phenomenon of the *pre*-sequence'.[34] A reports having heard the person in question as having articulated a typical pre-invitation utterance (paraphrazeable as: 'Are you doing anything tonight?') which conventionally establishes expectations of an ensuing invitation. Hearing an utterance as a pre-invitation thus established A's 'right to think' that an invitation was in the offing, perhaps even implied in the utterance itself. B, however, exhibits her doubt about such an implication and renders equivocal A's right to have thought that an invitation was involved. Nonetheless, although challenged in the present instance, A's entitlement to have thought what he did traded upon a conventional structure of conversation. Such structures, along with countless other life contingencies, furnish entitlements to co-conversationalists to take utterances in certain ways, even though the defeasibility of any given hearing may occasion its articulation in guarded ways.

There is an interesting, systematic undecidability (not always detected as such by co-participants) in utterances of 'I thought (that) . . .' occurring in members' accounts which has to do with the temporal relationship of the subject of the account to the moment of account-production. Take the following extract:[35]

(*B*)

1 A: Thought Pepper was gonna come over.

2 B: I dunno what could've happened.

(1.5 secs.)

3 A: Anyway they called ( ) couple times, two three times.

4 B: What day was that?.

A's first utterance contains: 'Thought' plus predicate, in which his use of 'thought' may signal his guarded orientation some time before the present moment (in the sense that he was not *sure* that Pepper would come over) or, conversely, it may be heard to index his *current* recognition of her non-arrival even though prior to this time he would perhaps have been prepared to say *un*guardedly that she would come over. He could hardly *now* be saying: 'Knew Pepper was gonna come over', even if *beforehand* he would have been prepared to say: 'I *know* Pepper's coming over tonight; she 'phoned to say so.' A similar inferential undecidability arises in fragment (*A*). Ordinarily, however, these undecidabilities are of no practical consequence. Whichever way such locutions are taken, it is clear that the employment of the expression 'I thought (that)' has nothing to do with the description of a mental experience and everything to do with the character of the information being disclosed. We may be articulating a prior guardedness or engaging in 'guardedness by hindsight', but we are not reporting upon a stream of occurrences in our heads. Although we may report upon a silent soliloquy[36] in saying: 'I was thinking (that) . . .', we may also employ this expression to preface the disclosure of an opinion we hold which at no particular time we have actually *recited* to ourselves. And the cogency of our disclosure of our thoughts does not turn upon their having been expressed in sentences inwardly articulated.

6 Phenomenological Residua

I have been attempting to make a case for understanding various aspects of our 'subjectivity' as interpersonally negotiable; for construing the social setting and its participants as primary in the ascription and ratification of the mental predicates discussed so far. Even if we feel secure in our private moments, once we make public disclosure of our thoughts, understandings, intentions, recollections, perceptions, motives and sensations, we place ourselves within a social orbit of appraisal and judgment; our subjectivity becomes analyzeable within a shared, situated frame of reference. We must 'live up to' the requisites of others, satisfy their contextual, presuppositional and biographical analyses, locate our cognition within the topic-frames of discourse, and become (albeit defeasibly) transparent. Our opacities are preserved only at varying interactional costs and on pain of perversity; we sustain our presumptively 'incorrigible' self-ascriptions against the circumstantially criterial rebuttals of our interactants only if we disdain the judgments afforded by our common culture. We may actively court, or not know enough to avoid, the ascription of ignorance of the concept, deceit, pretence, lying, joking, and a host of negative or down-grading counter-assertions wherever we fly in the face of the grammar of mental-predicate disclosure. We may, conversely, get away with flouting the conventionally-established terms in which we are entitled to avow our cognitive and experiential orientations, our sensations and our dreams. And yet, when we do so, we literally do not understand the meanings of our own words. I can, if I wish, say: 'I don't know whether this state of mind, in which I now am, is the expectation of an explosion or of something else'.[1] Yet in saying this I am making no literal sense, whatever may be my figurative intention. For, as Wittgenstein has remarked, the language-game in which the expression 'I have the expectation that . . .' has a part to play is one in which the expression is itself a verbal reaction, 'the movement of the pointer, which shows the object of expectation'.[2] Whatever my state of mind may be, I am disallowed by linguistic convention from articulating the *specific* uncertainty about what I expect embodied in the first expression (but I am allowed to articulate a *general* uncertainty about what *to* expect). If I vascillate about the likelihood of an explosion, this is not at all the same as, *per impossibile*, vascillating about my *expectation* of an explosion. And if I say: 'I expect it to explode in ten seconds', others will judge from my conduct whether I really mean what I say. (They may be misled, of course, and the bomb may claim us all because I was calmly anticipating my own suicide and failed to inform them of my intention; instead of grasping that possibility, they appraised my behavior to belie my claim.) Similarly, I can, if I wish, say: 'You disturbed me as I was intending to go away tomorrow', and I can hope that this will be understood as: 'You disturbed me as I was performing the mental act of intending to go away tomorrow', but others who speak English better than I, having grasped the use of 'intend', are highly unlikely to hear me complaining about the interruption of my 'mental act', but as complaining about being disturbed in the course of preparing myself to leave the next day, where they understand 'as I was intending to go away tomorrow' as *the reason for* my saying of them that they disturbed me, and *not* as specifying the *process that was disturbed*. For intending is not a process, however I may abuse the word.[3]

It is in these ways that our public language regulates our interpersonal assessment of 'subjective possibilities'. We each have a limited sovereignty over the disclosure of those possibilities, and often the practical sovereignty which we are permitted is a pseudo-sovereignty granted by misusing our linguistic resources and our reasoning. However, even as we narrow down the dimensions of the 'private', there remains a stubborn conviction that there, at the heart of human existence, lies a residue to which philosophers and psychologists have given various designators: the 'I', the 'ego', the 'self'.

In what follows, I seek to dispose of this 'nomological dangler', as Feigl would have it.[4] I shall start by trying to demonstrate that the concept of the 'I' or 'ego' has functioned in lay and psycho-philosophical theorizing as an explanatory fiction, a kind of metaphysical stop-gap for a misconceived *system* of explanation of human conduct. Then I shall try to show how this concept has functioned within the peculiar iconography of both the Freudian and the Husserlian miscomprehensions of consciousness. Finally, I shall draw out some positive theses about the concept of 'I', connecting these theses to what Gunderson has called an 'ontologically benign' view of subjectivity.[5]

The 'I' As Explanatory Fiction

George Herbert Mead went further than most other theorists of his day in pacifying the concept of self; he argued that our unspoken ratiocinations derive from our socialized resources (especially gestures and linguistic symbols), and that we can symbolize ourselves to ourselves—become objects or topics for our own reflection—only through acquiring the capacity to symbolize the roles played by others and to 'take the role of the other' in organizing our own conduct. We learn by communicating with others that symbols can arouse in ourselves the sort of responses which they can arouse in others, and we thereby become our own stimulators, establishing a conceptual distance from ourselves that enables us to reflect upon our own faculties and powers as we do upon those of other people.[6] Although this account has an immediate appeal and plausibility, for it grounds a once-metaphysical 'entity' within the sphere of social relations, it is developed into a system of explanation of actual social behavior. People are claimed to relate to one another by orienting to each others' socially-allocated roles and the rules or expectations afforded by such roles, and their personalities, systems of relevance and purpose and concrete courses of action are viewed as wholly derivative from the internalization of other's specific roles or from the adoption of the generalized social attitudes of the culture or subculture to which they belong. (This organized set of generalized social attitudes was termed by Mead 'the generalized other'.[7]) In this way, Mead established a closed system of explanation of personality, self-hood and social activity—an archetype of what Wrong has referred to as an 'oversocialized conception of man'.[8] However, he realized that, prior to the introduction of his distinction between the 'I' and the 'me', he had erected a theoretical framework within which creativity, novelty and innovation played no part. Until his discussion of the 'I', he had merely 'hinted that the self does not consist simply in the bare organization of social attitudes'.[9] Fundamentally, it was the dynamic role accorded to the 'I' as an hypostatized element of the personality or the self which saved Mead from reducing the 'human organism' to the level of cultural and 'judgmental dope',[10] in Garfinkel's felicitous phrase. Kolb comments on this move:

Mead gives no explicit explanation of the facts of social change

or of the fact that the actions of individuals never exactly correspond to the roles which they are expected to play, prior to
the introduction of the 'I' and 'me' concepts .... The 'I'
becomes accountable for everything that cannot be explained
by the organized set of roles which the individual takes over
in the process of social interaction.[11]

Mead invokes a kind of phenomenological 'evidence' for dividing
up 'the self' into the 'I' and the 'me'. Whereas the 'me' is
simply the set of organized social roles or social attitudes, 'the
"I" is not a "me" and cannot become a "me"',[12] except in
the restricted sense that 'I become a "me" in so far as I remember
what I said':[13]

It is because of the 'I' that we say that we are never fully
aware of what we are, that we surprise ourselves by our own
action. It is as we act that we are aware of ourselves. It is
in memory that the 'I' is constantly present in experience. We
can go back directly a few moments in our experience, and
then we are dependent upon memory images for the rest. ...
As given, it is a 'me', but it is a 'me' which was the 'I'
at the earlier time. If you ask, then, where directly in your
own experience the 'I' comes in, the answer is that it comes
in as a historical figure.[14]

No sooner does the 'I' serve to initiate action (as 'the response
of the organism',[15]) than it becomes available only as itself a role,
a feature of socialized attitudes. There is no way to grasp the
'I' apart from through the *mediation* of socialized resources identified
with the 'me'. Mead argues, 'It is what you were a second ago
that is the "I" of the "me". It is another "me" that has to
take the role. You cannot get the immediate response of the "I"
in the process'.[16]

Although there is much to confuse in this account, it is strongly
reminiscent of Sartre's contention that 'No-one would deny for
a moment that the *I* appears in a reflected consciousness ... there
is no *I* on the unreflected level'.[17] Whatever reified item is being
made to act as a referent for the concept 'I', it is clear that
during the course of purposeful practical action the objects of attention
or manipulation, of thought or of gaze, do not include anything
which we might take to be the 'I'. However, retrospectively, we
might conceive of ourselves as having been the subjects of such
a course of action, and we might conjure up a picture of ourselves
as the active agent and allow that picture to suggest to us that
we have located something to 'stand for' the 'I' in comments

such as: 'I did X'. We shall return to the phenomenological contro-
versy further on.

Mead moves on to employ his category of the 'I' in order
to inject an element of indeterminacy into his system. Having claimed
that the 'I' is the source of action, the mainspring or initiator
of responses, he remarks that 'this response of the "I" is something
that is more or less uncertain'[18] and he adds that 'The "I" gives
the sense of freedom, of initiative'.[19] More specifically:

> ... the 'I' is something that is never entirely calculable. The
> 'me' does call for a certain sort of 'I' in so far as we meet
> the obligations that are given in conduct itself, but the 'I' is
> always something different from what the situation itself calls
> for. The self is essentially a social process going on with these
> two distinguishable phases. *If it did not have these two phases there*
> *could not be conscious responsibility, and there would be nothing novel*
> *in experience.*[20] [italics mine].

Having theoretically filled minds with social roles and attitudes,
having explicitly argued for a view of mind 'as the individual
importation of the social process',[21] Mead is now confronted with
the need to supply a motor which could navigate, select, drive
and review the internalized collection of roles and attitudes, something
which could transform these abstract resources into concrete activities.
He realizes that he very nearly depicted human beings as passive
products of their socialization, as mere receptacles of social resources,
as total conformists to the dictates and requirements of the 'organized
set of roles'. (Note the reference to 'conscious responsibility': surely
this marks a recognition on Mead's part that by almost submerging
human individuality into the culture's pregiven roles and attitudes
he has theoretically excused everyone from any *personal* responsibility
for their actions.) With the 'I' concept, Mead can build into
his model of human conduct a transcendental element to 'account
for' the unpredictabilities of so much of that conduct.

> ... if one puts up his side of the case, asserts himself over
> against others and insists that they take a different attitude toward
> himself, then there is something important occurring that is not
> previously present in experience.[22]

Mead does not address himself in any detail to the question
of *how* the move is made from a model of mind as consisting
in abstract socialized resources to the innovative, unpredictable,
trans-experiential activities of the 'I', except to note that it is
the 'I' which inspires and guides *creative* conduct, whilst the 'me'

both feeds in resources and controls the otherwise random impulsivity of the 'I'. It is not clear to what extent the 'me' is being used to designate the prevailing and observable social situation within which the person is to act and to what extent the 'me' signifies the stored-up resources for action. Moreover, the 'I' is usually taken to refer to the basis of all action in the individual actor, *as well as* to the novel or unpredictable response of the actor in a given situation. It seems clear that Mead uses his 'I'-concept as a residual category in a variety of (occasionally contradictory) ways. But the overall thrust of his discussion goes counter to the strictly (social-) behavioristic perspective announced as Mead's general position, and it is probably his acknowledgement of human creativity, his recognition of the limits of social determinism and his (albeit confusing) 'phenomenology' of the self which contribute to his contemporary incorporation into phenomenology proper by scholars like Natanson.[23] Despite some attempts (e.g. by Young[24]) to biologize Mead's concept of 'I' by seeing it as rooted in the constitutional foundations of the human organism, we can perhaps see that there are several metaphysical aspects to it.

We could, I believe, paraphrase most of Mead's general theory of conduct in such a way that his category of the 'I' disappears, but we would need to rework much of the discussion of social roles, responses and mind. Mead does not conceptualize social situations as open to appraising judgments on the part of their participant actors with respect to what conduct is entitled, required or sanctioned therein; rather, he treats social situations in quasi-behavioristic terms as fields of environing stimuli eliciting responses from human organisms. He does not conceptualize people as rule-following subjects employing their resources according to grammatical, normative and other sorts of conventions, but as role-playing animals operating mechanically on the basis of their capacity to take the roles of others, with the addition of an incalculable determinant of creative conduct in the 'I'. It is his attachment to the deterministic language of behaviorism which compels him to speak of locating a basis for *responses* in the 'I' rather than to speak of people doing the various things they do appropriately, rationally, intelligently, or otherwise. Where creative conduct is concerned (and Mead does not go into details on the nature and range of conduct considered 'novel'), the explanatory power of the 'I'-concept is transparently restricted; indeed, with this notion, Mead effectively explains *away* creative conduct which, in his scheme, is quite residual and as such is handled in a residual way with this vague and confused construction. His successors, like Blumer[25] and Kuhn[26], either ignore the notion altogether or express serious reservations about its sense and utility. Its explanatory failure is instructive, however, in that it points up the serious limitations to any attempt at the *generalized* explanation of human action. The distinctions between the vast varieties of actual actions are simply overlooked; the more generic distinctions between speech-acts and non-verbal conduct and between two-party and *n*-party actions are absent; the parameters of novelty are nowhere specified (and the most continuous type of creative activity—the production and understanding of novel sentences/utterances—is ignored in the discussions of language). Mead did succeed, to some extent, in linking the individual subjectivity to the social order, but his conceptualization of the nature of that connection is ultimately unsatisfactory. Instead of persons using their resources according to their generative capacities, which remain to be described, we find references to egological source-points somehow being both initiators of all *responses* (which Mead does not distinguish from constructed, albeit routine, activity) as well as initiators of *new* lines of conduct, and yet undifferentiated theoretically with respect to these different functions.

It is singularly strange that social psychology and sociology have often furnished generalized explanations of human action which become quite vacuous when concretized for *particular* actions. For instance, treating all action as the product of orientations to role and informed by the manoeuvrings of the ego will not *illuminate* any particular, situated action performed by someone in the actual world. (Compare the cash-value of generalized physical theories in particular cases: the general relationships postulated in Boyle's law governing the behavior of gases do indeed illuminate the behavior of particular gases in particular environmental conditions.)

Another puzzling element in Mead's account is the juxtaposition of a purely *technical* conception of the 'I', in which various capacities are ascribed to it within the theoretical system being developed, and the attempt to specify its *experiential* dimensions as a feature of (reflective) awareness. From Mead's 'phenomenology' of the 'I' we cannot derive any of the properties ascribed to it in the theoretical account (e.g. its role as an unpredictable initiator of action; its character as a source of novel conduct). I am not aware, even retrospectively, of an 'I' within myself that ('uncertainly') generated my course of action; I only know/believe that I did something, where my use of 'I' is a speaker-specifying, self-ascriptive device or token and not the name of an entity, mental or otherwise, interior to me. Mead's experiential characterization of the 'I' is redundant; it is poor as experiential description, and useless as a buttress or warrant for his theoretical stipulations about behavior.

Perhaps Mead, like others, fell victim to the sort of impulse which besets theorists who stress the 'internalization' of social roles and attitudes. After depicting people as performing roles in everything they do, the theorist then faces a quandry which has been articulated by MacIntyre as not knowing

> what the identity of the individual consists in and how the real individual may be distinguished from his pretences and performances.[27]

MacIntyre poses this as a genuine problem for Goffman[28] whose dramaturgical assimilation of human conduct leads him into a similar trap. However, the 'problem' is a theoretical artefact; there is no *generalized* answer to the question of who someone *really* is—only particularized answers in particular contexts, just as there can be no truly generalized account (independent of acting contexts) of why someone behaved as he did, or why some class of persons do what they do. All such questions, about who people are and why they are doing what they are doing, must be answered (if the answers are not to be vacuous) in the light of the purposes—practical, engaged—informing the posing of the question, and in the light of the sociohistorical circumstances of the acting individuals concerned. Notice that the question: 'what is X's *real* identity' only logically arises in situations in which the inquirer has reasons to suspect that the category under which X is supposed to be operating (doctor, teacher, ambassador) is in fact *not* the category genuinely informing his behavior. So, we find that the 'doctor' is in fact a fake practitioner, the 'teacher' a strike-breaking outsider, and the 'ambassador' a foreign intelligence agent. But having found out these things, it still makes sense to say of these people that they are *also*, in other contexts and for other purposes, fathers, Republicans, churchgoers, bookworms, veterans and so on. In fact, as Sacks has shown so elegantly,[29] the problem of member-categorization is a practical-reasoning problem solved (for situated purposes) in social interaction in quite orderly ways. There are selection relevances and selection preferences for member-categorization that can be described for types of ordinary conversation.[30] It is the road to metaphysics and the terminus of meaningful inquiry to pose the problem of member-categorization *outside of* practical contexts, as if it were a general theoretical problem for the human sciences to resolve.

The proposition that human conduct can be understood generically in terms of roles and role-playing also has its dangers. Am I, for instance, to be understood as now playing the *role* of the author of a book or paper? If so, then this would strongly imply that I am not *really* the author of a book or paper, but masquerading as such. (Which might be a way of down-grading what I would describe myself as now doing, but hardly illuminating what I am doing; in my eyes I am certainly the author of this piece of work, whatever its demerits!) Sociologists and social psychologists have been too quick to take literally their own metaphorical constructions, and then turning around to find themselves faced with a paradox of their own creation. They forget the delicate grammar of the concepts they employ (such as 'role', 'I') and over-extend them to the point where their use leads to unpalatable conceptual consequences and puzzles. Only *on occasion* may I be described as taking on the role of such-and-such, unless the describer wishes to imply about me that I never behave naturally under my category-auspices, or that I am never who I seem to be.

It is plausible to suggest that social theorists are driven to metaphorical constructions because they conceive of their enterprize as *necessarily* explanatory in the general, scientific sense. If they were to re-conceptualize their purely technical task as one of analytical description (in the manner illustrated in my first chapter), they would not find any need to have recourse to metaphorical models of man. Fictional explanations require explanatory fictions. Mead's 'I' is a paradigmatic case in point.

Iconographies of Mind: Freud and Husserl

I am avoiding, in this work, any protracted discussion of Freud. This is in large part because I find myself unable to take his theory of mental functioning seriously enough to do it an expository justice, and in part because sociologists are not in general much influenced by his explanatory endeavors in their own work. However, no discussion of the 'ego' can omit reference to Freud's general position. Sketching this position is difficult, however, for, as Thalberg has commented:

> Freud's conception of the ego (*das Ich*) was unsettled prior to 1923. Frequently he seems to mean by 'ego' the whole person (1894, 1920). Other passages, occasionally in the same works, suggest that the ego is a component of one's mind, and that Freud is contrasting the ego with parts of which one is unconscious (1894, 1895, 1920). At times Freud makes the ego a delegate within us of morality, which censors our ideas. It keeps shameful items away from our 'consciousness' (1900). Here Freud cannot be contrasting our ego with parts of our mind which elude our awareness. A person is no more aware that his ego is engaged in censorship than he is of what it excludes from his consciousness. Finally, in his *Project* of 1895, Freud presents the ego as nothing but a sub-system of 'neurones' whose job it is to maximize

'discharge' of psychic energy from our whole homeostatic mental apparatus (1950).[31]

For Freud, the 'ego' is 'located' mentally between the primordial 'id' and the civilizing, socially-constituted 'super-ego'. Freud once compared his picture of their inter-relationship to the relationship of rider to horse. The 'ego' brings the influence of the external world to bear on the crude impulsivities of the 'id' (seeking to substitute the reality-principle for the pleasure-principle). The 'ego' is also in charge of much of the individual's motility, but the rider now must use borrowed forces and occasionally rest content with the superior power of the 'id' and merely guide it where it wants to go. The 'ego', then, is always in some contact with the 'id'. The 'super-ego' may also be in occasional conflict with the 'ego', since the 'super-ego' is a wholly external derivative imposed upon the individual through socialization. (Note that by picturing socialization in this way, Freud is seeking to build a constraint into his model against blind and passive introjection of culture and its norms on the part of individuals.) The 'ego' is that agency which takes into account both the impulse and the conflicting super-ego demands and designs and executes the act. In later work, the picture changes.

I believe that Freud's model constitutes a psychological iconography of the most bizarre and reifying kind in the history of the subject, but that it is quite intelligible as a metaphorical construction designed to come to terms in general with the common experiences of socialization and conduct. It comes to grief only because it encourages psychology to seek and construct fictional explanations rather than allow its conceptualizations to be constrained by the logic of ordinary concepts and the limits of generality in theorizing about human behavior in its specifically human aspect.

Given that Freud thought of the mind on the analogy of the brain (he was at the beginning a gifted neurologist), it is to be expected that his theorizing would take the form of a kind of spatial mapping of the zones of the mind, each with its structure and function described in very general terms. It is also natural that he would describe mental goings-on in terms of physical 'forces' and 'energies', employing hydraulic categories like 'displacement' and 'discharge', with barriers set up in the form of 'endo-psychic censors' repressing materials in the way that neural inhibition is effected by blockages and re-routings of electrical-chemical impulses. Indeed, the impulsivity of the 'id' seems to be based on the literal impulsivity of neural cells firing and nervous tissue conducting impulses here and there to be channelled or released or attenuated in the brain. Freud's topology of mind is **quite** directly informed by the topology of the brain, and eventually, as Thalberg observed, he lapses into undisguised reductionism, asserting that the 'ego' *is* a sub-system of neurones, and the mind a homeostatic apparatus.

I noted earlier that Freud's model of mind is not in general use by contemporary sociology (with the major exception of Jurgen Habermas). Burgess[32] and Eliot[33] have documented the early influences of Freud on American sociology, and Swanson[34] in his essay on Mead and Freud commented upon the affinity for sociological perspectives on socialization of the Freudian concept of the 'super-ego', although it is not clear why sociologists really required such an additional construct. Parsons[35] borrowed heavily from Freud in constructing his account of family socialization processes and the general theory of human action, but such incorporations were deemed intellectually unsatisfying by subsequent commentators, and the new generation of sociologists seems largely immune to Freudian influences. The early attempts to marry Freud to Marx, resumed by Marcuse in his *Eros and Civilization*,[36] failed to attain a consensus amongst critical theorists more impressed with the philosophical anthropology available directly from Marx himself in his early writings and with the elaborations provided by Lukács and Mészáros. The notion that within all of us there is a component able to generate action, organize what we think, and subsist in part unsusceptible to cultural and ideological influences—the Freudian 'ego'—was considered, and I believe correctly, to be a reactionary dogma as well as an unfalsifiable pseudo-scientific postulate. For most sociologists, especially those who are also in the Marxist camp, man consists in his social relations, and there is no meaningful category beyond the sociohistorical and the biological with which to analyze human conduct. Although Freud's 'ego' partakes of both the social and the organic, it is usually made to stand apart from either in metaphorical isolation and ontological functioning.

Again, we can perhaps detect in the Freudian scheme the sort of confusions that arise when the theorist seeks some generic answer to the question: what is it that accounts for my distinctive individuality as a person, rather than as a mere organism? What can account for my unique modes of orientation, my unique structure of relevances? Granted that I share many orientations and relevances with my fellows (indeed, I must if I am to enter into intelligible relationships with them, even as mortal enemy), there is nonetheless something quite differentiating about me apart from my particular organic constitution. In what does it consist? The answer cannot be: culture. This is because it is precisely cultural knowledge and norms that provide for my shared features of orientation and action. Social roles and attitudes are exactly trans-individual, and hence cannot be appealed to in order to 'explain' my idiosyncratic ways, my specific constellation of emotional and cognitive requirements, needs and aspirations. My speech is individuated not only by much manifest content, but also by tone, occasionality, accompaniments, stress, gesture and so on. Why?

I do not think that there is anything very fruitful to be gained in pursuing this question at the level at which it is being posed. This seems especially to be arguable in the light of the Freudian and Meadian reifications of the concept of 'I' and the subsequent confusions that beset their theorizing. However, we might profitably ask a reformulated question, *viz.* by what conventional procedures of reasoning do members ascribe activities to someone's unique individuality? What are the conventional presuppositions of the work of explaining actions in ordinary situations with reference to someone's personality? These ethnomethodological ways of posing the question are empirically meaningful. The other direction for empirical study would presumably be the neurosciences, and I understand from their literature that neither the theory nor the experimental and analytical technology are yet available to enable investigators to so specify brain functioning as to differentiate between individual personalities, with the exception of clearly *morbid*, organic cases such as brain-damaged or brain-diseased psychosyndromes.[37] Had Freud not sought to erect a *general* theory of the personality, we might have been spared the many confusions he introduced in to the study of conduct. And the practice of psychoanalysis might have been more harmlessly rhetorical, normative and hermeneutical, more transparently consisting of interpersonal devices and strategies of persuasion, than is now the case.

Husserl's iconography of consciousness is cut from quite different cloth. He had no general explanatory intentions, and his difficulties with the 'ego' derive from a wholly different problematic.

Seeking to ground all scientific claims in the pre-reflective sphere of mundane experience, Husserl sought to elucidate the basic concepts of experience and perception by bracketing all questions of the reality or unreality of external objects, events and persons, and to uncover the essential structures of our modes of experiencing and being aware of phenomena as they appear. We have already said something in a prior chapter about the conceptual miscomprehension of categories like 'appear' and the projection of qualified descriptions of real phenomena into a mental or 'phenomenal' realm (where 'it appears to be so-and-so' is taken to be a description of something phenomenal or mental, whereas it is a guarded or qualified description of something objectively present, or even, as in cases like 'it appears *as* a white dot on the horizon', a quite *un*guardedly objective description). What Husserl sought was a series of descriptions of how our conscious and 'intentional' acts of looking constitute the world of appearances *as* a world populated with the familiar objects, events and persons apprehended naively in our practical and pre-reflective affairs. Nothing was to be allowed to pass unanalyzed as the product of the constitutive work of our intentional (*noetic*) acts. But then, asked Husserl, what about the 'ego'? Can we treat the basic presupposition of every intentional act of consciousness as itself constituted by consciousness, or must we treat the ego as *transcendental*, as beyond the constitutive grasp of phenomenological description? He remarks:

> Difficulties arise just at one limiting point. Man as a natural being and as a person linked with others in a personal bond, the uniting bond of 'society', is suspended [or bracketed—JC], so too whatever possesses an animal nature. But how fares it then with the pure Ego? Is even the phenomenological Ego which finds things presented to it brought through the phenomenological reduction to transcendental nothingness? . . . So much is clear from the outset, that after carrying this reduction through, we shall never stumble across the pure Ego as an experience among others within the flux of manifold experiences which survives as transcendental residuum; nor shall we meet it as a constitutive bit of experience appearing with the experience of which it is an integral part and again disappearing. The Ego appears to be permanently, even necessarily, there, and this permanence is obviously not that of a stolid unshifting experience, of a 'fixed idea'. On the contrary, it belongs to every experience that comes and streams past. . . .[38]

Husserl reasons that the Ego lies behind every *cogito* (or intentional act of consciousness) and as such is resistant to the phenomenological reduction or bracketing of all objectivities *per se*. As such, the nature or essence of the Ego is impenetrable to phenomenological, constitutive analysis. It remains beyond the grasp of phenomenology, and is therefore transcendental. It is always a residual component of consciousness, but never open to constitutive analysis because it does not show itself as an experience or feature of any particular experience. It *stands behind* all experiences. Husserl's acceptance of a transcendental Ego meant that he conceded that objects were dependent for their various assignable characteristics upon something immune from phenomenological analysis. Since Husserl had started out in his philosophical quest by denying that consciousness has any self-generated contents, but rather that it has only integral, intentional relations with phenomena outside itself which it constitutes in various aspects (there is only 'consciousness *of* . . . '), the admission of an Ego in back of all acts of consciousness implies that consciousness itself must have some *content*, thus refuting the claim of phenomenology to be able to give descriptions of phenomena *in their own right* as constituted by intentional acts alone. For now we introduce something over and above intentional, constituting acts—we have an Ego which is not itself constituted by any intentional act of consciousness but which is rather presupposed by all such acts, and upon which the characteristics of objects are predicated.

It was Sartre who, in his *The Transcendence of the Ego*,[39] sought to refute Husserl's doctrine of the transcendental Ego and its implications for phenomenological description. He boldly asserts, contrary to Husserl, that there is only an Ego *for* consciousness, not behind it or presupposed by it. He tries to reintroduce the early Husserlian doctrine that consciousness as such is the realm of absolute priority, that it has no content, and that objects are *for* consciousness and not *in* consciousness. For Sartre, intentional acts *are* consciousness, whereas for Husserl they had become only *one* essential feature of consciousness. He argues:

> ... the phenomenological conception of consciousness renders the unifying and individualizing role of the *I* totally useless. It is consciousness, on the contrary, which makes possible the unity and the personality of my *I*. The transcendental *I*, therefore, has no *raison d'être*.[40]

Arguing apodictically, Sartre charges that my *I* is no more certainly given for consciousness than the *I* of other men.[41] It is only more 'intimate'.[42] There is no thematic unity to consciousness to be discovered by phenomenological reduction; in Sartre's terms,

> ... transcendental consciousness is an impersonal spontaneity. It determines its existence at each instant, without our being able to conceive anything *before* it. Thus each instant of our conscious life reveals to us a creation *ex nihilo*. Not a new *arrangement*, but a new existence.[43]

This 'impersonalization' of consciousness has troubled some commentators. For example, Spiegelberg, noting that Sartre was attempting to show that the Ego is not the immanent source of consciousness but rather its 'constituted object' (in reflection), comments:

> Sartre's attack on the pure ego, which he replaces by a stream of impersonal consciousness, actually volatilizes existence. By denying it a center and the dimension of inwardness he deprives it at the same time of its existential weight.[44]

Spiegelberg here raises a similar issue to the one faced by Mead, namely, to account for the idiosyncracies and particularities of individual orientations in the world given the initial postulation of a more-or-less homogeneous and impersonal collection of shared resources. Without his 'I', like Husserl without his 'pure Ego', Mead faced impersonalizing and volatilizing human existence. Whereas for Sartre, the Ego is viewed as a device for thematizing experience *post hoc*, for Husserl and Mead it was an ontological or quasi-ontological agent, a center or source; for the former a center of consciousness, for the latter a source of responses and creative action.

Sociologically, what are we to make of the 'I'? Does it pose for us any intractable difficulties standing in the way of our analytical explications? At this point, we must turn to consider some more positive theses, ones more amenable to our overall approach in this work, and see whether they can be defended.

The Concept of 'I' in Linguistic Philosophy

'I' is not the name of a person, nor 'here' of a place, and 'this' is not a name. But they are connected with names. Names are explained by means of them. It is also true that it is characteristic of physics not to use these words.[45]

Wittgenstein's reminder is immediately relevant to this discussion, for he was seeking to dereify the concept of 'I' by returning to examine its logical space—its parameters of reasoned use in ordinary language. Instead of conceiving of 'I' as an elusive residuum or a kind of opaque ontological mystery, we should pay very careful attention to the use of the concept in everyday linguistic activity. Like 'this' and 'now', they are indexical tokens specifying different items for attention depending upon the context of utterance: 'I' is speaker-specifying, 'this' an index word for utterance-topic, or an object/person/event under discussion or perceptual indication, 'now' betokening the moment (or range of moments) of actual utterance. Even this is too narrow, because there is a sense in which 'I', when it occurs in various types of utterance (e.g. 'I am in pain'), does not call attention to a particular person among a group of people; it is not susceptible to referential *failure*, and hence does not genuinely function in many of its uses as a referential expression or demonstrative pronoun. On the other hand, in saying something like: 'I have grown six inches', the word 'I' is being used as an object-expression. I can be wrong about the increase in the height of my body, and wherever the possibility of referential failure is provided for, the word is being used in its object-sense.

If I say: 'I have broken my arm' when I have just been in an auto accident and spot a broken arm next to my body which I take to be mine, then I have made a referential mistake of the sort which is unthinkable for cases in which 'I' is being used as subject, e.g., in expressions such as: 'I've a bad toothache'.

We feel then that in the cases in which 'I' is used as subject, we don't use it because we recognize a particular person by his bodily characteristics; and this creates the illusion that we use this word to refer to something bodiless, which, however, has its seat in our body.[46]

And yet we should not conclude that every case in which 'I' is used as *object* (broadly, its bodily or body-part applications) requires of the speaker that he recognize or identify anything about himself. As Hacker has pointed out, 'I am being looked at by him' involves no self-identification or recognition, but is *not* immune to error relative to the speaker. After all, I may be correct about his looking at a person, but wrong in thinking that the person in question is myself—he may be looking at someone behind me.[47] Moreover, my use of 'I' as *subject* presupposes, though does not consist in the exercise of, an ability on my part to identify a person. Identifying something as oneself presupposes the possession of a certain sort of knowledge which could not itself spring naked, so to speak, from one's psyche; it is socialized knowledge.

It is worth mentioning here that Ryle's treatment of what he termed 'the systematic elusiveness of "I"'[48] is deficient in the discrimination of the two basic modalities of use indicated by Wittgenstein ('I' as subject and 'I' as object). For Ryle, 'I'-sentences are analyzed in this early work exclusively in terms of second- or higher-order performances in which the speaker applies 'the method of inter-personal transaction' as a sort of observer of his own functioning.[49] It is necessary to supplement this account with some reference to the non-object uses of 'I' as in 'I feel faint', etc. Here, 'observation' is quite irrelevant, because it makes no sense to say of someone that he could be mistaken in his claim, when sincerely made, about feeling faint. Wittgenstein assimilates these latter cases to his non-cognitive thesis of avowals of psychological states, in which he argues that feelings, pains, etc. are had, not observed, and expressions of them using 'I' are not predicated upon observation (with the attendant risks of observational failure) but upon having them and *reacting to them verbally*. The *form* of the verbal reaction to a sensation will depend upon the speaker's having a prior grasp of the criteria for person-identification, but will not in the present instance depend upon the *application* of any such criteria. I must be able to understand other people's sincere utterances of 'I am in pain' as grounds for saying of them that they are in pain, just as I must know that observers of me, when I sincerely say 'I am in pain', can locate in my saying so grounds for asserting 'He is in pain'.

Although complex, and interwoven with other uses of language, the concept of 'I' is not mysterious in any psychological sense, and much of the mystery that has been spun around the notion derives from misconstruing its actual functioning in ordinary language. 'I' does not denote a spiritual locus of experiences somewhere inside me; it is not the name of an entity, although it can betoken a body or body-part in some of its applications in speaking. Because others cannot investigate me and use 'I' in their accounts of me, it should not be thought that there is therefore something necessarily hidden away eternally from our understanding of people. Following Gunderson, we have to realize 'why this makes no more difference (ontologically) than the fact that a submarine's periscope cannot locate itself in its own crosshairs makes an ontological difference between the nature of the periscope doing the sighting and the things it can sight'.[50] The problem in realizing that I, not just my body but other things about me, can become an object for investigation lies in part in my failure to understand that although I cannot treat myself as an object of investigation in every respect this does not mean that others cannot so treat me: 'once we are aware that the unpublic nature of my self vis-a-vis me does not show my self to be unpublic simpliciter, each of us is then in a position to see and describe ourselves by way of an acceptance of how others see and describe us. . . .'[51] The ensuing arguments about other people's descriptions of us can then be organized around meaningful issues (such as public evidence, fairness in appraisal, and so on) rather than around essentially metaphysical ones about the purely private Ego.

The Meadian, Freudian, Husserlian and Sartrean analyses of the concept of 'I' (which they all mistakenly construed as investigations of the properties of some *phenomenon*) each in its own way began from a specific sort of ontological assumption; Mead and Freud employed their ontologized version of 'I' for misguided explanatory purposes, whilst Husserl and Sartre did so for essentially speculative and mentalistic reasons. (They have all, in the process, developed strange ideas about mind and consciousness; in philosophical psychology, one category-error seems to beget several more.) It surely cannot be claimed for their analyses that they were self-consciously metaphorical. Such a 'defence' cannot be squared with the claims of each theoretician to be providing a literal and scientific account of mind. (Mead, Freud, Husserl and Sartre have each avowed such an aim in their writing; Mead the strict scientific inheritor and developer of scientific behaviorism and Darwinism, Freud the self-proclaimed scientist, Husserl the founder of phenomenology as a rigorous science, and Sartre the wayward early disciple of Husserl.)[52]

Rather than join in these traditions, I believe that any rational approach to the study of mind should break from them. Interpersonally recordable ascriptions, avowals, appraisals, disavowals and other speech events involving cognitive predicates are available for inspection. The ethnomethodological analysis of such public phenomena as self- and other-appraisals and ascriptions can proceed unencumbered by the argument that somewhere lurks a phenomenological residue called the 'I' which, if it were only public, could explain us all.

7 Affect and Social Context

Sociology has had little to say about the nature of 'affective' or emotional conduct, perhaps primarily because, following Max Weber's lead, it has generally been hived off theoretically from the bulk of 'rational' action in human affairs, downgraded to a sort of appendage to social relations and consigned to a permanently residual status. Mistakenly thought of as beyond the scope of social convention and constraint, affective states have been allowed to fall exclusively within the province of psychology. In its turn, psychology has generated a variety of ways of handling the phenomena of affect, but few of them have remained consistent with, or controlled by, the conceptual structure of emotion-concepts, and this has entailed a serious neglect of the socio-cultural dimensions integral to the very constitution of the phenomena under study. It will be argued here that such dimensions are *primary* in the consideration of affective states and conduct. Affect and rationality are much more closely inter-related than has been noted in the behavioral sciences, and both are throughout subject to socio-cultural and sociolinguistic analysis. Affective states have too frequently been identified with feeling-states, or with other 'contents of consciousness'; they have also been theoretically 'reduced' to biological impulses or other visceral, vasomotor and biochemical transformations, or to the perception of such changes on the part of the organism. In the ensuing discussion, these issues are taken up in order to show how the relationships that obtain between particular sorts of emotions and social contexts (prior to or concurrent with their display) are analyzeable. The socio-logic of affect and affective states is a hitherto underdeveloped area outside of philosophy, and so we must begin with the clues bequeathed to us by the philosophy of mind.

Emotions as Internal Episodes

In one form or another, the basic categories of emotion—e.g. anger, fear, grief, shame, happiness, guilt, disgust, regret, envy, pride, wonder, remorse, sadness, jealousy, embarrassment—will admit of combination with the concept of feeling; thus, we get 'feels angry', 'feels grief-stricken', 'feels ashamed', 'feels proud' and so on. Since we can also combine the notion of 'feels' with a wide range of sensation-concepts, as in 'I feel tired', 'she feels toothache', 'he feels hungry', 'she felt thirsty', 'I feel pain', the stage is set for the misassimilation of emotions to sensations (i.e. in the formal mode, the treatment of the categories of affect as if they functioned identically in our talk to the categories of sensation). This has been a pervasive mistake in the history of philosophical and psychological reflection on the subject. Hume, for instance, remarked:

> . . . when I am angry, I am actually possessed with the passion, and in that emotion have no more reference to any other object, than when I am thirsty, or sick, or more than five feet high.[1]

Clearly, this misses the point that we cannot even begin to *identify* the emotion we are dealing with unless we take into account how a person is appraising an object or situation. Although on some occasions it makes sense for us to say of someone that he knows his own emotion better than anyone else, we should not be able to sustain this as an invariant principle in our practical, judgmental affairs with other people; the reason why we may on some occasion reckon that a person knows his own emotion(s) better than we do is not because he has private access to internal feeling-states that define for him what his emotion is but because, as Bedford has remarked, 'it is hardly possible for a man to be completely ignorant, as others may be, of the context of his own behavior'.[2] This does not mean that a person is to be thought of as analyzing his own conduct and then *concluding* that he feels angry, jealous, etc., although this can happen when, e.g., someone is debating about whether or not he really feels jealous of another person. Rather, it is to be understood in terms of his routinely knowing (whilst others may not) some circumstances entitling him to be angry, jealous, sad or any of the affective states. If someone informs us that he *feels* angry, this may be treated as corroborative rather than indispensable testimony, but *the warranted ascription of anger does not depend necessarily upon a corresponding avowal, nor upon the presence of a particular feeling-state accompanying the anger displayed.* Wittgenstein observed that emotions are not genuinely localizable in the ways in which sensations can be, although the expression-behavior of emotions (such as a tightening of the face, a rapid pulse, etc.) implies some characteristic sensations. 'But these sensations are not the emotions.'[3] He goes on to note that he would 'almost like to say: One no more feels sorrow in one's body than one feels seeing in one's eyes'.[4] It is a further variant of the fallacious doctrine of perceptual introspectionism, already discussed in the case of sensations themselves, which leads us to think that emotions are internal events. Various sensations may be bound up with syndromes of, e.g., fear, anxiety, grief and so on, but they cannot be thought of as *constituting* these emotions.

Melden has articulated the basic issue succinctly:

> When we ask ourselves whether someone is angry, our question is not whether such and such events are transpiring in the hidden chamber of his mind; nor do we, when we feel angry, turn our attention inward from the things that provoke us, the persons with whom we are angry, and the circumstances in which we show, display and vent our anger.[5]

Because people can sometimes feign or suppress their felt anger and other affective states, it is a short step to the argument that there is a 'something' absent in the case of the pretence and present in the case of the stoically undisplayed anger, where the natural candidate for this 'something' is a sensation or feeling-state. However, if we treat self-reports like 'I feel angry' as circumstantially justified or unjustified *expressions of* anger, instead of as descriptions of internal events or states, then the 'something' that may be present or absent is nothing hidden in the chamber of the mind or body, but is some justifying or entitling (set of) circumstance(s). A sensation or feeling-state could arise and be avowed intelligibly in ways that are unoccasioned by the social and historical circumstances of a meaningful environment, whereas, by contrast, the appropriate application of affect-concepts to describe someone's state *depends upon* specific arrays of meaningful circumstances. What distinguishes grief from remorse and disappointment from shame is not a determinate inner feeling but responses, actions, appraisals and situations in the social world. It is not just that we cannot locate any neatly discriminable feeling-states uniformly correlated with (let alone constitutive of) the variety of emotions which leads us to propose that emotions and sensations are different sorts of phenomena; rather, it is that emotions cannot be hived off completely from the 'weave of life';

> 'Grief' describes a pattern which recurs, with different variations, in the weave of our life. If a man's bodily expressions of sorrow and of joy alternated, say with the ticking of a clock, here we should not have the characteristic formation of the pattern of sorrow or of the pattern of joy.
> 'For a second he felt violent pain.'—Why does it sound queer to say: 'For a second he felt deep grief'? Only because it so seldom happens?[6]

Not only do emotions characteristically have meaningful objects or situations as their occasions, but such objects or situations *make emotions intelligibly present*. This is not a psychological point, but a logical one. It is not that it is impossible to experience some feeling previously associated with being ashamed in the absence of the recognition that one is open to criticism of some kind; the only argument being made here is that the *rational* avowal or ascription of shame is conceptually tied to the recognition on the part of the person of some responsibility for the object or situation of the shame, and a susceptibility to personal criticism for it. In Bedford's terms, changing the example:

> ... the decision whether to say that the driver of a car which has broken down for lack of water is indignant, or merely annoyed or angry, depends on whether the radiator is empty through (let us say) the carelessness of a garage mechanic who undertook to fill it for him, or through his own carelessness ('annoyed with myself' but not 'indignant with myself').[7]

If the driver were to state that he was *jealous* of the situation, or *elated* by it, we should not understand his claim, even if he went on to say that this was how he actually felt. We simply do not know our emotional state or the emotional state of another by accepting the recognition of a sensation to stand for the emotional state. A man is not the final court of appeal in his own case; Bedford reminds us that 'those who are jealous are often the last, instead of the first, to recognize that they are'.[8] And any such ratified recognition will hinge upon the appraisal of the specific meaningful circumstances operative in the particular case. Any affect-avowals made outside of the situated bounds of circumstantial justification or entitlement can lead to derogatory inferences as to the avowing agent's psychological condition; indeed, various self-imputed mental disorders rest upon the agent's recognition of a mis-match between his rational judgment of a situation's affect-affording features and his actual disposition to avow a specific emotion. (For example: 'I know there's no reason to be afraid of television sets; but I just can't help myself . . .') More commonly, however, ascriptions of affective disorders are undertaken by third parties (or in the third-person), because it is usually found that irrational affective states are occasioned by a delusional version of the world taken to be true. *If* any television set had the property of radiating harmful energies or of receiving one's thoughts and broadcasting them to the rest of the audience, we too may feel afraid of the object.

An emotion, unlike a sensation, may be described as reasonable or unreasonable, appropriate or inappropriate. A sensation, unlike an emotion, may be *had* as well as felt. We may, however, say something like: 'I had a pang of regret this afternoon' (where we cannot say that we had an anger or an envy), and this appears to be both a case in which we say we 'have' an emotion and also one in which the phrase 'of regret' describes the sensation of the 'pang'. However, whilst it would make no sense to ask a man who reported having had a 'pang' whether it was really reasonable or justified, it does make sense to ask a man who reported having had a 'pang of regret' whether or not it was reasonable or justified. And this shows us that a wholly different language-game is being played with the word 'pang' in the two cases; 'the pang of regret is justified, if it is, not as a feeling, but because his regret is justified'.[9] Moreover, notice that we can intelligibly suggest to people that they abandon certain emotions on rational grounds, that we can argue them out of their anger, shame, embarrassment, disappointment, fear etc. in ways that are not open to us in the case of sensations. In this sense,

> . . . our capacity to experience certain emotions is contingent upon learning to make certain kinds of appraisals and evaluations. And learning how to make these appraisals and evaluations involves more than simply learning to identify some items of observation, whether 'private' or 'public'. That is, it is not like learning to identify headaches, toothaches, tables, or even moving trains. Rather, it is learning to interpret and appraise matters in terms of norms, standards, principles, and ends or goals judged desirable or undesirable, appropriate or inappropriate, reasonable or unreasonable, and so on.[10]

(It might be remarked here that we probably do not learn to 'identify' headaches and toothaches as private phenomena, either; the argument has already been presented earlier.) Standards of judgment enter into the picture in the case of emotions; to feel some emotion is to feel in some way *about* someone or something, as Pritchard notes.[11] And it is not to feel a certain way about anything physiological, unless one is, e.g., distressed or worried or panic-stricken about a physiological matter. The James–Lange theory of the emotions, according to which an emotion is a feeling of some visceral, vasomotor or other kind of internal, physical event(s), entirely confuses this point. Whilst it is undoubtedly true that biochemical and physiological transformations of various kinds occur during or after various emotions are felt, this fact can only be established experimentally, and that presupposes an *independent* set of criteria for identifying the emotions in question; thus, emotions are not *identical* to feelings of any such kind.[12] It is nonsensical to say that an angry person is angered *by* any bodily factors, except in special circumstances where these form the object or focus of his appraisal and attention. It looks as though there might be an exception to the claim that emotions are not identical to sensations of physical changes in the case of disgust. Here, one might think of the case in which a person is disgusted with the scene left by a murderer, where he experiences genuine nausea. But note that nausea is *not* identical to disgust, and the disgust which is felt in the given case is justified not by the nausea but by the immorality and inhumanity of the act whose results are witnessed. One may be disgusted with the corruption of a politician, but no nausea need be present as a warrant for the avowal of the emotion.

Schachter and Singer conducted a series of experiments that tended to show how mere physiological arousal is insufficient to induce a subject to report that he is experiencing a specific emotion, even though the arousal was almost identical to that present in certain sorts of emotional states.[13] The experimenters injected epinephrine into volunteer subjects, a substance known to produce physical transformations similar to those found in persons undergoing various emotional reactions or in various emotional states. Some were told of the nature of the physiological reaction they would have, whilst others were told that there would be no experienced reaction whatsoever. Each subject was placed in a room with an actor who pretended to be either angry or euphoric. Those subjects who had been correctly informed about the reaction they would have to the injection did not become either angry or euphoric, whereas those who were told that they would not have a reaction tended to take on the apparent emotion of the actor.[14] Those who did not know the physical basis for their feeling-state sought some way of accounting for it, and their taking on the apparent emotion of the actor in the room with them seems to have been a function of their appraisal of their sensation *in the light of* the available social information. Similar phenomena are discussed in some of Becker's work on drug use.[15] The development of severe anxiety in cases where a novice has taken LSD-25 had usually been attributed to the pharmacological action of the drug itself. Becker, however, noted that since such apparent drug-induced anxiety states or anxiety-psychoses were generally restricted to neophyte users, some other explanation might be sought out. He proposes that when a drug user finds his subjective state altered in such a way as to fit his pre-conceptions of insanity or 'loss of mind', then such an account of the experience may occasion panic. Even long-term users may experiment with a higher dosage than usual and experience effects unlike any previously known. Unless there are others present to counteract the 'loss-of-mind' interpretation of the experience, e.g., by redefining it as desirable rather than frightening, then panic may occur on the part of the user. Becker notes that those accompanying a drug-user whilst he is under its effects typically speak reassuringly about the drug's effects, instruct the user (if he is new to the drug) in how to compensate for perceptual distortion, and generally normalize the situation. 'Experienced users prevent the episode from having lasting effects and reassure the novice that whatever he feels will come to a timely and harmless end.'[16] He concludes:

... the most likely interpretation we can make of the drug-induced psychoses reported is that they are either severe anxiety reactions to an event interpreted and experienced as insanity, or failures by the user to correct, in carrying out some ordinary action, for the perceptual distortions caused by the drug. If the interpretation is correct, then untoward mental effects produced by drugs depend in some part on their physiological action, but to a much larger degree find their origin in the definitions and conceptions the user applies to that action.[17]

The unavailability of anxiety-neutralizing definitions of the drug-using is claimed here to be decisive in the case of putatively drug-induced anxiety and panic.

Emotions, then, are not mere eruptions independent of appraisals and judgments, beliefs and conceptualizations. They are not to be identified with sensations nor with physiological changes *per se*. They are generally amenable to reasoned dissuasion and inculcation. Moreover, emotions such as fear or jealousy may be cited as motives that commonsensically explain actions. Mischel has pointed out that to say that jealousy was a man's motive for some particular action

... is not to say anything about the physiological arousal that energized his behavior, nor is it to say that he was in an emotional state ... and we often use 'fear', 'jealousy', and so on, not to explain actions, but to signify emotional states that explain *a failure to act appropriately* ...[18]

To say, for instance, that a man acted out of resentment is to relate his currently problematic conduct to the way in which he has appraised the situation in relation to prior social experiences; it is to assert of him that he knows or believes that someone or some institution or group has done something that has affected him adversely and that his present behavior is informed by that knowledge or belief. Conversely, one could use the category to account for the absence of some otherwise conventionally required conduct on the part of a person. It is most routinely the case that emotion-concepts function in accounts that explain action that is in some way considered untoward or problematic within a situation, or that explain the absence of some otherwise obligatory or preferred course of action. Where actions are not 'noteworthy' *in situ*, by virtue of their situatedly clear motivational status, the categories of affect are rarely invoked in regard to conduct. Indeed, as Parsons long ago indicated, there are entire classes of actions which are undertaken according to the convention of preferred affective-neutrality.[19]

Nothing in this account of emotions argues against the claim that we can *experience* emotions. However, it is clear that, as Kenny remarks, 'only beings who are capable of manifesting a particular emotion are capable of experiencing it'.[20] For example, emotions which can only be manifested by the use of language (e.g. remorse for a crime committed long ago, a longing for the arrival of a friend from a distant place, etc.) can be experienced only by language-users. As Meldon observes:

> No matter how much a dog may cringe with its tail between its legs when caught in the act of dragging its bone across the family's prize oriental rug, it does not feel guilt or shame. And no matter how endearingly it then proceeds to lick the hands of its master, it is not feeling remorse or asking to be forgiven for a shameful performance.[21]

Whatever it is that the dog feels (fear? affection?) the ascription of categories such as guilt, shame, or remorse, apply only by analogical extension; warranted ascriptions of such categories properly depend upon the recognition by the offender of some standards of conduct, some rules applicable to him in the situation, and the understanding that violations are not merely unpleasant if uncovered but wrong.[22] It becomes clear that the capacity to experience genuinely either shame, or guilt, or remorse, hinges upon a mastery of a natural language involving cultural knowledge and reasoning conventions.

Because of the connections between emotion-ascriptions and ascriptions of recognitions and appraisals of various kinds, such ascriptions are mundanely analyzeable for what they presuppose on the part of the ascriber. Were I to ascribe jealousy to you on the basis of your annoyance about your wife's having gone to lunch with another man, I should be betraying something about my *own* assessment of the emotional possibilities inherent in the situation, as well as making a claim about yours. The common retort of: 'What is there to be jealous (afraid, ashamed, embarrassed, etc.) about?' marks the disjunction that can arise when the ascription is being disavowed by reference to a discrepant analysis of the situation in question. However, there are (logical) limits to the possibilities of disjunctive emotion-affording appraisals. Without common ground, we could not teach emotion-concepts nor recognize and avow emotions in intelligible ways. Types of situation are paradigmatically linked to the emotions they afford *by convention*. The link is neither deterministic nor biological, but socio-cultural. It is, in a broad sense, moral; a person may be found morally deficient not to be, e.g., upset by the death of his father, moved by an act of extreme courage, angry at a miscarriage of justice—given, that is, that he concurs in the relevant description of the situation. Indeed, we may appeal to the conventional emotion-affording properties of a situation as grounds for claiming of someone that he is *hiding* his emotion, *concealing* his true feelings, in cases where his behavior does not (appear to) express the appropriate emotion in the situation. Moreover, since various forms of conduct may be characteristic *both* of an emotional state and of a reaction to a sensation or physiological process (e.g. crying), we require knowledge of the circumstances in order to disambiguate the behavior on many occasions. If a person cries we can only know whether this is emotional behavior or pain-behavior if we know whether the circumstances occasioning the behavior were emotion-affording or pain-causing. In some instances where a person has displayed what for a clinician is 'inappropriate affect', it has been found that the person has been reacting to an undetected source of acute physical discomfort which he has been unwilling to disclose. In other instances, children have been known to masquerade their emotional responses by claiming some slight physical injury or discomfort as the grounds for their crying, moodiness or irritability. Successful concealment of the circumstances informing behavior can thus incur observers' errors in ascribing either emotion or physical sensation to an individual.

The psychologistic model of the emotions as internal episodes, then, fails to do justice to the constitutive connections between emotion-avowals and -ascriptions, and conduct, context, appraisal, belief and social convention. This model can never illuminate, only distort, our appreciation of the variegated ways in which emotions figure in the 'weave of our lives'.

Social Organization of Emotional Displays and their Treatment

In what follows, I shall sketch out, in a preliminary way, some suggestions for investigating the social structures of emotional displays and their treatment in various sorts of social interactions. An extract of data will be presented and discussed in terms of the analytical distinctions and issues raised above. Because there are no leads in the research literature on the study of actual emotional displays in natural settings, I am following a time-worn tradition of focussing upon an intuitively deviant case in order to illuminate conventional reasoning more sharply. The data is taken from an actual occasion in which two mental health social workers, a prospective mental patient already known to all present as psychiatrically diagnosed to be a hebephrenic schizophrenic, and her mother, are speaking together. The diagnostic category of hebephrenic schizophrenia has no set extensional domain but broadly signifies a state of alternating emotional behavior, in the absence of clear object or cause, on the part of the patient.

Data extract

1 *First Mental Health Social Worker* (hence: MW01): What d'ya want to tell me today? You were telling me a bit about yourself last time Sheila; tell me some more about yourself
2 *Sheila* (*Prospective Patient*): laughs.
3 *Mother of prospective patient* (hence: MPP): Go on then! (Pause 2.0 secs.) What's funny?
4 *Sheila*: begins crying and looking imploringly at assembled company.
5 *MPP*: *Don't*. (1.5 sec.) Shut up! What's there to be unhappy about?
6 *Second Mental Health Social Worker* (hence: MW02): Perhaps she's feeling ill.
7 *MPP*: Nah ... she often cries ... just like that when there's no reason to.

8 *Sheila*: begins to laugh, then breaks into sobbing.

9 *MWo1*: Why are you crying, Sheila? Don't ya feel well today?

10 *Sheila*: sobs even louder. (Duration of 5 secs.)

11 *MWo2*: Tell us what's troubling you.

12 *Sheila*: begins to laugh loudly and looks delighted.

13 *MWo2*: Are ya laughing at me?

14 *Sheila*: No.

15 *MWo1*: Are ya laughing at *me*? (Sheila begins laughing louder) What is it? (Sheila laughs more) Ya keep laughing at us what *is* it?

16 *Sheila*: Dunno

17 *MWo1*: Ya do ... don't wanna say, though, do you.

18 *Sheila*: No.

19 *MWo2*: Why not?

20 *MPP*: Why not? (1.5 secs.) Minute ago you were crying.

21 *MWo1*: Is it those awful voices again?

22 *Sheila*: Mmmm.

23 *MWo1*: What are they saying now?

24 *Sheila* (still laughing): They co;:hm ta tanta::hlize me (breaks into sobs).

25 *MWo1*: What do they say that's upsetting ya now?

26 *Sheila*: They scream at me ... sometimes they tease me (laughs).

Sheila's alternating elation and distress is not observably synchronized with any interactional events, and poses a problem for the assembled participants in locating the possible object or objects for these fluctuating emotional displays. Ordinarily, the location of an object that makes an emotional display intelligible does not necessarily cast light on the cause of the display—I can be elated *at* being complimented but *because* I am drunk, or angry *at* little things *because* I am suffering from dyspepsia, where to know its object is not thereby to understand its cause.[23] Where the object of the display cannot be determined at all, or when determined is found to be irrational, issues of causality *do* become specifiable (albeit in defeasible ways). Thus, locating Sheila's auditory hallucination as the object of her emotional displays enables co-participants to find her apparently objectless and bizarre alternations of affect to be intelligible, and serves to specify the cause of her affective state in her mental disorder. Similarly, if co-participants had remained unable to locate the object of Sheila's emotional displays, then again her longer-term, overarching condition of mental disorder could appropriately have been invoked as their possible cause. (There is, however, an interesting argument that would postulate affective psychiatric disorders as *consisting in* such bizarre affective alternations, rather than as the *cause* of them.)

Notice that the first reaction to Sheila's display of elation consists in an enquiry about it. Her mother, in utterance 3, asks her what is funny, searching for an object for the display. In doing so, she is presupposing that nothing in the interaction so far entitles or justifies the display. In turn 4, Sheila begins crying and looking imploringly at the co-participants. Again, her mother expresses her puzzlement by asking what there is 'to be unhappy about'. Her mother is clearly orienting to Sheila's behavior as emotional and raising questions directed to locating the object or objects of the behavior so constituted. However, in utterance 6, the second mental health social worker orients to Sheila's behavior in terms of her possible *physical* condition, thereby constituting it as ambiguous between emotion and sensation-reaction. No observable circumstances have yet been determined which could enable co-participants to settle upon a consensual orientation to her behavior: it could be *either* a display of emotions or pain-behavior interspersed with laughter. In utterance 7, Sheila's mother says that the present display (sobbing, looking unhappy) can be assimilated to prior cases in which there has been 'no reason' to behave in this way. If accepted by coparticipants, this would provide for construing Sheila's conduct as *emotion-like* behavior. After the ensuing bout of sobbing, however, the first mental health worker, in utterance 9, reverts to the physiological possibility by asking the girl whether she feels well, a locution signalling a primarily physical concern. After more sobbing, the second mental health worker asks the girl, in utterance 11, for what is troubling her. Formally ambiguous with respect to physical or life-circumstantial matters, the notion of 'troubling' her reopens an orientation to Sheila's conduct as potentially emotional in nature. The subsequent laughter on her part, and the cessation of distress-behavior, reorients everyone present to a search for an object rather than a cause.

The alternating displays occasion alternating sorts of search-procedures on the part of co-participants; where the conduct is construed (albeit tentatively) as emotional, objects are sought; where it is constituted (again tentatively) as a sensation-reaction, causes (of a physiological sort) are presupposed in the questioning. The opacity of the possible object or objects of the behavior construed as emotional provides for the persistence of the ambiguity it seems to have; where no object can be located in the meaningful environment for a display of this kind, the conventional options for conceptualizing the display appear to include construing it as something *other than* emotional.

In utterance 15, the first mental health worker responds to Sheila's sustained and heightened laughter by pressing hard for an explanation of its object. The laughter is being taken, not as a reaction to anything physiological (such as a tickling or other animating sensation of that sort) but now as firmly affective behavior. When Sheila says in utterance 16 that she does not know what she is laughing at, this is flatly contradicted by the mental health worker in utterance 17, and the contradiction is resolved by adding a reason for her denying knowledge of the object of her laughter, a reason that takes the form of an ascription of intentional concealment on her part. Sheila acknowledges that the ascription is warranted by agreeing in utterance 18 that she does not want to disclose the object of her laughter. (Note that one can often *agree* by saying 'No'—the token is not self-evidently negating.) Eventually, it is proposed by the same mental health worker that 'those awful voices' form the object of the emotional displays. Once concurred in as the object, it is revealed that changes in what the voices say occasion changes in Sheila's overt conduct. Now a synchrony has been located, as the object of the displays is rendered transparent.

Ordinarily, emotionlike displays may be related synchronously to features of an ongoing meaningful environment or, where nothing therein observably entitles or justifies the display, to features of the agent's undisclosed thoughts or, further, to something physical, which thereby transforms the perception of the behavior and constitutes it as non-emotional. The sort of search procedures that are initiated by someone's betraying the marks of some emotion in situations devoid of conventionally entitling objects will depend upon the analysis of the probability that the conduct is occasioned by (i) undisclosed objects or (ii) physical stimuli. Since to suggest that someone is not disclosing something may be dispreferred in most ordinary situations, one would expect that the first search-preference would construe the conduct as occasioned by some physical stimuli wherever such a possibility would make sense. This would, as noted, logically entail the temporary abandonment of seeing the conduct *as* emotional. Having located an object for conduct constituted as emotional, questions about causation can be raised. In some instances, as in the above, the *kind* of object located *can* be informative as to the causation of the emotional display. (Note that 'causation' is here being construed singularly and locally; no causal propositions about affect can take the form of law-like statements of necessary and sufficient antecedent conditions for the display of a type of emotion. It has already been argued here that emotions may be rational or irrational, appropriate or inappropriate, justified or unjustified, in their contexts, and hence are normatively explicable rather than mechanically predictable phenomena.)

No matter how distant in time from the ongoing interaction is the object of an emotional display, it is rendered relevantly present in virtue of the device of postulating the operation of the memory and current reflection. For specific displays, some object is *requiredly* available and knowledge of it is ascribable to agents of the displays. Laughter is such a display. Where laughter is not seeable as physically occasioned, the agent is conventionally accountable for its object. Claimed ignorance of the object of laughter is unacceptable as an account, and may be warrantably disbelieved unless the agent makes out that his laughter consisted of imitation of others or that it was undertaken as a pretence of some kind. The latter two possibilities are contextually investigable, and may be employed as derogatory accounts for laughter where the known-in-common situation is consensually devoid of laugh-entitling features. In such ways, laughter may be construed in a setting as *devoid of genuine emotion*. Where it is treated as the expression of genuine emotion, then its object must either be contextually presupposed or tacitly available, or construed as available in the undisclosed but potentially discloseable thoughts of the person doing the laughing.

People normally have to deal with more complex emotions than fear, elation and other forms of affect which do not require any linguistic capacity on the part of those who manifest them: human emotions include a large range whose objects are 'abstract'. Characteristically, even those emotions warrantably ascribable to non-linguistic creatures are tied, in their human displays, to conceptually-constituted abstract phenomena, although of course humans can *re*act with fear or elation directly in a way that is unmediated by linguistic constitution. Those emotions constituted by the orientation of the person to a *conception* of an event or situation can be transformed by alterations in the conception of that event or situation. Thus, Henslin has illustrated some of the ways in which the emotion of guilt, constituted by four different orientations to the suicide of a relative or close friend,[24] can be 'neutralized' by adopting changed conceptualizations of the suicided person, the nature of the suicide itself, and/or the factors thought to 'explain' the suicide.[25] Henslin's is one of the only genuinely sociological approaches to the study of affect and its transformation available in the human sciences, and is itself admittedly a first approximation. We are becoming more prepared to investigate affect independent of psychobiological speculations, but its social construction and organization remain largely unanalyzed.

One word of caution should be noted here. It should not be thought that, because specific emotions can be transformed or eliminated by reconceptualizations of their objects (events, situations, etc.), there are no normative constraints oriented to by members in such transformations. We may say of someone who does not seem to recognize situatedly relevant normative constraints on his reconceptualization that he is 'not facing facts', or that he is 'making excuses'. Various sorts of situations have features socially pre-designated as fearful, hateful, provocative, frightening and the like, and once any given situation has been oriented to socially as belonging to a class of such situations, the possibility is open for a member's *re*conceptualization of it to be judged in some way untoward. Moreover, the categorization of a member as 'stoic' or 'hard-headed' in the face of some situation which conventionally entitles or justifies some specific emotion may be withdrawn if it is found that the member has not construed the situation along the convention-relevant dimension. Ascribed deviations from expressions of normatively required emotions are typically implicative for the ascription of personality; often more so than conformities.

There is a high degree of commonsense predictability involved in gauging the emotional responses or reactions to various classes of utterances and actions in everyday life. So much so, in fact, that we routinely ascribe the apparent affective consequences of an action to the actor as a part of his action itself, as when we say, e.g., 'he alarmed her', 'he frightened them', 'she angered him'. Such act-consequence elisions were even referred to as a class of actions *per se* by Austin in his category of 'perlocutionary acts'.[26]

Here I must leave the subject, in the hope that enough has been said to stimulate its further development.

8 The Metaphysics of Mental Illness

One conceptual dilemma which has had practical repercussions beyond the confines of scholarly debate in philosophy and the human sciences is that surrounding the notion of 'mental illness'. A polarization of views has taken place, which, in this particular field, has been unproductive, confusing and politically consequential. In the ensuing discussion, I shall try to disentangle some of the contending claims and isolate what I argue to be the defensible positions. In so doing, I shall need to examine the notions of 'illness', 'diagnosis' and 'definition'. Hopefully, such elucidation should cast some light upon the intelligibility of psychiatric praxis and its grounding in ordinary reasoning, but will leave open the question of how to resolve some of the better-informed disputes about its transformation as a social institution.

If we can get clear about the logical status of the concept of mental illness, then our ethnographies of psychiatric reasoning and our moral argumentation about the future of psychiatry can proceed unencumbered by some of the misassimilations and inferential mistakes that presently confound the field. Since I have already tackled some of the issues to be addressed again here (in my *Approaches to Insanity* (1973)), I shall keep the discussion reasonably brief, although it will be found that, on at least one score, I am correcting my own earlier over-simplification of the logical grammar of 'schizophrenia'.

Is Mental Illness Really 'Illness'?

When a psychiatrist declares that a person is 'mentally ill', what is he doing? This question has been answered in various, often wholly contradictory, ways. Some have claimed that the psychiatrist is employing a 'metaphor'[1] in order to refer to what are literally describable as 'problems in living'[2] or 'transformations of social identity',[3] but that he tends to take the metaphor literally, thereby (allegedly) misassimilating the mental to the physical domain of discourse in virtue of the invocation of the idea of 'illness'. The diagnostician using the expression 'mental illness' in his work is said to be a kind of naive realist with respect to 'mind':

> Contemporary users of the mental illness concept are guilty of illicitly shifting from metaphor to myth. Instead of maintaining the metaphorical rhetoric 'it is as if there were states of mind' and 'it is as if some states of mind could be characterised as sickness', the contemporary mentalist (sic) conducts much of his work as if he believes that minds are 'real' entities and that, like bodies, they can be sick or healthy.[4]

In a somewhat different vein, R. D. Laing proposes that the diagnostician who ascribes 'mental illness' to a person is in fact imputing 'a hypothetical disease of unknown aetiology and undiscovered pathology'.[5] One of the original proponents of this view, whose work has formed a critical resource for Laing and his colleagues, is Ludwig Binswanger. For Binswanger, psychiatric diagnoses of 'mental illness(es)' consist in the reification of the 'psyche':

> ... psychopathology accepts (the reduction of human existence down to the categories of natural science) in order to find that 'connection' with biology which, as noted, *alone warrants the concept of illness in the medical sense and the possibility of a medical diagnosis and a causal therapy.*[6] (my italics)

The biological 'connection', thought to be integral to the meaning of 'illness', is alluded to again in Sarbin's claim that 'assigning persons to the class "ill" carries the meaning of objective signs and symptoms of a recognised or named disease in addition to subjectively experienced discomfort'.[7]

In sharp contrast to these proposals is the position (developed from direct argument with them) that the use of the phrase 'mental illness' (or 'mental disease') does not entail nor logically presuppose any ontological or biological referent (whether 'state' or 'entity'). In Engelhardt's view:

> Diseases such as cancer, tuberculosis, and schizophrenia thus exist, but as patterns of explanation, not as things in themselves or as eidetic types of phenomena ... evaluation enters into the enterprise

of medical explanation because accounts of disease are immediately focused on controlling and eliminating circumstances judged to be a disvalue ... the concept of disease is as much a mode of evaluating as explaining reality.[8]

We must, argues Engelhardt, 'abandon ontological hypostatization of disease and nosological realism'[9] and explicate the concept of 'disease' as a pragmatic explanatory and evaluative device without ontological commitments. From this, it would seem that the psychiatric diagnostician's use of 'mental illness', although perhaps capable of being misconstrued as committing him to ontological hypostatization (or nosological realism), actually functions to evaluate and explain, in a purely pragmatic and practical way, 'the world of appearance',[10] which would consist for him in the (proto-)patient's talk and conduct. A similar position is adopted by Moore,[11] who argues:

> To the extent that common and psychiatric discourse about mental illness can be paraphrased so as to avoid the hypostasis of an entity named by the phrase, then any criticism that complains that there is no such *thing* as mental illness is beside the point; for orthodox psychiatry and common understanding can happily agree, but still use the phrase to make significant (albeit non-referring) statements.[12]

Of course, even when so paraphrasable, much commonsense and psychiatric discourse about mental illness can *still* be referential, only the referent will not be a hypothetical and hypostatized mental entity, but a person's crazy conduct in its (various) circumstances. As Linsky long ago pointed out,[13] the way in which a speaker refers is a contextual matter and cannot simply be pre-determined by stipulating some fixed properties of a referent for any referring expression.

Moore devotes much critical attention to the thesis of Thomas Szasz, and attempts to demonstrate that Szasz's position that 'mental illness is a myth' hinges upon a restricted and inaccurately formulated conceptualization of 'illness' *per se*. For Szasz, the term 'bodily illness' refers to physiological occurrences:[14] 'we call people physically ill when their body functioning violates certain anatomical and physiological norms'.[15] In this sense, a physician's medical diagnoses are 'value-neutral' and unaffected by socio-cultural normative standards and preferences. By contrast to this, Szasz claims, the psychiatric diagnostician's use of the phrase 'mental illness' constitutes an illegitimate extension of the concept from this value-free, physiological context and serves only to gloss over normative appraisals of conduct in scientific or medical terms. Against this, Moore observes:

> The first thing one wants to say is that 'illness' was a word in the English language long before anyone knew very much about anatomy or physiology, and thus the meaning of the word cannot be a matter of statistical deviation from a physiological or anatomical norm.[16]

Furthermore, there are many persons who have anatomical defects but remain perfectly healthy—indeed, you may recover from an illness but retain a physiological abnormality: by Szasz's reasoning, you would still be ill! It is clear that deviation from a physiological norm 'is in itself neither a necessary nor a sufficient condition of being ill'.[17] Illness is a culturally-relative state, an avowable and/or ascribable state of pain and/or serious incapacitation: it is not to be identified with its physiological *causes* (if there be any) nor is it to be treated as a strict synonym for 'disease', a concept with which it is only partially interchangeable. (Disease may be predicated of a specific bodily organ; illness is predicable only of persons or whole organisms.)

Contrary to Binswanger, Szasz and Sarbin, the concept of 'illness' does *not* entail any reference to a biological or physiological state, but rather operates as a signal for states of personal incapacity which might or might not have some biological foundation. However, it is quite unjustified to conclude from all this that there are *no* relevant and important distinctions to be made between the activity of psychiatric diagnosis and that of medical diagnosis. Sociologists have, for some years, been aware of the peculiarly wide latitudes in psychiatric diagnostic variability contrasted with the variability tolerated within physical medicine. In the former case, a biochemical or neurological screening can, at least in principle, be effected to rule out various psychodynamic or 'functional' diagnoses and rule in diagnoses of physical illness (e.g. paresis, senile dementia, brain tumor, etc.) but there are no determinate tests available to rule *in* a psychodynamic or functional diagnosis of, e.g., 'schizophrenia'. As Temerlin has pointed out, on the basis of a study showing how, by controlling contextual, social information, one can vary the probabilities of a given functional diagnosis:

> The basic problem ... is the difficulty of separating *diagnoses* of mental illness from mental illness itself, if it exists, because there is no operational criterion of mental illness which is independent of psychiatric diagnosis, and with which psychiatric diagnosis

might be correlated in a validity study.[18]

The question which I am seeking to raise here, then, is the following: does the absence of generalized, context-independent criteria for mental illness (of the 'functional' kind) signify that psychiatric diagnoses are predicated upon an unjustifiable subjectivity?

It is certainly true that the absence of context-independent criteria (either biological *or* behavioral) has wrought havoc in psychopathology as an organized inquiry into the 'causes' of various mental illnesses;[19] it is also clear that this absence has been of little consequence for the development of an array of psychotropic drugs available for the treatment of persons diagnosed psychiatrically.[20] The focus here is upon neither of these areas, but rather upon the practical, daily work of psychiatric diagnosis as a part of the organized systems of psychiatric work.

Psychiatric Diagnosis as Practical, Situated Work

Lay and professional ascribers of mental illness are not necessarily, in virtue of their ascriptive categories, committed to a somatic version of causality nor even to the assumption that such categories necessarily 'describe' or 'explain' anything. (Szasz and Scheff both seem to share the view that to use the phrase 'mental illness' is *eo ipso* to betray a commitment to a physicalist model of insanity and its aetiologies; Engelhardt, on the other hand, seems to construe psychiatric diagnoses of, e.g., schizophrenia, as constituting explanatory statements.) The psychiatric clinician is not a disinterested scientist, and it is only the attempt to conceive of his role in this inappropriate way that has prompted the various critiques of his practices. For as soon as we abandon the idea that this practice is everywhere to be informed by scientific rationalities as 'sanctioned ideals of conduct',[21] we start to *see* more clearly what it consists in as a set of rational activities in their own right. It is only with reference to such an idealized version of psychiatric practice that Kolb could argue that:

> ... answers supplied by a psychiatrist in regard to questions of rightness or wrongness of an act or of 'knowing' its nature almost constitute a professional perjury.[22]

A brief exposure to actual psychiatric work would reveal at once that *any* determination of insanity or mental illness begins (and usually ends) with judgments about the 'wrongness' of the talk and/or conduct of the person in question, seen against a background of observed and reported social events in his recent biography, and must also include some assessment of the person's cognition of his own conduct—of 'knowing' its nature. For what other forms of judgment will be relevant? Similarly, Sobeloff's assertion that, when 'forced' to adopt 'the vocabulary of morality and ethics', the psychiatrist 'is speaking in what to him is a foreign language and in an area in which he claims no expertise',[23] is strangely naive. Unless we are arbitrarily to restrict the vocabulary of morality and ethics, the psychiatric diagnostician is to be found employing it all the time in order to accomplish his practical task; how else are we to characterize the vocabulary of judgments such as 'inappropriate affect', 'unreasonable behavior', 'failure to react normally' and the rest of what van den Berg has called the 'vocabulary of denigration'?[24] Psychiatric determinations, just as lay insanity-ascriptions, are thoroughly normative, even where the diagnostician or ascriber does not openly articulate or even recognize his participation in the normative order of action-description and appraisal.

There has been a range of studies of practical, psychiatric activities, many of them focussing (at least in part) upon the work of psychiatric diagnosis. Scheff,[25] Mechanic,[26] Daniels,[27] Strauss *et al.*,[28] Phillips and Draguns,[29] Braginsky *et al.*,[30] and Rosenhan[31] have all contributed to our understanding of the social-organizational contingencies within which psychiatric decisions are made—in courts, hospitals, military situations and clinics. Nearly all of these studies are critical of the conduct of practical psychiatry, detailing its *ad hoc*, normative and often idiosyncratic features. As empirical studies of psychiatry at work, they illustrate (often dramatically) the wide variety of constraints and considerations routinely confronted by clinicians. Let us sample some of the claims made by these researchers: Scheff, for instance, claims that

> Typically one or more of the following kinds of ambiguity might occur (in the diagnostic process): the alleged symptoms are not so extreme and perhaps have some grounds, as for elation, for example, Moreover, the amount of information at the disposal of the diagnostician may be extremely limited and of uncertain reliability: garbled accounts of alleged incidents by hostile or confused family members are frequently the chief source of information. . . . Frequently, there is confusion because of conflicts between different accounts of the symptoms: the family may have one version, the patient another, and the diagnostician's own observations may suggest still another. Many of the patients seen by clinicians have been forced or tricked into the hospital; the clincian must unravel the 'illness' from the reactions of the patient to coercion and/or duplicity.[32]

Mechanic observes that many busy clinicians simply 'assume illness' on initial contact with a prospective patient:

> Both the abstract nature of the physician's theories and the time limitations imposed upon him by the institutional structure of which he is a part make it impossible for him to make a rapid study of the patient's illness or even to ascertain if illness, in fact, exists.[33]

Daniels notes that, for the combat psychiatrist, the significance of 'symptoms' is typically dependent upon the combat history of the person with whom they are associated; in wartime, the psychiatrist operates with a significantly shifted baseline for assessing 'tolerable' and 'intolerable' experiences, often applying the criterion that no single encounter in combat can in itself suffice to engender mental incapacity and attempting to sustain the fighting strength in the face of suspected malingering: '(symptoms) mean nothing without combat experience, something else when a soldier has little combat experience, and something else again when he has a history of nine or ten months of honorable and efficient service'.[34] These priorities are in sharp contrast to those prevailing in the context of routine court incompetency hearings, in which, according to Scheff's study,[35] psychiatrists tend to err on the side of commitment rather than release when confronted with borderline cases. This error-preference also operates in mental hospital settings, according to a study by Rosenhan in which eight sane persons gained secret admission to twelve mental hospitals:

> Despite their public 'show' of sanity, the pseudopatients were never detected. Admitted, except in one case [where the diagnosis was 'manic-depressive'—JC], with a diagnosis of schizophrenia, each was discharged with a diagnosis of schizophrenia 'in remission'. The label 'in remission' should in no way be dismissed as a formality, for at no time during any hospitalization had any question been raised about any pseudopatient's simulation . . .[36]

What do these studies actually tell us about psychiatric diagnosing as a practical accomplishment? The most obvious difficulty in evaluating them is the absence of detailed, interactional data from which we might observe for ourselves the displayed characteristics of the 'symptoms' and attendant contextual data witnessed by the diagnosticians as the bases for their decisions about the presence of mental illness. However, there is no reason to doubt that psychiatric judgments are contextually variable; in fact, there are no general rules which could guide the clinician in a search-procedure for contextually relevant information and, because *any* appraisal about human conduct is context-dependent, this will mean that mental-illness determinations depend upon the ways in which the operation of an organizational milieu provides for its own possibilities of looking and judging, including the ways in which it facilitates the presentation of candidate patients and accounts about them.

It was very easy, but quite unwarranted, to pass from observations such as these to claims that mental illness is a 'myth'. Clearly, there are no constant criteria organizing the judgments of every psychiatrist irrespective of his sphere of operations, and the contextually-embedded search procedures for and ways of looking at diagnostically relevant data are incapable of generalization; there can be no pre-established relevance criteria for such data because psychiatric diagnoses are predicated upon social and moral contingencies relating *both* to a person's conduct *and* to the context within which the diagnosis is being made. However, the contextual constitution of normative judgments about conduct cannot in itself be used as the basis for an argument for the non-existence of the phenomena about which such judgments are produced. We know that appraisals of 'intelligence' are subject to contextual constitution and incapable of genuine operationalization. They are, like mental-illness judgments, normative. Yet no-one, to my knowledge, has argued that there is no such thing as intelligence. Of course, the phenomena of intelligence and mental illness are not *ostensively* definable like stones and tables; but only by reifying the notion of 'phenomenon' could we arrive at a position which argued for their non-existence.[37] The occasional contestability of judgments about either is not sufficient grounds for the sort of *general* scepticism which has developed in recent years. It may well be true, however, that judgments of 'intelligence' and 'schizophrenia' are too contextually variable to permit generalized research strategies into their 'causes'; the 'validity' of any such categories can only be a *situated* validity. There is an argument about this which deserves closer examination.

Researchers in psychology and psychopathology have occasionally sought to measure the 'discriminatory power of the concept of schizophrenia'. Since the discriminatory power of any concept cannot be determined independently of the discriminatory abilities of its users in actual situations of use, the study of the 'validity' of the concept of 'schizophrenia' becomes interwoven with the study of psychiatrists' diagnostic 'consistency'. But how is one to distinguish between 'consistent' and 'inconsistent' diagnostic applications? A preferred answer to this question has been to invoke a fixed definition, sometimes claimed to capture the 'essential characteristics' of the phenomena categorized by the concept, and check each case of application with the characteristics contained within the definition. This procedure is subject to a number of rather obvious difficulties. Firstly, definitions themselves must be interpreted and 'matched' to actual cases, which adds yet another 'discriminator' to the users of the concept, this time usually the researcher himself who is doing the interpreting, matching and judging. Secondly, it is to treat formal definitions as if they furnished strict recognition rules by themselves; as if they embodied all and only all of the relevancies involved in judging. Not only is this a total misconception of the logical status of definitions, it omits any consideration of the 'open-textured' property of many of the concepts in which a researcher usually has an interest (such as 'schizophrenia' itself).[38] Thirdly, and most importantly for the present argument, failure in the validation of a category by such a procedure encourages the misguided criticism of diagnostic practice that it should 'work better' if *more exact* definitions of its taxonomic items were forthcoming. It is as if precise, fixed definitions of such items were a prerequisite for proper diagnostic practice; as if a diagnostician's relevant knowledge were somehow incomplete because he could not adduce such definitions and show a consistent reliance upon them. However, such an objection is as facile as claiming that a person who could not define 'red' is therefore incapable of discriminating red objects, or that someone who might give a rough approximation of the 'meaning' of the concept of 'game' had thereby exhausted his practical knowledge of games. Wittgenstein remarked:

> What does it mean to know what a game is? What does it mean to know it and not be able to say it? Is this knowledge somehow equivalent to an unformulated definition? So that if it were formulated I should be able to recognize it as the expression of my knowledge? Isn't my knowledge, my concept of a game, completely expressed in the explanations that I could give? That is, *in my describing examples of various kinds of game*; showing how all sorts of other games can be constructed on the analogy of these; saying that I should scarcely include this or this among games; and so on.[39]

Alan Blum, himself drawing upon Wittgenstein's discussions of knowledge, definitions and language-use, proposes two points which bear directly upon this issue:

1. The diversity of behavior named mental illness resists distillation in a formula or a fixed meaning or calculus.
2. We cannot use the formula exclusively because it has to be interpreted, which requires us to move beyond the list, which

presupposes settling the very questions that the list is supposed to resolve.[40]

Definitions are *not* enabling devices at all; they are not what facilitate the work of psychiatric diagnosis. It is not the 'flexibility' in definitions of mental disorders which permits the contextual variability of diagnosing and propensities to diagnose. To claim that definitions of psychiatric taxonomic devices are 'indeterminate' presupposes a standard of 'determinacy', but there cannot be any over-arching standard here as there can sometimes be in physical medicine, and to use the latter as a yardstick for judging the former is like using a rule of chess to judge a move in football.

Only by considering 'mental illness' out of its contexts of practical appraisal with their attendant organizational contingencies could one entertain the idea that strict rules and definitions could somehow *regiment* the practice and ensure uniformity and consensus. Above all, psychiatric diagnoses are devices for pragmatic use in ward and treatment allocation, for which they serve as gross indicators. They are sometimes used in inter-psychiatrist communication (and psychiatrist/referral-agent communication) as warrants for action of certain sorts but rarely as summaries of the patient's observable characteristics. For the latter, full descriptions are routinely preferred; psychiatrists know the limits to the information actually conveyed about a patient with the use of a single, 'functional' descriptor like 'schizophrenic'. The use of such terms by themselves is generally restricted to written records, which are typically truncated documents by comparison with the fuller discussions which can be heard at case conferences. The idea that psychiatrists are generally ignorant or stupid about the utility of their concepts in practical activities is the unfortunate result of much of the 'theorizing' around the quite limited observations produced by the 'labelling'-theory researchers whose work we have sampled. That there are economic, political, juridical, temporal and ideological pressures to which some clinicians succumb is a well-documented and socially important fact; but to conclude from a documentation of abuses to the non-discriminability of mental illness or to its 'non-existence' is to indulge in a distracting and potentially harmful metaphysics.

Psychiatric diagnoses are not poor cousins of physical diagnoses, for they do not belong to that family of practices, however 'medical' are some of the consequences. Rather, they are members of that cluster of ascriptive practices in which assessments of conduct and beliefs are made. It is clear that professional clinicians do not have a monopoly upon the sensible ascription of mental illness, although they do play a critical part in the ratification or otherwise of those ascriptions already effected. Except for special cases in which psychiatrists are brought in to adjudicate upon a person's insanity (e.g. courts of law) they are rarely the first people to make an ascription. Initial ascriptions are lay affairs, most routinely conducted by family co-members, peer group personnel, G.P.'s and social workers in various combinations around the prospective patient. For many, the path to the psychiatric examination is decided for them by others who have found them sufficiently disturbed or bizarre to require specialist attention, and then usually as a last resort.[41] Although lay referral agents conventionally speak of the referred person as 'mentally ill', 'insane', 'disordered' or some vernacular equivalent, not using terms such as 'schizophrenia' very much, they often find that the psychiatrist's more erudite terminology translates without residue into their own commonsense scheme of interpretation which they had employed in the first place to make the referral of the patient in question.[42] Indeed, on those occasions when a clinician is asked to 'put that into simple English', he typically reiterates the mutually known features of the patient's conduct, adding perhaps some details about the projected course of treatment. Lay persons, then, are very unlike the 'scientific illiterate' discussed by Winch in the following passage:

> A scientific illiterate, asked to describe the result of an experiment which he 'observes' in an advanced physics laboratory, could not do so in terms relevant to the hypothesis being tested. . . .[43]

If we substitute for 'the results of an experiment' something like 'the symptoms of the patient'; for 'in an advanced physics laboratory' something like 'in various ordinary situations', and for 'the hypothesis being tested' something like 'the diagnosis being considered', we can begin to see how different is the relationship between commonsense knowledge and psychiatric determinations from the relationship between commonsense knowledge and determinations in physics. My point is that the lay person who has an ordinary mastery of his natural language is able to describe the symptoms of the patient in ways quite relevant to the determination of a diagnosis, whilst the physics illiterate cannot describe what he is observing in ways relevant to the physics hypothesis. Psychiatric reasoning about the presence or absence of a (functional) mental illness is constituted out of lay psychological reasoning; the functional categories themselves are a response to mundane social and moral requirements, and not to the development of some esoteric branch of knowledge. Sometimes, through judicious screening, a clinician will be able to locate a physical lesion and alter an initial perception of a functional mental illness to one of organic disease; here, specialized skills and technology *are* required. However, it is useful to bear in mind the fact that mental-illness determinations do not invariantly require any esoteric knowledge or equipment—relocating the mundane grounds of the concept of 'mental illness' helps us better to understand the meaning of the concept and to resist the temptation to construe it as the exclusive province of psychiatry as a profession. We can thereby see how strange it is to propose that 'there is no such thing', or that we should 'alter our ways of talking'. We can often *see* mental illness, sickness or disorder without special training and certainly without making biological commitments either to aetiology or therapy. And we can ascribe mental illness without the least hint of pejorative intention: it is hardly a logical contradiction to feel sympathy and to excuse persons whom we consider mentally ill; the concept itself is not to blame for the uneducated prejudices of *some* of its users, nor for the theoretical flights of fancy of others. Of course there is no reason to believe that advances in our biochemical and neurophysiological knowledge will provide us with strict correlates in the brains and bodies of persons diagnosed as 'schizophrenic' on the basis of varying contingencies and presenting conduct—the concept of 'schizophrenia' simply cannot be used to generate a sample of persons with invariant patterns of conduct and belief, let alone constant *biological* properties. But this need in no way concern the pragmatic clinician, just as the absence of any common property in all and only all cases where we appropriately confer the category 'intelligent' upon someone does not undermine its mundane functions even though it creates nightmares for naive operationalists. Perhaps the cultural impulse toward generality, toward regimenting our practical affairs with instrumental and determinate rules, leads us to balk at the contextual sensitivity and discretion with which psychiatric judgments have to be made; but there are no algorithms by which we can escape our human, moral responsibilities *and* our failures and abuses in this field. Indeed, the move to standardize and impersonalize such judgments, besides being largely unworkable and generally misguided, reduces the area for particularistic attention and concern essential to the humane organization of psychiatry as a practical, moral enterprise.

We need to be vigilant about psychiatry; some of its practitioners must be brought to account for the abuses conducted in its name—especially now, in the Soviet Union[44]—and we must keep watch against its slick manipulation by interest groups, lawyers and the peddlers of contemporary pseudo-phenomenological mysticism. We need to take full social responsibility for the state of our psychiatry because the art of diagnosis is an art of cultural and civic competence which we share and make possible. We must not allow the activities of psychiatrists to escape decipherment into the mundane, practical terms which inform them. Above all, we should strip the subject of its metaphysics. Psychiatry is practised in heterogeneous contexts as a form of social control and custodial ideology; humanizing its operations will not be done by disengaged polemic against its categories nor by promulgating panaceas.

Concluding Remarks

The basic arguments presented in these essays sought to pacify some of the problems associated with subjectivity—showing how much more can be said about human conduct without reference to the 'contents' of the consciousness of individuals in specific cases than might have been thought possible. Subsidiary arguments were also designed to show to what extent the ascription and avowal of mental-conduct categories turn upon essentially *public* grounds (and in particular upon the conventional consequentialities for social interaction of making such ascriptions and avowals). Although our analytical interest remains in *conventional* actor-orientations and reasoning-procedures, these are conceptualized as properties of the culture, rather than imputed directly by the analyst to the minds of individuals in particular settings whose actions form the data-base for analysis. In this way, the pit-falls of mentalist metaphysics and psychologism are avoided, and a fresh area of investigation is opened up: the description of the ways in which the culture permits us to ascribe and avow mental-conduct categories and expressions in our interpersonal affairs.

I have also sought to argue that such investigations are not indirect attempts to study mind: they *are* studies of mind. It has been proposed that there is no sense to the claim that wherever and whenever a mental-predicate avowal or ascription is properly made there corresponds to it an inscrutable and private mental 'contents' that gives it its meaning. I have *not* claimed that there cannot be instances in which people conceal or refrain from disclosing the thoughts they have or the intentions they have formed, but

153

I have argued (i) that wherever and whenever any undisclosed thought or intention is entertained its non-disclosure does not *entail* the essential inaccessibility to others of the thoughts and intentions involved, and (ii) that 'thought-concealment' and 'intention non-disclosure' etc. are themselves defeasibly ascribable predicates (in the ways that members have of invoking them) whose uses are subject to culturally-conventional, public grounds and constraints that are analyzeable.

It is not that the 'phenomenology' of so many of our mental states and processes is difficult to articulate—it is that for so many of our mental-predicates there is *no* correspondingly essential state or process available for phenomenological (eidetic) investigation. I have tried to show this in the case of 'intending' amongst others. I have argued that our analysis of intending and intention must start from the observation that when I declare my intention (which is the primary use of the concept), I cannot be thought of as reporting upon a mental state or process, but rather as making a move in a language-game of personal commitment to future states of affairs, akin to saying 'I promise ...' Hunter, in his analysis of what it is to 'tell' someone something,[1] remarked that the language-game of telling others about one's thoughts, attitudes or intentions is organized conventionally in such a way that the pursuant conversation centers 'not on what has been happening to me but, one might say, on the upshot of what I have said: not on the thinking by me of something, but on *what* I have thought, not on my intending but on what I intend'.[2] For example, it would sound very peculiar if, when I tell you what I intend to do about something, you replied by asking me how long my intending took; or if you suggested that I take steps to avoid intending quite so often, or if you observed that it is annoying when such intentions happen. A descriptive semiotics of such language-games as stating or divining intentions and dealing with them reveals that:

> The moves we make do not necessarily or even generally convey information, but rather *affect* the other person: amuse, intrigue, comfort, warn, embarrass, threaten him; or appeal to him, for sympathy, encouragement, advice, or just to make some decisive move. There is not always a sense in which such tellings may be true or false, but even when there is, we say them not because they are true, but because they play a useful role in the linguistic exchange that is taking place.[3]

Hunter's stress on 'upshot', on 'going on from there', on 'affecting' rather than merely informing, in connection with various mental-predicate avowals is fully commensurate with my concern for how the available consequentialities of a mental-predicate avowal or ascription inform its use and what is done with its use by hearers in interaction situations. It also thoroughly demystifies sensation-avowals, for they can now be thought of (as argued earlier) in terms of their communicative functions instead of as purely descriptive expressions employed as labels for inner goings-on (which poses the intractable problem of how any such label for a putatively unobservable object could be learned). Such utterances are designed in the light of conventional 'uptake-potentials', under whose auspices they are acquired. However, the assessment of my *truthfulness* or sincerity by others (where this does become an interactional relevance) is contingent upon commonsense knowledge about the conventional relationships between conduct, circumstances and mental-conduct (or sensation) claims and the situated analysis that is made of the particulars at hand. Aspects of this commonsense knowledge and the conventional features of such situated analytical work on the part of recipients of mental-conduct accounts have been examined in these essays. Indeed, the refutation of specific forms of mentalistic theorizing attempted here depends upon the results of such an examination for various predicates-in-use (e.g. reading, hearing, thinking, being jealous, etc.). There is, then, nothing wrong with employing mental-conduct concepts in everyday life and in analytical work, as long as their logical status is understood (i.e. the constraints upon their proper employment). Sociologists, social and cognitive psychologists and theoretical linguists have typically misconstrued the level of abstraction at which an investigation of mind and subjectivity has to be carried out (especially where they seek to warrant specific sorts of direct imputations of 'mental contents' to members/subjects for explanatory purposes) and they have thereby missed the opportunity for an exploration of the language and culture in terms of the reasoning and communicative 'logic' of cognitive, experiential and related predicates. Such an exploration (tentatively begun in these essays and elsewhere) would constitute a semiotics of subjectivity. The range of 'uses' to be investigated vary from the mundane ('having a motive', and the subsequent varieties of motives avowable and ascribable, as well as conventionally open to members' presupposition-analyses) to the relatively complex and circumscribed ('having a mental illness', 'hallucinating' and so on). Since the informal logic of our concepts of phenomena settle for us what the phenomena could be, these essays have for the most part been preoccupied with the conceptual structures of mental constructs. The ways we have, as ordinary concept-users, of avowing, ascribing, disavowing, and infering 'subjective' states and orientations become topics for analytical reflection.

However, analytical reflection does not purport to provide any transcendental characterizations, a sort of 'perfect speech' (whatever that could be), about its topics. Moreover, there is no attempt made to provide explanations of *why* members, on various occasions, have the thoughts, intentions, motives, sensations, emotions etc. which they do have, since, as has been argued, any such explanation must be defeasible in character and, if generalizing, vacuous in content. The theoretical aim of locating 'social determinants' of specific sorts of thoughts, beliefs, knowledges, interpretations or attitudes held by members, individually or collectively, has only resulted in the provision of unilateral imputations of reasoning-orientation to societal members, often in the form of *ad hominem* excusing or justifying conditions. There are no such things as social 'forces' triggering or coercing cognitive orientations—only social procedures (which may or may not be followed) and culturally-conventional orientations (which may be violated or ignored). Bypassing members' rationality and structures of relevance leads to idle stipulation and not analytical reflection. That the limits to what I can think, believe, and reason are established (ongoingly) by my currently available stock of socialized concepts and reasoning-practices is clear, but it should not be concluded from this that whatever I *do* think, believe, and reason is caused by, programmed into me by, my social circumstances or social-structural location. Such circumstances serve me as resources, and serve others as informational grounds for their understandings and appraisals of me and of my conduct, but they are not the determinants of what I think, believe or reason, nor of how I think, understand and interpret the world. For whilst I may have particular *reasons* for some of the things I think, believe, claim to know and understand, there is no sense in the assertion that I am socially caused to think, believe or reason that so-and-so is or is not the case. (And it is a strange form of intellectual snobbery to think that this holds true only for intellectuals.) No matter how compelling the arguments may be as they arise within my social milieux for thinking, believing or reasoning that so-and-so is the case, I can act irrationally and not heed the arguments, or I can demonstrate creativity and originality by transcending the stock of available ways of conceiving the matter; in either case, there is clearly no question of my being determined to think, believe or reason in this way or that, and no amount of reference to brain physiology can undermine this claim. No argument (and *a fortiori* no social 'force') can so operate on me as to bypass my rationality or lack of it. If I possess rationality, this will mean that I have mastered the culturally-available informal logic for acting and reasoning; it will not mean that my specific acts and utterances are the output of some anonymous social programming. I am responsible for what I think, etc., and this responsibility cannot be sloughed off onto others, and certainly not onto mere sociological abstractions. My actions *express* thoughts, beliefs and ways of reasoning; they display or exhibit them (sometimes ambiguously, and sometimes clearly). They are not, therefore, purely *contingent* effects of thinking, etc., in certain ways, nor are they contingent antecedent causal conditions. Wherever social scientists treat 'cognitive states' as dependent variables (by which they usually mean treating ideas, beliefs and attitudes as such), an explicit or implicit form of causal model is assumed (along with a typically reifying view of the components of subjectivity). The implications for the non-biological human sciences of taking the anti-reductionist position seriously, as I have tried to in these essays, are thoroughly dereifying. For not only is it common to hear sociologists and psychologists still talking of motives or thoughts or intentions as antecedent 'mental conditions' causally related to actions, it is also still sadly common to hear talk of such 'conditions' as observable only 'indirectly', since they are thought to lurk inside the head. This misleading way of approaching the analytical task then encourages idle speculations about how best to impute or ascribe such determinate 'conditions' to the subjects of any inquiry. The discussions presented here are attempts to contribute to the reorientation of the field away from such unfortunate theoretical commitments and towards analytical problem-areas that do not require them. As soon as this step is taken, a fresh look at subjectivity becomes possible in the project of a semiotics of mental-predicate uses and practical subjectivity-determinations in organized daily life. The *substantive* explanation of actions and social relations becomes, therefrom, an unavoidably normative or ideological undertaking with its own standards of discourse—itself, perhaps, an analytically rich subject-matter for study in its own right at the level at which we are now proposing sociology should work.

Further into the future, one might even consider the possibility of more meaningful neurophysiological models of human organic functioning which make reference to the biochemical mechanisms which facilitate memory and perception. Yet it is clear that current attempts to read back into the organization of the brain a set of more or less determinate rules formulated by analysts on the basis of principles ordained by defective semantic and cognitive theories are doomed to the fate of perpetual undecidability. There is simply a normative 'barrier' to the formulation of objective standards for grammaticality, semantic intelligibility, intelligence and the ascription of many of the relevant mental predicates for which correlates are so earnestly sought in the functioning of the brain.

The semiotics of subjectivity here being outlined and proposed is obviously a search for a level of orderliness not usually considered outside philosophy and linguistics, and it must, at least initially, be parasitic upon them. Ethnomethodology, with its emphasis upon the achieved orderliness of ordinary actions, is fully commensurate with such a semiotics, broadly conceived. It is time that disciplinary barriers between the students of mind were eroded; the intellectual promise of such an erosion in this field is, in my view, considerable. The intellectual cost of going it alone is one we have paid too long already.

Notes

Introduction

1 Stanley Cavell, 'The Claim to Rationality: Knowledge and the Basis of Morality', Unpublished Doctoral Dissertation, (Harvard University, 1961–2) p. 90.

2 *Ibid.*, p. 244. Cavell provides some excellent examples of anomalous uses of language based upon violations of the normatively-ordered signalling functions of ordinary expressions.

3 Zeno Vendler, 'Linguistics and the *A Priori*' in Colin Lyas (ed.), *Philosophy and Linguistics* (Macmillan: St. Martin's Press, 1971) p. 257.

4 It is, of course, fallacious to believe that logico-grammatical, as opposed to conventionally normative, analyses are restricted to any *one* natural language. As Vendler notes, '. . . a foreigner, with a language radically different from English, might try to understand what we mean by *to know*. And, if he is successful, then he too will see that one cannot know something erroneously, precisely because he has succeeded in reconstructing in his own language a conceptual model sufficiently similar to the linguistic environment of the English word. This is like showing in Riemannian geometry that the internal angles of a Euclidean triangle must total 180 degrees. It is difficult but not impossible. Wittgenstein's policy shows full awareness of the situation: he did not prohibit the translation of his work, but insisted that the original text should accompany the translation.' (*ibid.*, p. 261).

5 D. C. Dennett, *Content and Consciousness* (Routledge & Kegan Paul, 1969) p. 9.

6 *Ibid.*, p. 6.

7 See my 'Beliefs and Practical Understanding' in George Psathas (ed.), *Recent Studies in Ethnomethodology* (forthcoming). For a short comment

on beliefs and social structure, see my review of Russell Keat &
John Urry, *Social Theory as Science* (1975) in *The Sociological Review*,
Vol. 24, No. 3, August 1976, pp. 624–7.

Chapter 1

1   Alfred Schutz, 'Concept and Theory Formation in the Social Sciences',
Journal of Philosophy, Vol. 51 (April 1954) pp. 266–7.
2   Peter Winch, *The Idea of a Social Science and Its Relation to Philosophy*
(Routledge & Kegan Paul, 1958) p. 87.
3   *Ibid.*, p. 123.
4   A. Schutz, *op. cit.*, p. 267. (I should note here, anticipating my line
of argument in the text, that I am unhappy with the use of 'determine'
in this formulation.)
5   See Albert J. Reiss Jnr., 'The Social Integration of Queers and Peers'
in John H. Gagnon & William Simon (eds.), *Sexual Deviance* (Harper
& Row, 1967).
6   On ascriptions of suicide, see Jack D. Douglas, *The Social Meanings
of Suicide* (Princeton University Press, 1970) and J. Maxwell Atkinson,
'Societal Reactions to Suicide: The Role of Coroners' Definitions'
in Stanley Cohen (ed.), *Images of Deviance* (Penguin, 1971). On the
ascription of delinquency, see Aaron V. Cicourel, *The Social Organization
of Juvenile Justice* (John Wiley, 1968). On the ascription of alcoholism,
see Craig MacAndrew, 'On the notion that persons given to frequent
drunkenness are suffering from a disease called alcoholism' in S. Plog
& R. Edgerton (eds.), *Changing Perspectives in Mental Illness* (1969).
On the ascription of mental illness, see T. J. Scheff, *Being Mentally
Ill: A Sociological Theory* (Aldine, 1966) and J. Coulter, *Approaches
to Insanity: A Philosophical and Sociological Study* (Halsted: John Wiley,
1974), Part II.
7   Hanna F. Pitkin, *Wittgenstein and Justice: On the Significance of Ludwig
Wittgenstein for Social and Political Thought* (University of California
Press, 1972) pp. 254–5.
8   See note 6 above.
9   David Sudnow, *Passing On: The Social Organization of Dying* (Prentice-
Hall, 1967) esp. chapter 4, 'Death and Dying as Social States of
Affairs'.
10 H. F. Pitkin, *op. cit.*, p. 256.
11 Alan R. White, *The Philosophy of Mind* (Random House, 1967) p. 52.
12 Gilbert Ryle, *The Concept of Mind* (Hutchinson, 1949) chapter 8.
13 Norman Malcolm, 'Scientific Materialism and the Identity Theory'
in C. V. Borst (ed.), *The Mind/Brain Identity Theory* (Macmillan: St.
Martin's Press, 1970) pp. 174–5.
14 Steven Lukes, 'Methodological Individualism Reconsidered' in Alan
Ryan (ed.), *The Philosophy of Social Explanation* (Oxford University
Press, 1973) p. 128. It should be noted here that Lukes was speaking
of the claim that quasi-mechanical, psychological forces are the sole
causal influences at work on behavior. I do not see how one can

move intelligibly from a metaphor like 'psychological forces' to neuro-physiological phenomena which, when they *are* forces, are clearly electro-chemical in nature. David McClelland at least sustains the same conceptual level in his wistful yearnings for 'a "psychic X-ray" that would permit us to observe what was going on in a person's head in the same way that we can observe stomach contractions or nerve discharges in a hungry organism'. (from his *The Achieving Society* (D. van Nostrand, 1961) p. 39). A. R. Louch's discussion of McClelland in his *Explanation and Human Action* (Basil Blackwell, 1966) chapter 6, is particularly relevant here.

15 J. L. Austin, *How To Do Things With Words* (ed. J. O. Urmson, Oxford University Press, 1962).

16 J. L. Austin, 'A Plea for Excuses' in his *Philosophical Papers* (eds. J. O. Urmson & G. J. Warnock, Oxford University Press, 1970) p. 201.

17 A. R. Louch, 'The Very Idea of a Social Science', *Inquiry*, Vol. 6, No. 4, Winter 1963, p. 285.

18 MacIntyre's early paper, 'A Mistake About Causality in Social Science' (in Peter Laslett & W. G. Runciman (eds.), *Philosophy, Politics and Society*, 2nd Series, Basil Blackwell, 1964), was a sustained argument against the practice of treating beliefs and actions as discrete phenomena which could be related together causally in Humean terms. Peter Winch's *Idea of a Social Science*, op. cit., constituted a broader assault on the idea of a causal sociology. The article under discussion in the text is MacIntyre's more recent paper, 'The Idea of a Social Science' in B. R. Wilson (ed.), *Rationality* (Basil Blackwell, 1974), in which he rescinds his earlier position and subjects Winch's book to criticism for its abandonment of causality as a model for sociological explanation.

19 Alasdair MacIntyre, 'The Idea of a Social Science', p. 116.

20 *Ibid.*, p. 117.

21 *Ibid.*

22 MacIntyre assumes that an hypnotic state, and hypnotic suggestion, are distinguishable from other states and ordinary suggestions by the degree to which the former have a sort of automaticity. For an excellent defense of a non-mechanistic interpretation of hypnosis and posthypnotic behavior, see T. X. Barber, 'Toward a Theory of Hypnosis: Posthypnotic Behavior', *Archives of General Psychiatry*, Vol. 7, 1962, pp. 321–342, and T. X. Barber, N. P. Spanos & J. F. Chaves, *Hypnotism: Imagination and Human Potentialities* (Pergamon Press, 1974).

23 Erving Goffman, *Asylums: Essays on the Social Situation of Mental Patients and Other Inmates* (Penguin, 1968).

24 A. MacIntyre, 'The Idea of a Social Science', p. 120.

25 *Ibid.*

26 *Ibid.*, p. 122. MacIntyre admits as an instance of a causal generalization the proposition that 'Isolated living of a certain kind tends to lead to acts of suicide' (p. 126). I think we need to examine closely the meaning to be given to the expression 'tends to lead to'—surely this could only mean something like 'tends to be associated with',

because even *if* suicided persons had all left reliable suicide notes or other evidence to indicate that their social isolation was their reason for killing themselves, we should still be without any grounds for saying that there was more than a certain *probability* that similar circumstances would figure as *reasons for suicide*. I do not see why we should accept a tendency-(probability)-statement as an example of a causal generalization. There is surely a conceptual sleight-of-hand in reformulating a probabilistic projection such as 'in conditions *xyz*, there is a probability of *n* that ϕ will occur' into a causal statement such as 'conditions *xyz* cause ϕ to occur with a probability of *n*', where $n = <1$. (Many isolated people like to live like that!)

27 Don Zimmerman & Melvin Pollner, 'The Everyday World as a Phenomenon' in Jack D. Douglas (ed.), *Understanding Everyday Life: Toward the Reconstruction of Sociological Knowledge* (Aldine, 1970).

28 The example is taken from Michael Polanyi, *Personal Knowledge* (University of Chicago Press, 1958) chapter 4.

29 See Stanley Cavell, 'Must We Mean What We Say?', reprinted in Colin Lyas (ed.) *Philosophy and Linguistics* (Macmillan: St. Martin's Press, 1971). Austin's discussion of sureness, certainty and knowledge in his paper, 'Other Minds' (in his *Philosophical Papers*, op. cit.) is a classic analysis of the sort which explicates such linguistic commitments and bounded, conventional implications.

30 I am indebted to Wes Sharrock (University of Manchester, England) for this aphorism which, I gather, derives from a remark of Henry Elliott's.

31 On measurement by fiat in science, see Warren Torgerson, *Theory and Method of Scaling* (Wiley, 1958); for a fuller development, see Aaron V. Cicourel, *Method and Measurement in Sociology* (Free Press of Glencoe, 1964) especially chapter 1.

32 John Goldthorpe, 'A Revolution in Sociology?' (review article), *Sociology*, Vol. 7 (1973).

33 Erving Goffman, 'The Moral Career of the Mental Patient' as reprinted in Earl Rubington & Martin S. Weinberg (eds.), *Deviance: The Interactionist Perspective* (2nd Edition: Macmillan, 1973) p. 102.

34 This term belongs to Austin; see his *How To Do Things With Words*, op. cit. The illocutionary force of an utterance is the action performed in its use. (For some illuminating discussion of Austin's typology of locution/illocution/perlocution, see Mats Furberg's *Saying and Meaning* [Basil Blackwell, 1971]).

35 Harvey Sacks, *Lecture 6*, U. C. Irvine Mimeo Lecture Series, October 24, 1967, p. 9.

36 Harvey Sacks, *Lectures 1* and *2*, April 4 and 6, U. C. Irvine Series, Spring 1972. For the further exploitation of this technical construct in the development of a model of conversational turn-taking, see H. Sacks, E. A. Schegloff & Gail Jefferson, 'A Simplest Systematics for the Organization of Turn-Taking for Conversation', *Language*, Vol. 50, No. 4, Part 1, December 1974.

37 See H. Sacks, *Lecture 2*, April 6, 1972, and also E. A. Schegloff, 'Notes on a Conversational Practice: Formulating Place' in David

Sudnow (ed.), *Studies in Social Interaction* (Free Press, 1972).

38 For further development of this notion, see E. A. Schegloff & H. Sacks, 'Opening Up Closings' in Roy Turner (ed.), *Ethnomethodology* (Penguin, 1974).

39 H. Sacks, *Lecture 1*, April 4, 1972, p. 25.

40 For documentation of this point, see James Schenkein, *Getting to the Reason*, unpublished Ph.D. thesis, U.C.L.A., 1970.

41 The data and much of the analysis presented derives from chapter 3 of my unpublished doctoral thesis, *The Operations of Mental Health Personnel*, University of Manchester, England, 1975.

Chapter 2

1 R. Brown, *Words and Things* (Free Press, 1968).

2 J. D. Bransford & N. S. McCarrell, 'A Sketch of a Cognitive Approach to Comprehension', in W. B. Weimer & D. S. Palermo (eds.), *Cognition and the Symbolic Processes* (Lawrence Erlbaum Associates, 1974), follow Roger Brown's conceptualization of the problem.

3 Gilbert Ryle, *The Concept of Mind* (Penguin University Books ed., 1973) p. 163.

4 Ludwig Wittgenstein, *Philosophical Investigations* (trans. G. E. M. Anscombe; Basil Blackwell, 1968) para. 332.

5 *Ibid.*, paras. 154–5.

6 *Ibid.*, para. 180.

7 J. L. Austin, 'Performative Utterances' in his *Philosophical Papers* (eds. J. O. Urmson & G. J. Warnock; Oxford University Press, 1970).

8 Norman Malcolm, 'Knowledge of Other Minds' in G. Pitcher (ed.), *Wittgenstein: The Philosophical Investigations* (Macmillan, 1968) p. 377 (italics added).

9 L. Wittgenstein, *op. cit.*, para. 371.

10 J. L. Austin, *How To Do Things With Words* (ed. J. O. Urmson; Oxford University Press, 1973 ed.) pp. 156–8. ('The whole point of a commissive is to commit the speaker to a certain course of action. Examples are: promise, covenant, contract, undertake, bind myself, give my word, am determined to, intend, declare my intention, mean to . . . (etc.)'—p. 156).

11 A. R. Louch, *Explanation and Human Action* (Basil Blackwell, 1966) p. 112.

12 *Ibid.*, p. 114.

13 Alfred Schutz, *The Phenomenology of the Social World* (trans. G. Walsh & F. Lehnert; Northwestern University Press, 1967) pp. 30–1. Schutz also makes the strange observation that: '"intended meaning" is . . . essentially subjective and is in principle confined to the self-interpretation of the person who lives through the experience to be interpreted. Constituted as it is within the unique stream of consciousness of each individual, *it is essentially inaccessible to every other individual* . . . (moreover) the point is that the meaning I give to your experiences cannot be precisely the same as the meaning you give to them when you

proceed to interpret them.' (*ibid.*, p. 99). The first general assertion about 'intended meaning' is clearly solipsistic; surely intended meanings can be sincerely disclosed on occasions? The inaccessibility thesis here has clear affinities with Schutz's narrow notion of 'ordinary observation'—but we can often see what a man's action is intended by him to amount to in context. (See the discussion in my text.) The second general remark about the ascription of meaning to lived experiences is similarly mentalistic, and stems in part from a failure to unpack the sense of 'meaning' being employed. If we inhabited this Schutzian world of wholly discrepant meaning-identifications, no-one could ever learn a public language within which to express his experiences. Whilst we often interpret the *significance* of *some* of our experiences differently, this cannot be an invariant problem, and should not be misassimilated to 'meaning' *tout court* to result in a variant of the long-discredited 'private-language argument', so ably laid to rest by Wittgenstein and his interpreters. See, e.g., P. M. S. Hacker, *Insight and Illusion: Wittgenstein on Philosophy and the Metaphysics of Experience* (Oxford University Press, 1975) esp. chapter 8.

14 A. Schutz, *op. cit.*, p. 30.

15 A. Schutz, 'Concept and Theory Formation in the Social Sciences' in Maurice Natanson (ed.), *Philosophy of the Social Sciences* (Random House, 1963) p. 243.

16 Stanley Cavell, 'Must We Mean What We Say?' in Colin Lyas (ed.), *Philosophy and Linguistics* (Macmillan, 1971) pp. 322–3, note 33.

17 C. S. Chihara & J. A. Fodor, 'Operationalism and Ordinary Language: A Critique of Wittgenstein' in G. Pitcher (ed.), *op. cit.*, p. 413. These writers refer to Wittgenstein as a 'logical behaviorist' and remark: 'if "inner states" require "outward" criteria, behavioral criteria are the only plausible candidates' (p. 401). This is an inaccurately narrow understanding of what Wittgenstein meant by 'criteria', and would obviously be behavioristic. As Hacker has pointed out, 'criteria for *p* [e.g. "He's in pain", or "He understands"—JC] are dependent upon an indeterminate range of circumstances and are essentially defeasible. The behavioral criteria, for, e.g., the occurrence of a given mental state, are criteria only in certain circumstances.' (*op. cit.*, p. 296.)

18 L. Wittgenstein, *op. cit.*, p. 227.

19 John W. Cook, 'Human Beings' in Peter Winch (ed.), *Studies in the Philosophy of Wittgenstein* (Routledge & Kegan Paul, 1969) p. 135.

20 Immanuel Kant, *Critique of Pure Reason* (trans. N. Kemp Smith; Macmillan, 1929) p. 147.

21 J. F. M. Hunter, '"Forms of Life" in Wittgenstein's *Philosophical Investigations*' in E. D. Klemke (ed.), *Essays on Wittgenstein* (University of Illinois Press, Urbana, 1971) p. 283.

22 See, e.g., J. J. Franks, 'Toward Understanding Understanding' in W. B. Weimer & D. S. Palermo (eds.), *op. cit.*, p. 241: 'In pattern recognition, as in language, there is essentially an infinitude of possible instances of any perceptual/cognitive class. Grammars are formulated as generative recursive systems to characterize the unbounded set of potential sentences. Likewise, in pattern recognition, an adequate charac-

terization of our knowledge would seem to involve some sort of generative recursive structures.' For relevant discussion of this problem in pattern-recognition studies from a standpoint similar to the one defended in this paper, see Keith Gunderson, 'Philosophy and Computer Simulation' in O. P. Wood & G. Pitcher (eds.), *Ryle* (Macmillan, 1971).

23 J. Fodor & J. J. Katz, 'What's Wrong with the Philosophy of Language?' in Colin Lyas (ed.), *op. cit.*, p. 270.

24 J. F. M. Hunter, *Essays After Wittgenstein* (University of Toronto Press, 1973) chapter 7.

25 *Ibid.*, p. 251. (Unless we want to know how to express *p* in the *best* way for such-and-such an occasion, which is besides the point.)

26 J. J. Katz, *The Philosophy of Language* (Harper & Row, 1966).

27 J. F. M. Hunter, *Essays After Wittgenstein*, p. 164.

28 Keith Gunderson, 'Philosophy and Computer Simulation', p. 333.

29 Bernard Harrison, *Meaning and Structure: An Essay in the Philosophy of Language* (Harper & Row, 1972). For Harrison's position on Katz's latest formulation of a Chomskian semantics of a natural-language, see his cogent critical review of Katz's *Semantic Theory* (Harper & Row, 1972) in *Mind*, Vol. 83, No. 332 (October 1974).

30 B. Harrison, *Meaning and Structure*, p. 93.

31 This constitutes the 'projective' mechanism in the theory, enabling it to deal with novel utterances. *Ibid.*, chapter 7, esp. p. 119 *et seq.*

32 *Ibid.*, p. 118.

33 *Ibid.*, p. 127. It should be pointed out that Harrison has recently changed his position on the question of 'knowledge of the rules' and 'rule-following'. (Personal communication, December 1975) In further work, he seeks to avoid strong 'psychological reality' claims.

34 W. V. Quine, 'Methodological Reflections on Current Linguistic Theory' in D. Davidson & G. Harman (eds.), *Semantics of Natural Language* (D. Reidel Co., Boston, 1972).

35 G. J. Warnock, *The Object of Morality* (Methuen University Paperbacks, 1971) p. 48.

36 Zenon W. Pylyshyn, 'Mind, Machines and Phenomenology: Some Reflections on Dreyfus' "What Computers Can't Do"', *Cognition*, Vol. 3, No. 1, 1974–75, esp. p. 65.

37 See, *inter alia*, George Lakoff, 'Presupposition and Relative Well-Formedness' in D. D. Steinberg & Leon A. Jakobovits (eds.), *Semantics: An Interdisciplinary Reader in Philosophy, Linguistics and Psychology* (Cambridge University Press, 1971). See also R. Stalnaker, 'Pragmatics' in D. Davidson & G. Harman (eds.), *op. cit.*

38 This insight, and its subsequent elaboration, belongs to Harvey Sacks. See his paper, co-authored with E. A. Schegloff and Gail Jefferson, 'A Simplest Systematics for the Organization of Turn-Taking for Conversation', *Language*, Vol. 50, December 1974.

39 William Labov, 'Rules for Ritual Insults' in David Sudnow (ed.), *Studies in Social Interaction* (Free Press, 1972). Labov's own analysis of the subsequent interchange is unsatisfactory: he proposes that '... younger members of a social group may not be able to find

the proposition being asserted . . . the unstated proposition being asserted here . . . is presumed to be part of the communal *shared* knowledge . . .' (*ibid.*) However, Linus' 'failure' does not consist in his not having grasped an asserted proposition—rather, he did not assign an appropriate *presupposition* to Violet's utterance. It is not clear how anyone can assert an 'unstated' proposition, as Labov puts it. He alternates confusingly between 'proposition' and 'unstated proposition'. Yet what is being asserted (or proposed) by Violet in the extract is: 'You're younger than me', and that which remains unstated or tacit is the presupposed convention which is the feature of unevenly distributed background knowledge. The same assertion could, in other contexts, take different assignable presuppositions: imagine it uttered by a tired parent to his children who are asking him to join them in their fifth beach-ball game. Assignable presuppositions are clearly indexical—i.e., contextually varying.

40 On the phenomenon of 'adjacency pairs', see H. Sacks, *Lecture 1*, Spring 1972, April 4 (University of California at Irvine, mimeo).

41 H. Sacks, 'Everyone Has To Lie', extended lecture, 1968; in R. Blount & R. Sanchez (eds.), *Ritual, Reality and Innovation in Language Use* (Seminar Press, 1974).

42 Paul & Carol Kiparsky, 'Fact' in D. D. Steinberg & L. A. Jakobovits (eds.), *op. cit.*

43 George Lakoff, 'Presupposition and Relative Well-formedness'.

44 Gilbert Ryle, *The Concept of Mind*, pp. 173–7.

45 The concept of 'defeasibility' is elaborated by H. L. A. Hart in his celebrated discussion of 'The Ascription of Responsibility and Rights' in Anthony Flew (ed.), *Logic and Language* (1st & 2nd Series) (Doubleday-Anchor, 1965).

46 As originated and developed by Harold Garfinkel in his *Studies in Ethnomethodology* (Prentice-Hall, 1967) and elsewhere. For Garfinkel, the problem of social order is posed as an analytical problem of describing the methods by which members of a culture construct their social interactions and social circumstances and generate practical understandings and accounts of them.

47 For a treatment of 'belief' (in which the notion of presupposition is further elaborated), see J. Coulter, 'Beliefs and Practical Understanding' in G. Psathas (ed.), *Recent Studies in Ethnomethodology* (forthcoming).

48 Alan F. Blum & Peter McHugh, 'The Social Ascription of Motives', *American Sociological Review*, Vol. 36 (February 1971).

49 *Ibid.*, p. 103.

50 *Ibid.*

51 *Ibid.*, p. 107. See also discussion by S. Cavell, *op. cit.*, of the ascription of the category 'voluntary'.

52 Blum & McHugh, *op. cit.*, p. 103.

53 *Ibid.*

54 *Ibid.*, p. 106.

55 *Ibid.*

56 On the notion of a standardized relational-pair, see H. Sacks, 'Initial Investigation of the Usability of Conversational Data for Doing Soci-

ology' in D. Sudnow (ed.), *Studies in Social Interaction*.

57 H. Sacks, *Lectures 12 & 13* (November 14 & 16, 1967), U. C. Irvine, mimeos.

58 A 'formative' hearing-rule is one extracted *in situ* by a member from any serially organized features of discourse. (A formative rule in mathematics is one for completing a series such as 2, 6, 10, 14.) It stands in contrast to what Dorothy Smith has called a 'standard-pattern rule', which is known *in advance* of an occasion rather than extracted from within an occasion, and which would consist in complete knowledge. A typical instance of standard-pattern rule-application is completing a series of letters identified as belonging to the alphabetical arrangement [e.g. *hijklmn*] which could not be done accurately without complete knowledge of the alphabetical arrangement. The exploitation of this distinction for analytical purposes concerning rules and norms of reasoning and conduct has been initiated by Dorothy Smith in her brilliant paper, 'K. is Mentally Ill' (forthcoming).

59 See Gail Jefferson, 'A Case of Precision Timing in Ordinary Conversation: Overlapped Tag-Positioned Address Terms in Closing Sequences', *Semiotica*, Vol. IX, No. 1, 1973.

60 H. Sacks, *Lectures 12 & 13*.

61 E. Schegloff & H. Sacks, 'Opening Up Closings' in Roy Turner (ed.), *Ethnomethodology* (Penguin, 1974) p. 258. On adjacency-pairing, the authors write: 'by an adjacently positioned second (utterance), a speaker can show that he understood what a prior aimed at, and that he is willing to go along with that ... and, inspection of a second by a first (speaker) can allow the first speaker to see that while the second thought he understood, indeed he misunderstood'. (p. 240). (See text for examples of adjacency pairs).

62 J. Coulter, *Approaches to Insanity: A Philosophical and Sociological Study* (John Wiley, Halsted, 1974) Part 2.

63 J. Coulter, 'Perceptual Accounts and Interpretive Asymmetries', *Sociology*, Vol. 9, No. 3 (September 1975).

64 See Michael S. Moore, 'Some Myths About "Mental Illness"', *Inquiry*, Vol. 18, No. 3 (Autumn 1975).

65 The ensuing discussion is adapted from my unpublished Ph.D. thesis, 'The Operations of Mental Health Personnel', University of Manchester, U.K., 1975, chapter 6.

66 Gilbert Ryle, *The Concept of Mind*, p. 257.

67 H. Sacks *et al.*, 'A Simplest Systematics . . .'.

68 From a transcription of a conversation between a probation officer and a juvenile client.

69 J. Coulter, 'The Operations of Mental Health Personnel', chapter 6.

70 G. H. Mead, *Mind, Self and Society* (ed. C. W. Morris; University of Chicago, Phoenix, 1967) p. 223, note 25.

Chapter 3

1 Noam Chomsky, *Cartesian Linguistics* (Harper & Row, 1966); Chomsky,

Language and Mind (Harcourt, Brace & World, 1968), and Chomsky, *Reflections on Language* (Pantheon Books; Random House, 1975).

2 Noam Chomsky, 'Linguistics and Philosophy' in Sidney Hook (ed.), *Language and Philosophy: A Symposium* (New York University Press, 1969) p. 88.

3 Chomsky, *Reflections* . . . , p. 30. (It should be noted that one can only cross-reference so easily between Chomsky's recent writings on these matters because he has so scrupulously sustained theoretical consistency in adumbrating his position on them).

4 This is paraphrased from Chomsky's *Reflections* . . . , pp. 30–3.

5 See Chomsky, *Language and Mind*, along with J. J. Katz's paper, 'Mentalism in Linguistics' (mimeo: n.d.).

6 John Searle, 'The Rules of the Language-Game', *Times Literary Supplement*, September 10, 1976.

7 Noam Chomsky, *Aspects of the Theory of Syntax* (M.I.T. Press, 1965) p. 27. See also his 'Linguistics and Philosophy', *op. cit.*, p. 63: '. . . one can describe the child's acquisition of knowledge of language as a kind of theory construction. Presented with highly restricted data, he constructs a theory of the language of which this data is a sample (and, in fact, a highly degenerate sample, in the sense that much of it must be excluded as irrelevant and incorrect—thus the child learns rules of grammar that identify much of what he has heard as ill-formed, inaccurate and inappropriate)'.

8 Gilbert Ryle, 'Mowgli in Babel', *Philosophy: Journal of the Royal Philosophical Society*, Vol. 49, No. 187, January 1974, pp. 9–10.

9 Stephen Toulmin, *Human Understanding Vol. 1: The Collective Use and Evolution of Concepts* (Princeton University Press, 1972), chapter 7: 'The Apparent Invariants of Thought and Language'.

10 *Ibid.*, pp. 463–5.

11 *Ibid.*, p. 465.

12 *Ibid.*, pp. 467–8.

13 Nelson Goodman, 'The Emperor's New Ideas' in S. Hook (ed.), *Language and Philosophy* p. 141.

14 Karl Popper, 'What is Dialectic?' in his *Conjectures and Refutations* (Routledge & Kegan Paul, 1963).

15 See Noam Chomsky, 'A Review of B. F. Skinner's *Verbal Behavior*', *Language*, Vol. 35, No. 1 (1959) pp. 26–58. Reprinted in J. A. Fodor & J. J. Katz (eds.), *The Structure of Language: Readings in the Philosophy of Language* (Prentice-Hall, 1964) pp. 547–78.

16 A. R. Louch, *Explanation and Human Action* (Basil Blackwell, 1966) p. 56. Chomsky's view of mind or intelligence as a 'quality space' of cognitive structures *underlying* particular capacities or abilities prompted these observations about the concept of intelligence, but it should be clear that Chomsky himself does not *assert* any clear conception of intelligence at all.

17 Noam Chomsky, 'Some Empirical Assumptions in Modern Philosophy of Language' in S. Morgenbesser, P. Suppes & M. White (eds.), *Philosophy, Science, and Method: Essays in Honor of Ernest Nagel* (St. Martin's Press, N.Y., 1969) p. 277.

18 Chomsky, *Reflections* . . . , p. 35.
19 Chomsky, 'Some Empirical Assumptions in Modern Philosophy of Language'.
20 *Ibid.*, p. 280. Our 'tacit theory' is acquired by induction restricted by innate principles, once again.
21 *Ibid.*
22 *Ibid.*
23 Ludwig Wittgenstein, *The Blue and Brown Books* (Harper Colophon ed., 1965) p. 119 *et seq.*
24 *Ibid.*, p. 119.
25 *Ibid.*, p. 120 (Parenthetical phrases added).
26 *Ibid.*, p. 121.
27 Ludwig Wittgenstein, *Philosophical Investigations* (trans. G. E. M. Anscombe; Basil Blackwell, 1968) para. 160.
28 *Ibid.*, para. 165.
29 *Ibid.*, para. 167.
30 *Ibid.*, para. 171.
31 Paul Feyerabend, 'Wittgenstein's Philosophical Investigations' in K. T. Fann (ed.), *Ludwig Wittgenstein: The Man and his Philosophy* (Dell Publishing Co., 1967) p. 224, note 9. It is often forgotten that the Husserlian phenomenological program was a form of investigation into the *a priori* conceptual frameworks of everyday life, and that the essentialistic inquiries sought to specify the common 'intentional act(s) of consciousness' peculiar to each phenomenon 'named' by a concept. The total failure of this program to generate adequate conceptual analyses of knowledge, belief, understanding, hope, remorse and a host of other conceptualized phenomena of the mundane world was due in large measure to its stipulation that such phenomena had 'essential properties' determinable by free (phantasy) variation. It is strange to find Chomsky siding with an Husserlian view of a (mental) concept after having presumably read Wittgenstein's strictures against essentialism in the *Philosophical Investigations*, esp. paras. 65–80. He nowhere offers a critique of Wittgenstein's general position on common nouns and proper names, a position lethal for orthodox phenomenology.
32 Paul Feyerabend, *op. cit.*, pp. 222–3.
33 Chomsky, 'Some Empirical Assumptions . . .', p. 279.
34 *Ibid.*, pp. 279–80.
35 *Ibid.*, p. 285, note 20.
36 *Ibid.*, p. 279. Chomsky wrongly ascribes this meaning to Wittgenstein's use.
37 For this rendering of Wittgenstein's notion of 'criterion', I am relying on what I consider to be the best account by far: P. M. S. Hacker's 'The Problem of Criteria', chapter 10 of his *Insight and Illusion* (Oxford University Press, 1975).
38 In this way, we can avoid the labels of established theory (e.g. 'behaviorism', 'mentalism', 'phenomenology') and set out to discover, from instances of reasoned usage, *how* such concepts as reading are, for those instances, functioning as descriptive/ascriptive devices in ordinary accountings of events. This enterprise, as I conceive of it, is explicative

and not geared to theory-construction.

Chapter 4

1 David Pears, *Wittgenstein* (Fontana Modern Masters, 1971) p. 148.
2 Pears (*op. cit.*) refers to this thesis as 'C-subtle' in his discussion
   of Wittgenstein's views on sensations (chapter 8). I am unhappy
   with his treatment of Wittgenstein here, however, because he does
   not take up the issues revolving around the misuse of the concept
   of 'reference', and thereby does Wittgenstein's position some disservice.
3 L. Wittgenstein, *On Certainty* (Basil Blackwell, 1969) para. 130.
4 L. Wittgenstein, *Zettel* (Basil Blackwell, 1967) para. 332.
5 See the excellent exegesis of this issue in P. M. S. Hacker, *Insight
   and Illusion: Wittgenstein on Philosophy and the Metaphysics of Experience*
   (Oxford University Press, 1975) pp. 237–8.
6 This example is taken from Norman Malcolm, 'Wittgenstein's *Philosophical Investigations*' in George Pitcher (ed.), *Wittgenstein. The Philosophical
   Investigations* (Macmillan Modern Studies in Philosophy, 1970) pp. 83–4.
7 L. Wittgenstein, *Philosophical Investigations* (Basil Blackwell, 1968) para.
   293. Cf. para. 304: 'We have only rejected the grammar which tries
   to force itself on us here'—*viz.* the inappropriate language-region of
   material-object categorization.
8 L. Wittgenstein, *Philosophical Investigations*, op. cit., para. 244. Cf. para.
   274: 'Of course, saying that the word "red" "refers to" instead
   of "means" something private does not help us in the least to grasp
   its function; but it is the more psychologically apt expression for
   a particular experience in doing philosophy. It is as if when I uttered
   the word I cast a sidelong glance at the private sensation, as it
   were in order to say to myself: I know all right what I mean by
   it.'
9 P. M. S. Hacker, *Insight and Illusion*, pp. 267–8.
10 *Ibid.*, p. 268.
11 J. F. M. Hunter, 'The Concept of Pain' in his *Essays After Wittgenstein*
   (University of Toronto Press, 1973) p. 131.
12 Gilbert Ryle, *The Concept of Mind* (Penguin University Books ed.,
   1973) p. 194.
13 J. F. M. Hunter, 'The Concept of Pain', pp. 120–1.
14 Norman Malcolm, 'Wittgenstein's *Philosophical Investigations*', p. 84.
15 I believe that this argument would meet the sort of objection raised
   by Feigl: 'Even if we *learn* the use of subjective terms in the way
   indicated, once we have them in our vocabulary we *apply* them to
   states or conditions to which we, as individual subjects, have a "privileged access"'. (H. Feigl, 'Mind-Body, *Not* A Pseudo-Problem' in
   Jordan M. Scher (ed.), *Theories of the Mind* (Free Press, New York,
   1962)).
16 'Now one would like to think that one can still formulate a logical
   implication by taking a description of pain-behavior and conjoining

it with the negation of every proposition describing one of those circumstances that would count against saying he is in pain. Surely, the conjunction will logically imply "He is in pain".' But this assumes there is a *totality* of those circumstances such that if none of them were fulfilled, and he was also pain-behaving, then he *could not but* be in pain. There is no totality that can be exhaustively enumerated, as can the letters of the alphabet. It is quite impossible to list six or nine such circumstances and then to say "That is all of them . . ."— the list is not infinite but *indefinite*. Therefore, entailment-conditions cannot be formulated; there are none.' (Norman Malcolm, 'Wittgenstein's *Philosophical Investigations*', pp. 85–6.)

17 L. Wittgenstein: 'If, however, one wanted to give something like a rule here, then it would contain the expression "in normal circumstances". And we recognize normal circumstances but cannot precisely describe them. At most, we can describe a range of abnormal ones.' (*On Certainty*, Basil Blackwell, 1969, para. 27).

18 L. Wittgenstein, *Zettel*, paras. 118–119.

19 Gilbert Ryle, *The Concept of Mind*, p. 239.

20 S. S. Stevens, 'On the Psychophysical Law', *Psychological Review*, Vol. 64, 1957, pp. 153–181.

21 W. V. Quine, 'Methodological Reflections on Current Linguistic Theory' in Gilbert Harman & Donald Davidson (eds.), *Semantics of Natural Language* (D. Reidel Publishing Co., Humanities Press, 1972) p. 449. The ambiguity of inferences about experiential 'space' and semantic 'space' recurs frequently in psychological experimentation based upon self-reporting.

22 P. M. S. Hacker, *Insight and Illusion*, p. 280.

23 J. L. Austin, *Sense and Sensibilia* (reconstructed from Austin's MSS notes by G. J. Warnock: Oxford University Press, 1964) p. 43. Cf. Anthony Quinton, 'The Problem of Perception' in G. J. Warnock (ed.), *The Philosophy of Perception* (Oxford University Press, 1967) chapter 3.

24 J. L. Austin, *ibid.*, p. 38.

Chapter 5

1 Locke developed this view in his *Essay Concerning Human Understanding* (ed. A. C. Fraser, 1894 republished in N.Y., 1959). Note, *inter alia*, the following observations: 'Besides articulate sounds, therefore, it was further necessary that (man) should be able to use these sounds as signs of internal conceptions; and to make them stand as marks for the ideas within his own mind, whereby they might be made known to others, and the thoughts of men's minds be conveyed from one to another' (*Essay* III, i, 1–2). 'The chief end of language in communication being to be understood, words serve not well for that end, neither in civil nor philosophical discourse, when any word does not excite in the hearer the same idea

which it stands for in the mind of the speaker' (*Essay* III, ix, 4).
'. . . there comes, by constant use, to be such a connection between
certain sounds and the ideas they stand for, that the names heard, almost
as readily excite certain ideas as if the objects themselves, which are apt to
produce them, did actually affect the senses' (*Essay* III, ii, 6). '. . . the
ideas they (words) stand for are their proper and immediate signification'
(*Essay* III, ii, 1). 'Man, though he have great variety of thoughts,
and such from which others as well as himself might receive profit
and delight; yet they are all within his own breast, invisible and
hidden from others, nor can of themselves be made to appear . . .
it was necessary that man should find out some external, sensible
signs. Whereof those invisible ideas, which his thoughts are made
up of, might be made known to others. . . . Thus we may conceive
how words . . . came to be made use of by men as the signs of
their ideas' (*Essay* III, ii, 1). Treating all words as if they functioned
as *names* do is an error that dates back to St. Augustine (possibly
beyond), and the conception of words as all 'standing for' something
goes along with the naming conception of meaning, so vehemently
and successfully undermined by Wittgenstein and his successors in
analytical philosophy. The description of Lockean theories of meaning
as 'synchronous act theories' is due to Jonathan Bennett. See his *Locke,
Berkeley, Hume: Central Themes* (Clarendon Press, Oxford, 1971) esp.
pp. 1–11.

2   J. Bennett, *op. cit.*, pp. 5–6.
3   Ludwig Wittgenstein, *Philosophical Investigations* (trans. G. E. M. Anscombe, Basil Blackwell, Oxford, 1968) para. 329. See also his remarks
on p. 176.
4   *Ibid.*, p. 217.
5   *Ibid.*, p. 18.
6   *Ibid.*, p. 33.
7   *Ibid.*, para. 676.
8   *Ibid.*, para. 674.
9   *Ibid.*, p. 217.
10   Note that the description of someone's 'having to think before he
understands' is a description which has criteria in specific and very
restricted situations only.
11   See note 3 above.
12   Alan R. White, *The Philosophy of Mind* (Random House, N.Y., 1967)
pp. 98–9.
13   Ludwig Wittgenstein, *The Blue and Brown Books* (Harper, 1965) p.
7. Just as the king-of-which-the-rules-of-chess-treat has no *ontological*
status, but is a construct from the relevant pieces and the rules of
play, so also are we to treat the notion of a thought as an abstract
construct from the very diverse things we call thoughts for practical
communicative purposes. To look for a location of thought, considered
in a generic sense, or to seek for a place where thinking is done
(other than in studies, sitting-rooms, offices, cars and countless other
locations in the world), is to misunderstand the logical status of the
concept.

14 L. Wittgenstein, *Zettel* (eds. G. E. M. Anscombe & G. H. von Wright; trans. G. E. M. Anscombe, Basil Blackwell, Oxford, 1967) para. 110.

15 *Ibid.*, para. 123.

16 Gilbert Ryle, 'Thinking and Reflecting', in *The Human Agent* (Royal Institute of Philosophy Lectures, No. 18, 1966–67) and 'The Thinking of Thoughts', *University of Saskatchewan University Lectures*, No. 18, (1968).

17 Alan R. White, *op. cit.*, p. 97.

18 P. M. S. Hacker, *Insight and Illusion: Wittgenstein on Philosophy and the Metaphysics of Experience* (Oxford University Press, 1975) p. 243. Again, Wittgenstein is directing our attention to the fact that any so-called 'inner' process stands in need of 'outward' criteria if a concept of it is to figure in our functioning language-games; consider the ways in which a child might be trained in, might acquire, the use of the word 'think', or the expression, 'X is thinking'.

19 F. N. Sibley, 'Ryle and Thinking' in O. P. Wood & G. Pitcher (eds.), *Ryle* (Macmillan Modern Studies in Philosophy, 1971) p. 102. Sibley has some cogent critical remarks to make about Ryle's recent work on thinking, but I do not believe that anything in the present essay goes beyond what is uncontroversial in Ryle's account. On the specific point Sibley makes, compare Wittgenstein's comment in *Phil. Investig.*, para. 335: 'Now if it were asked: "Do you have the thought before finding the expression?" What would one have to reply? And what, to the question: "What did the thought consist in, as it existed before its expression?"'

20 L. Wittgenstein, *The Blue and Brown Books*, p. 5.

21 F. N. Sibley, *op. cit.*, p. 94. Compare with the arguments made by Justus Hartnack in his excellent paper, 'On Thinking', *Mind*, Vol. LXXXI, No. 324, October 1972. On this issue, there seems to be a clear consensus between Wittgenstein, Ryle, White, Sibley and Hartnack. I can find no cogent counter-arguments. In *Zettel* (*op. cit.*), Wittgenstein observes that in our pre-theoretic language-games in which ascriptions of thinking are involved we are not bound to any imagist doctrine about thinking: (paras. 93–4): 'If a normal human is holding a normal conversation under normal circumstances, and I were to be asked what distinguishes thinking from not-thinking in such a case—I should not know what answer to give. And I could *certainly not* say that the difference lay in something that goes on or fails to go on while he is speaking.

The boundary-line that is drawn here between "thinking" and "not thinking" would run between two conditions which are not distinguished by anything in the least resembling a play of images. (For the play of images is admittedly the model according to which one should like to think of thinking.)'

22 See, e.g., J. Fodor, *The Language of Thought* (T. Crowell, 1975). Fodor's search for something like a unitary 'model' of thinking and thoughts consistent with his computer-analogy paradigm leads him to operationalize these concepts in ways which prevent his conceptualization from dealing with them adequately.

23 L. Wittgenstein, *Remarks on the Foundations of Mathematics* (eds. G. H.

174 *The Social Construction of Mind*

von Wright, R. Rhees & G. E. M. Anscombe: trans. G. E. M.
Anscombe; M.I.T. Press 1972) paras. 131 & 133, p. 41e.

24 David Pears, *Wittgenstein* (Fontana Modern Masters, 1971) p. 168.
25 Steven Lukes, 'Some Problems About Rationality' in Bryan R. Wilson
(ed.), *Rationality* (Basil Blackwell, 1974) pp. 209–10. I do not see
why Lukes thinks Winch's position in any way implies the possibility
of a functioning natural language lacking such basic logical constants.
What Winch actually says about logical rules is as follows: 'One
is inclined to think of the laws of logic as forming a *given* rigid
structure to which men try, with greater or less (but never complete)
success to make what they say in their actual linguistic and social
intercourse conform. One thinks of propositions as something ethereal,
which just because of their ethereal, non-physical nature, can fit together
more tightly than can be conceived in the case of anything so grossly
material as flesh-and-blood men and their actions. In a sense one
is right in this; for to treat of logical relations in a formal systematic
way is to think at a very high level of abstraction, at which all
the anomalies, imperfections and crudities which characterize men's
actual intercourse with each other in society have been removed.
But, like any abstraction not recognized as such, this can be misleading.
It may make one forget that it is only from their roots in this
actual flesh-and-blood intercourse that those formal systems draw such
life as they have; for the whole idea of logical relation is only possible
by virtue of the sort of agreement between men and their actions
discussed by Wittgenstein in the *Philosophical Investigations*.' (*The Idea
of a Social Science and its Relation to Philosophy* [Routledge & Kegan
Paul, 1958] pp. 125–6). The 'agreement' to which Wittgenstein alluded
in his *Investigations* was not an intellectual or propositional agreement
in opinions, but in basic judgments and responses to training. These
background agreements in judgment are not predicated upon a shared
logic, but are what make any logicality possible in human cultures.
(see Wittgenstein's *Investigations*, paras. 241–2).
26 Example taken from actual transcription data.
27 Peter McHugh, 'A Common-Sense Conception of Deviance' in Jack
D. Douglas (ed.) *Deviance and Respectability: The Social Construction of
Moral Meanings* (Basic Books, N.Y., 1970) p. 69. In this, McHugh
draws upon the work of Chaim Perelman, *The Idea of Justice and
the Problem of Argument* (Humanities Press, N.Y., 1963) esp. pp. 112–13.
28 Example taken from actual transcription data.
29 N. Cameron, 'Reasoning, Regression and Communication in Schizoph-
renics' in Max Hamilton (ed.), *Abnormal Psychology* (Penguin, 1967)
p. 165. This classic paper is rich in such analyses involving strategic
contextualization unencumbered by the economy convention.
30 I owe this point to Lena Jayyusi.
31 Example taken from actual transcription data.
32 J. S. Bruner *et al.*, *A Study of Thinking* (John Wiley, N.Y., 1956).
33 Gilbert Ryle, *The Concept of Mind* (Penguin University Books, 1973
ed.) pp. 17, 20, 26–7, etc.
34 Harvey Sacks, *Lecture 9*, November 2, 1967 (U. C. Irvine: mimeo).

35 Transcript fragment used by permission of Jay Meehan.
36 See Roger Squires, 'Silent Soliloquy' in *Understanding Wittgenstein: Royal Institute of Philosophy Lectures*, Vol. 7, 1972–73 (Macmillan, 1974).

Chapter 6

1 L. Wittgenstein, *Zettel* (eds., G. E. M. Anscombe & G. H. von Wright; Trans. G. E. M. Anscombe: Basil Blackwell, 1967) para. 53.
2 *Ibid.* Cf. 'Is "I hope ..." a description of a state of mind? A state of mind has duration. So "I have been hoping for the whole day" is such a description; but suppose I say to someone: "I hope you come"—what if he asks me "For how long have you been hoping that?" Is the answer "For as long as I've been saying so"? Supposing I had some answer or other to that question, would it not be quite irrelevant to the purpose of the words "I hope you'll come"?' (*ibid.*, para. 78). It is the all-too-rapid projection of mental states on the basis of a highly selective and often unrepresentative sample of uses of such concepts as 'hope' which accounts for much of the mystification surrounding the concept of mind.
3 *Ibid.*, paras. 45–51.
4 H. Feigl, 'The "Mental" and the "Physical"', *British Journal of Psychology*, Vol. XLVII, 1956, p. 428, as amended in usage by J. J. C. Smart in his paper, 'Sensations and Brain Processes' in V. C. Chappell (ed.), *The Philosophy of Mind* (Englewood Cliffs, N.J., 1962).
5 Keith Gunderson, 'Asymmetries and Mind-Body Perplexities' in M. Radner & S. Winokur (eds.), *Minnesota Studies in the Philosophy of Science*, Vol. IV (University of Minnesota Press, Minneapolis, 1970) p. 273.
6 G. H. Mead, *Mind, Self and Society* (ed. C. W. Morris; Phoenix Books, University of Chicago Press, 1967 ed.).
7 *Ibid.*, p. 154 et seq.
8 D. Wrong, 'The Oversocialized Conception of Man in Modern Sociology' in L. A. Coser & B. Rosenberg (eds.), *Sociological Theory* (Macmillan, 1964).
9 G. H. Mead, *op. cit.*, p. 173.
10 H. Garfinkel, *Studies in Ethnomethodology* (Prentice-Hall, 1967) pp. 66–8.
11 William L. Kolb, 'A Critical Evaluation of Mead's "I" and "Me" Concepts' in J. G. Manis & B. N. Meltzer (eds.), *Symbolic Interaction* (Boston: Allyn & Bacon, 1967) p. 242.
12 G. H. Mead, *op. cit.*, p. 174.
13 *Ibid.*
14 *Ibid.* Mead claims: 'The "I" of this moment is present in the "me" of the next moment. There again I cannot turn around quick enough to catch myself.' (*ibid.*) It is quite unclear, of course, what it is that Mead finds himself unable to catch!
15 *Ibid.*, p. 175.
16 *Ibid.*, p. 174. Amongst other difficulties created by this passage is understanding what could be meant by: 'you cannot *get* the immediate

response of the "I"' (italics mine). Does this mean 'see'? 'think out'? 'anticipate'? What? If it means 'see', then we are back with a peculiar sort of perceptual introspectionism; if it means 'think out' or 'anticipate', then there is surely something wrong here, since I often think out and anticipate my responses to situations in advance of having to deal with them, in company with most people. If Mead is trying to describe conduct which does not have any determinable and introspectable antecedent (like most spontaneous talk and conduct), then he is surely making things unnecessarily mysterious. If something is spontaneous, then it is no wonder that it is not reflected upon prior to its performance or execution!

17 Jean-Paul Sartre, *The Transcendence of the Ego: An Existentialist Theory of Consciousness* (Trans. & Annotated by F. Williams & R. Kirkpatrick; Noonday Press, Farrar, Straus & Giroux, 1957) p. 48.

18 G. H. Mead, *op. cit.*, p. 176. Note that this is difficult to square with the assertion that 'The "I" is the response of the organism to the attitudes of the others...' (p. 175). Does this imply that *every* such response of the person must be uncertain? And yet of many attitudes we *are* certain in our practical affairs, and our responses show this.

19 *Ibid.*, p. 177.

20 *Ibid.*, p. 178. Given the equation of the 'I' with the organism's responses to the attitudes of the others, such a conception of the 'I' as 'always something different from what the situation calls for' (in text) would entail that *all* our responses are inappropriate. Such a view of human conduct is clearly absurd, and obviously the product of Mead's confusion about his own concept.

21 *Ibid.*, p. 186.

22 *Ibid.*, p. 196.

23 Maurice Natanson, *The Social Dynamics of George H. Mead* (Public Affairs Press, Washington D.C., 1956).

24 Kimball Young, *Personality and Problems of Adjustment* (N.Y., 1940) p. 178.

25 Herbert Blumer, 'Society as Symbolic Interaction' in J. G. Manis & B. N. Meltzer (eds.), *Symbolic Interaction, op. cit.*, and H. Blumer, *Symbolic Interactionism: Perspective and Method* (N.J., 1969), chapter entitled: 'The Social Implications of the Thought of G. H. Mead', *inter alia*.

26 Manford H. Kuhn, 'Major Trends in Symbolic Interaction Theory in the Past Twenty-Five Years' in Manis & Meltzer (eds.), *op. cit.*

27 Alasdair MacIntyre, 'The Self as Work of Art', *New Statesman*, March 28, 1969.

28 Erving Goffman, *The Presentation of Self in Everyday Life* (Doubleday-Anchor, 1959).

29 Harvey Sacks, 'Initial Investigation of the Usability of Conversational Data for Doing Sociology' in David Sudnow (ed.) *Studies in Social Interaction* (Free Press, 1972) and his 'On the Analyzability of Stories by Children' in Roy Turner (ed.), *Ethnomethodology* (Penguin, 1974).

30 Four such category-selection preferences explicated by Sacks are: (i) 'For any population N, on any occasion of categorizing Members

... the task may be complete if each Member of the population has had a single category applied to him' (Sacks, in D. Sudnow, *op. cit.*, p. 34): (ii) 'If some population of persons is being categorized, and if a category from some device's collection (e.g. 'father' from the device/collection 'family'—JC) has been used to categorize a first Member of the population, then that category or other categories of the same collection *may* be used to categorize further Members of the population' (*ibid.*, p. 33): (iii) 'Prefer hearer-recognitionals' (Sacks & Schegloff, 'Two Preferences in the Organization of References to Persons in Conversation and their Interaction' in U. Quasthoff (ed.), *Sprachstruktur-Sozialstruktur* (Suhrkempf-Verlag, 1975): (iv) 'Where recognition cannot be achieved via minimal reference-forms, the latter preference may be subordinated to the recognition preference'. (*ibid.*)

31 Irving Thalberg, 'Freud's Anatomies of the Self' in Richard Wollheim (ed.) *Freud* (Anchor Books, 1974) pp. 148–9. Thalberg's references in parentheses in the citation are as follows: 1894: Freud, 'The Neuro-Psychoses of Defence'; 1895: Freud, with J. Breuer, *Studies on Hysteria*; 1900: Freud, *The Interpretation of Dreams*; 1920: Freud, *Beyond the Pleasure Principle*. In constructing my own discussion, I have relied upon: Freud, *The Ego and the Id*, as well as various subsidiary references.

32 E. W. Burgess, 'The Influence of Sigmund Freud upon Sociology in the United States', *American Journal of Sociology*, Vol. 45, 1939.

33 T. D. Eliot, 'Interactions of Psychiatric and Social Theory Prior to 1940' in A. M. Rose (ed.), *Mental Health and Mental Disorder, A Sociological Approach* (W. W. Norton & Co., Inc., N.Y., 1955).

34 Guy E. Swanson, 'Mead and Freud: Their Relevance for Social Psychology' in Manis & Meltzer (eds.), *Symbolic Interaction*.

35 Talcott Parsons, *Family Socialization and Interaction Process* (Free Press, 1960).

36 Herbert Marcuse, *Eros and Civilization* (Beacon Press, Boston, 1955).

37 Bernard Rimland argues: '... concerning our virtually complete ignorance of how the normal brain operates (a famous neurophysiologist was quoted recently as saying, "We know *zero* about how the brain really works"), it would seem presumptuous to label any given case "psychogenic"—even if we were sure that some cases were psychogenic. Each of the ten billion neurons in the human brain is far more complex than any transistor or vacuum tube. We don't know how a neuron works, and we certainly have no instrument for determining the adequacy of even one of these neurons.' ('Psychogenesis versus Biogenesis: The Issues and the Evidence' in S. Plog & R. Edgerton (eds.), *Changing Perspectives in Mental Illness* (Holt, Rinehart & Winston, 1969) p. 708).

38 Edmund Husserl, *Ideas: General Introduction to Pure Phenomenology* (Collier-Macmillan, 1972 ed.: Original German ed., 1913) p. 156.

39 See note 17 above.

40 J.-P. Sartre, *op. cit.*, p. 40.

41 *Ibid.*, p. 104.

42 *Ibid.*

43 *Ibid.*, pp. 98–9.

44 Herbert Spiegelberg, 'Husserl's Phenomenology and Sartre's Existentialism' in J. J. Kockelmans (ed.), *Phenomenology: The Philosophy of Edmund Husserl and Its Interpretation* (Doubleday-Anchor, 1967) p. 266.

45 L. Wittgenstein, *Philosophical Investigations* (Trans. G. E. M. Anscombe; Basil Blackwell, 1968) para. 410.

46 L. Wittgenstein, *The Blue and Brown Books* (Harper Colophon ed., 1965) p. 69.

47 P. M. S. Hacker, *Insight and Illusion: Wittgenstein on Philosophy and the Metaphysics of Experience* (Oxford University Press, 1975) p. 269.

48 Gilbert Ryle, *The Concept of Mind* (Penguin University Books, 1973 ed.) pp. 186–9.

49 *Ibid.*, p. 189.

50 K. Gunderson, 'Asymmetries and Mind-Body Perplexities', p. 305.

51 *Ibid.*

52 In grouping these thinkers together, it should not be inferred that I am considering them *all* as 'phenomenologists' in any strict sense. Nonetheless, all dealt in what I call phenomenological residua in their treatment of the concept of 'I'.

Chapter 7

1 David Hume, *Treatise of Human Nature*, 1739, L. A. Selby-Bigge, ed., Oxford University Press (Clarendon), 1888, Book II, Pt. iii, Section 3. Cited in Abraham I. Melden, 'The Conceptual Dimensions of Emotions' in Theodore Mischel (ed.), *Human Action: Conceptual and Empirical Issues* (Academic Press, 1969) p. 201.

2 Errol Bedford, 'Emotions' in V. C. Chappell (ed.), *The Philosophy of Mind* (Prentice-Hall, 1962) p. 113.

3 Ludwig Wittgenstein, *Zettel*, eds. G. E. M. Anscombe & G. H. von Wright; trans. G. E. M. Anscombe (Basil Blackwell, Oxford, 1967) para. 488.

4 *Ibid.*, para. 495.

5 Abraham I. Melden, 'The Conceptual Dimensions of Emotions', p. 206.

6 L. Wittgenstein, *Philosophical Investigations*, Trans. G. E. M. Anscombe (Basil Blackwell, 1968) p. 174.

7 Errol Bedford, *op. cit.*, p. 118.

8 *Ibid.*, pp. 112–13.

9 *Ibid.*, p. 121. Note that this shows that the phrase 'of regret' does not *name* the feeling in the way in which 'of giddiness' may be thought to name the sensation.

10 Michael S. Pritchard, 'On Taking Emotions Seriously', *Journal for the Theory of Social Behavior*, Vol. 6, No. 2, October 1976, p. 219.

11 *Ibid.*, p. 218. It would seem that occurrences of what can be termed 'diffuse' depression or anger contradict this claim. However, perhaps the main reason why such states puzzle us both as their bearers and as their observers is indeed their apparent objectlessness. In fact, arguments can revolve around avowals of such states on precisely this issue: it may be claimed that a person avowing a diffuse anger with no determinable object is not really angry at all because there is nothing

about which he may be said to be angry, or he may be considered to have exaggerated his feeling or misinformed us of its true nature. Nonetheless, we do seem able to acknowledge such states in ourselves and in others on occasion, although clearly as holding actions. We can later accept some specification of an object or objects for these states, and this is a task performed with differing degrees of creativity by psychotherapists.

12 A. I. Melden, *op. cit.*, p. 205. Melden goes on to remark that the body changes suggested by James and Lange are *unnoticed* by us when we are, e.g., afraid or angry. In this way, they cannot be compared to our perception of such physiological occurrences as an accumulation of saliva in the mouth or the tightening of the skin of our neck, which in turn are neither necessary nor sufficient to constitute anger or fear.

13 Stanley Schachter & J. Singer, 'Cognitive, Social and Physiological Determinants of Emotional State', *Psychological Review*, Vol. 69, 1962, and Stanley Schachter, 'The Interaction of Cognitive and Physiological Determinants of Emotional States' in Leonard Berkowitz (ed.), *Advances in Experimental Social Psychology* (1964) and in P. Leiderman & D. Shapiro (eds.), *Psychobiological Approaches to Social Behavior* (Stanford University Press, 1964).

14 See discussion in R. Harré & P. F. Secord (eds.), *The Explanation of Social Behavior* (Littlefield Adams & Co., Totowa, N.J., 1973) p. 272 *et seq.* Schachter and Singer conclude that: 'Given a state of physiological arousal for which an individual has no immediate explanation, he will label this state and *describe his feelings in terms of the cognitions available to him*' (1962, p. 398). (Italics added) I do not think that we have in the Schachter-Singer findings sufficient basis for an *arousal-label theory* of emotion, as Shibles has claimed (W. Shibles, *Emotion: The Method of Philosophical Therapy* (The Language Press, Wisconsin, 1974) pp. 129–32). Such a claim would be an over-extrapolation, insensitive to the multivariate nature of emotions and to the absence of uniform arousal levels corresponding to their warranted avowal in ordinary situations. Nonetheless, the experiments do show that a physiologic action, by itself, does not predispose invariantly to a recognition on the part of a subject that he is experiencing the 'same thing' independent of appraisals and the features of social settings.

15 Howard Becker, 'History, Culture and Subjective Experience: An Exploration of the Social Basis of Drug-Induced Experiences', *Journal of Health and Social Behavior*, Vol. 8, No. 3, September 1967; reprinted as 'Interpreting Drug Experiences' in Earl Rubington & Martin S. Weinberg (eds.), *Deviance: The Interactionist Perspective* (Macmillan, 1973). See also H. S. Becker, 'Becoming a Marijuana User', *American Journal of Sociology*, Vol. 70, 1953. (Variously reprinted, as in H. S. Becker (ed.), *Outsiders*, Free Press, 1963.)

16 H. S. Becker, in Rubington & Weinberg (eds.), *op. cit.*, p. 306.

17 *Ibid.*, p. 305.

18 Theodore Mischel, 'Epilogue', in T. Mischel (ed.), *Human Action, op.*

cit., p. 263. Italics mine.

19 Talcott Parsons, *The Social System* (Free Press, 1951).

20 Anthony Kenny, *Action, Emotion and Will* (Routledge & Kegan Paul, 1963) p. 62.

21 A. I. Melden, 'The Conceptual Dimensions of Emotions' in T. Mischel (ed.), *op. cit.*, pp. 215–16.

22 *Ibid.*, p. 215.

23 Anthony Kenny, *op. cit.*, p. 74.

24 James M. Henslin, 'Guilt and Guilt Neutralization: Response and Adjustment to Suicide' in Jack D. Douglas (ed.), *Deviance and Respectability: The Social Construction of Moral Meanings* (Basic Books, 1970). 'The major areas of guilt evidenced by these respondents concerned (i) not being aware of the suicidal intent, (ii) feeling that they should have been able to prevent the suicide, (iii) feeling that perhaps they had done something to cause the suicide, and (iv) noncausal actions that were regretted.' (p. 200).

25 Henslin lists thirteen 'guilt-neutralizing techniques' (p. 204) on the basis of his data, concluding with a shortened set: these are (i) the guilty person defines others and/or impersonal factors as the causal agents that led to the suicide; (ii) he defines the suicide as inevitable, and (iii) he defines the suicide in positive terms. (p. 222, *ibid.*) In a footnote (n. 22, p. 228), Henslin adds 'denial that the death was by suicide can prevent guilt, as can a strong negative conception of the deceased'.

26 J. L. Austin, *How To Do Things With Words* (ed. J. O. Urmson; Oxford University Press, 1973 ed.) pp. 101–31. Lena Jayyusi pointed out the oddness of treating act-consequentialities as types of acts in her unpublished Master's Dissertation 'Theory and Method in the Study of Communication' (University of Manchester, England, 1972), Chapter on 'Speech Acts'.

Chapter 8

1 This is the position first articulated in T. Szasz, *The Myth of Mental Illness* (Harper & Row, 1961). See also T. R. Sarbin, 'The Scientific Status of the Mental Illness Metaphor' in S. Plog & R. Edgerton (eds.), *Changing Perspectives in Mental Illness* (Holt, Rinehart & Winston, 1971), and T. J. Scheff, 'Schizophrenia as Ideology' in his edited collection, *Labeling Madness* (Spectrum, Prentice-Hall, 1975).

2 This euphemistic rediscription is Szasz's way of conceptualizing those phenomena categorized by psychiatrists and others conventionally as mental illnesses. See T. Szasz, *op. cit.*

3 This is Sarbin's similarly euphemistic redescription. See T. R. Sarbin, *op. cit.*

4 *Ibid.*, p. 19.

5 R. D. Laing, *The Politics of Experience (and the Bird of Paradise)* (Penguin, 1968) p. 87.

6 Ludwig Binswanger, 'The Case of Ellen West: An Anthropological-Clini-

cal Study' (trans. W. M. Mendel & J. Lyons) in Rollo May, Ernest
Angel & Henri F. Ellenberger (eds.), *Existence: A New Dimension in
Psychiatry and Psychology* (Simon & Schuster ed., 1958) p. 331. Cf.
his claim elsewhere: 'Where we speak of disease symptoms and make
a diagnostic judgment, quite a different frame of reference appears
to be in force. It is neither a cultural nor a purely natural-scientific-biolo-
gical one, but a medical one; it is the reference system of medical
pathology. If we judge abnormal social behavior—a cultural fact—psychiatrically as a pathological phenomenon, we have left the area of
purely biological judgment and entered the area of judgment of biological
purpose, just as if we had to deal with physical abnormal behavior'.
From his 'Insanity as Life-Historical Phenomenon and as Mental Disease: The Case of Ilse' in *ibid.*, p. 229. This seems a more defensible
claim to make.

7 T. R. Sarbin, *op. cit.*, p. 19.
8 H. Tristram Engelhardt Jnr., 'The Concepts of Health and Disease'
   in H. T. Engelhardt Jr. & S. F. Spicker (eds.), *Evaluation and Explanation
   in the Biomedical Sciences* (D. Reidel Publishing Co., 1975) p. 136.
   Developing this view, Engelhardt writes: 'Disease as an explanatory
   account is bound to the circumstances of that account. In short,
   explanatory accounts are not things; things are what explanatory
   accounts explain and disease is a mode for explaining things—in particular, ill humans'. (*ibid.*)
9 *Ibid.*, p. 134. This discussion is very useful in exposing the myth
   that for every case in which a 'disease' is warrantably said to be
   present there are only neutral, value-free determinations being made,
   irrespective of context and cultural conventions.
10 *Ibid.*
11 Michael S. Moore, 'Some Myths about "Mental Illness"', *Inquiry*,
   Vol. 18, No. 3, Autumn 1975.
12 *Ibid.*, p. 236.
13 Leonard Linsky, *Referring* (New York, 1967).
14 T. Szasz, *Ideology and Insanity: Essays on the Psychiatric Dehumanization
   of Man* (Doubleday-Anchor, 1970) p. 19.
15 *Ibid.*, p. 23.
16 M. S. Moore, *op. cit.*, p. 248.
17 *Ibid.*, p. 249. Alvan R. Feinstein has drawn attention to the existence
   of 'diseases' (e.g. carcinoma of the lung) which can be present prior
   to, independently of, a person's being 'ill' (—his category for such
   conditions is *lanthanic* diseases: see his 'Boolean Algebra and Clinical
   Taxonomy', *New England Journal of Medicine*, Vol. 269, October 31,
   1964, and his *Clinical Judgment* (Williams & Wilkins Co., Baltimore,
   1967), esp. pp. 145–8.) For further support of Moore's contention,
   consider the following: '. . . in African communities when air travel
   did not exist and where malaria was common, having sickle cell
   trait was not a disvalue at all. Individuals with sickle cell trait have
   increased immunity from malaria when compared with other people.
   In such African communities the same condition was of positive value,
   and would not have been considered a disease state. . . . In our

culture, individuals with sickle cell trait may be considered to have a disease, for they may not survive sudden accidental depressurization of an airplane . . .' (from Loretta Kopelman's 'On Disease: Theories of Disease and the Ascription of Disease.' in Engelhardt & Spicker (eds.), *op. cit.*) Kopelman is critical of Engelhardt's claim that in ascribing disease we are *thereby explaining* something. Her argument is surely sound.

18   M. K. Temerlin, 'Suggestion Effects in Psychiatric Diagnoses', *Journal of Nervous and Mental Disease*, Vol. 147, 1968, p. 358.

19   See my *Approaches to Insanity: A Philosophical and Sociological Study* (Martin Robertson, 1973) chapter 1.

20   For an excellent discussion of the history of various psychotropic drugs and the separation of psychopharmacology from organic-aetiological inquiry in psychopathology, see Leon Eisenberg, 'Psychiatric Intervention', *Scientific American*, Vol. 229, No. 3, September 1973.

21   Harold Garfinkel, 'The Rational Properties of Scientific and Common Sense Activities' in his *Studies in Ethnomethodology* (Prentice-Hall, 1967) p. 277. I have taken the liberty here of writing in 'conduct' in place of Garfinkel's use of 'choices' to simplify the discussion.

22   Laurence Kolb, as quoted in Herbert Fingarette, *The Meaning of Criminal Insanity* (University of California Press, 1972) p. 99.

23   Simon Sobeloff, 'Insanity and the Criminal Law: From McNaghten to Durham and Beyond', *American Bar Association Journal*, Vol. 41, 1955, p. 877. Quoted in H. Fingarette, *op. cit.*, p. 99.

24   van den Berg, as quoted in R. D. Laing, *The Divided Self* (Pelican, 1965) p. 27. This is perhaps too strong a characterization; however, it does not *entail* anything about subsequent treatment and attitudes toward the patient on the part of the clinician.

25   T. J. Scheff, *Being Mentally Ill: A Sociological Theory* (Aldine, 1966) and his 'Introduction' to his edited collection, *Mental Illness and Social Processes* (Harper & Row, 1967). See also T. Scheff (ed.), *Labeling Madness*, op. cit.

26   David Mechanic, 'Some Factors in Identifying and Defining Mental Illness' in T. J. Scheff (ed.), *Mental Illness and Social Processes*.

27   Arlene K. Daniels, 'The Philosophy of Combat Psychiatry' as reprinted in E. Rubington & M. S. Weinberg (eds.), *Deviance: The Interactionist Perspective* (Macmillan, 1973), from 'Normal Mental Illness and Understandable Excuses: The Philosophy of Combat Psychiatry', *American Behavioral Scientist*, Vol. 14, No. 2, Nov/Dec 1970, and her 'The Social Construction of Military Psychiatric Diagnoses' in H. P. Dreitzel (ed.), *Recent Sociology Vol. 2: Patterns of Communicative Behavior* (Macmillan, 1970).

28   Anselm Strauss *et al.*, *Psychiatric Ideologies and Institutions* (Free Press of Glencoe, 1964). See also L. Schatzman & Anselm Strauss, 'A Sociology of Psychiatry', *Social Problems*, Vol. 14, No. 1, Summer 1966.

29   L. Phillips & J. G. Draguns in *Annual Review of Psychology*, Vol. 22, 1971.

30   B. M. Braginsky, D. D. Braginsky & K. Ring, *Methods of Madness:*

The Mental Hospital as a Last Resort (Holt, Rinehart & Winston, 1969).

31 David L. Rosenhan, 'On Being Sane in Insane Places', *Science*, Vol. 179, 1973.

32 T. J. Scheff, 'Introduction' to his edited collection, *Mental Illness and Social Processes*, p. 6.

33 D. Mechanic, in *ibid.*, p. 26.

34 A. K. Daniels, 'The Philosophy of Combat Psychiatry', p. 139.

35 T. J. Scheff, *Being Mentally Ill*, esp. pp. 114–15.

36 D. L. Rosenhan, *op. cit.*, p. 252.

37 B. M. Braginsky *et al.* argue that 'schizophrenia' 'is a term without a referent and lacking any it cannot even be said to have outlived its usefulness, because there is no reason to think that it ever had any'. (*Methods of Madness*; op. cit., p. 164.) But a psychiatrist could certainly point to the crazy behavior of a patient and claim to be referring to his schizophrenia, even though the behavior referred to might have little or nothing in common with that of another patient so diagnosed. The category can be *situatedly* referential for various purposes, whilst still lacking a consistent or *fixed* 'referent' independent of context and purpose. It is further quite fallacious to deny *any* 'usefulness' to a concept incapable of ostensive definition. The referential comparability problem is a problem only for a limited range of theoretical, research purposes; see D. Bannister, 'The Logical Requirements for Research into Schizophrenia', *British Journal of Psychiatry*, Vol. 114, 1968. At this juncture, I should point out that in my own treatment of some of these issues (*Approaches to Insanity*, op. cit.) I did not distinguish clearly enough between the pragmatic consideration of 'schizophrenia' as a disease or illness and the biogenic-theoretical claims that 'schizophrenia' is uniformly a *brain disease.*

38 The 'open-textured' nature of a concept is, in the terms of F. Waismann who first used it systematically, its property of extension to cover phenomena not prescribed in any pre-formulated rules for the use of the concept. It is not to be confused with the relational concept of 'vagueness'. See Waismann's classic paper, 'Verifiability' in Anthony Flew (ed.), *Logic and Language* (Anchor Books, 1965).

39 Ludwig Wittgenstein, *Philosophical Investigations* (Basil Blackwell, 1968) para. 75.

40 Alan F. Blum, 'The Sociology of Mental Illness' in Jack D. Douglas (ed.), *Deviance and Respectability: The Social Construction of Moral Meanings* (Basic Books, 1970) p. 35.

41 For some documentation, see M. R. Yarrow *et al.*, 'The Psychological Meaning of Mental Illness in the Family' in Rubington & Weinberg (eds.), *Deviance: The Interactionist Perspective*, op. cit., and Kathleen Smith *et al.*, 'The "Last Straw"; Decision Incidents Resulting in the Request for Hospitalization in One Hundred Schizophrenic Patients', *American Journal of Psychiatry*, Vol. 120, 1963.

42 Field-notes gathered during one year's research into the organization of psychiatric activities in a large city in England during 1970–71. I have analyzed some of these materials in an unpublished doctoral dissertation entitled: *The Operations of Mental Health Personnel* (University

of Manchester, 1975).

43 Peter Winch, 'Understanding a Primitive Society' in B. R. Wilson (ed.), *Rationality* (Basil Blackwell, 1974) p. 82.

44 See Zhores and Roy Medvedev, *A Question of Madness* (Penguin, 1971), and the excellent summary of more recent evidence by Clayton Yeo, 'The Abuse of Psychiatry in the USSR: The Evidence', *Index on Censorship*, Vol. 4, No. 2, Summer 1975.

Conclusion

1 J. F. M. Hunter, 'Telling', *Essays After Wittgenstein* (University of Toronto Press, 1973).

2 *Ibid.*, pp. 96–7.

3 *Ibid.*, p. 113.

Subject Index

(Italicized numerals refer to the Notes)

Name Index

(Italicized numerals refer to the Notes)